SAVAGE

A JOURNEY THROUGH THE OPIOID EPIDEMIC

Stephen J. Sacchi

D1598607

CENTRAL PARK SOUTH PUBLISHING

Publisher: Central Park South Publishing
website: www.centralparksouthpublishing.com

Publisher's Note: True Story, Non-Fiction.

Book Layout – alienartifacts

SAVAGE – A Journey Through the Opioid Epidemic by Stephen J. Sacchi -- 1st ed. © 2020

ISBN 978-1-7352964-8-7

Dedication

I'd like to dedicate this to anybody who suffers from similar afflictions as my own. I promise if you confront your demons you will not only discover a better way of life, but that life is indeed worth living.

One - Early Days

I grew up on the south shore of Staten Island, a suburban paradise within the city limits of New York City. Almost all of my friends' parents moved here from Brooklyn after they made something of themselves. They figured they'd raise a family in what was supposed to be a safer and quieter section of the city. It was like a social experiment gone horribly awry. They accidentally raised a bunch of spoiled brats with a tough city attitude.

My generation of Staten Islanders were supposed to conquer the world. We were the children of the Brooklyn baby boomers who went out and accomplished the American dream. We were oozing with white privilege. We had every opportunity to grow into doctors or lawyers. We collectively rejected our birthright and instead embraced the opioid epidemic. Some of the opioid epidemic's finest all stars were all drafted from the south shore of Staten Island. Now in our 30's, many of us are still out there getting high. Plenty of us are dead. Very few of the survivors who are now clean have proceeded to make anything of themselves. Years of drug abuse set us back so far behind the curve it's downright humiliating. I know plenty of people still living with their parents without a clue in the world as to how to transcend the stupidity of our youth. I'm just barely living like an adult myself.

I think it's worth noting that I didn't come from a so-called dysfunctional family. I was deeply loved and provided for. Perhaps too much. I'm not anxious to admit that I was probably a bit spoiled myself. There was no trauma, no abuse, and no tragedies. My father, Steve, is a computer communications engineer. He designs and sells software that makes text messaging and things of that nature not only possible, but more efficient. He's the sweetest guy in the world. He doesn't smoke, doesn't drink, and doesn't gamble. He doesn't have a vice that I can think of. Nothing prepared this poor man for the trouble my brother and I would one day bestow upon him. My mother, Brenda, on the other hand, was a bit of a disciplinarian. Growing up I resented her for it and would often find myself at odds with her. She was a smoker and although she wasn't an alcoholic or a problem drinker, she would drink from time to time unlike my father. I've seen my father drink one alcoholic beverage in my lifetime and it was a Pina Colada for Christ's sake. I have a little brother, Johnny, and we were your run of the mill happy home. Sure there were issues, but Johnny and I were raised in as good a home as any.

Growing up I was a smart kid and an even better student. I was also a bit of an outsider. A misfit if you would. I went to a Catholic school called Our Lady Help of Christians. It was a small school with a church right across the parking lot. My graduating class had only sixteen students. I was shy at first and the other children didn't seem to care for me. It wasn't until the fourth grade that I started making friends. The other kids didn't care for me but they absolutely despised an annoying child named Gerard. At recess one afternoon, Gerard started imposing his antics on me. There I was walking around the schoolyard, sad, lonely, and minding my own business when he came along to harass me. I had tried my hand on the soccer team around that time and one thing I learned in soccer is the sensitivity of the shin. They made us wear shin guards because of it.

At first, I defied them on the first day because I thought shin guards must be for girls. I already had a target on my back and I didn't need any added abuse if shin guards weren't for the cool kids to wear. I found out the hard way that this wasn't something one could be too cool for. One kick to the shin and practice ended early for me. In the schoolyard during recess however, nobody was wearing shin guards. I took this knowledge and used it to my advantage. I kicked Gerard right in his shin and then punched him in the face which subsequently made him cry. The other children hoisted me up in the air and started chanting my name because their disdain for Gerard ran that deep. From that day on, I had a host of friends. When we went into the cafeteria for lunch after recess, they completely embraced me. I never sat alone again after that day.

Now that the other kids were talking to me, I would talk about the few things I actually knew anything about and, at that time, it was movies. Jim Carrey's movies to be more specific. I started doing impressions of "Ace Ventura" and "Cable Guy." I had all the lines memorized and my impressions were spot on.

The other kids were enamored. I learned two important lessons that day. Beating somebody up can garner respect from your peers and being funny will help maintain that respect. The seed was planted for an exaggerated sense of humor to be my defense mechanism. Unfortunately, I've carried these insights a little too far into adulthood. Sometimes humor is a powerful asset but it often becomes a liability when you never seem to take anything seriously.

When I was ten years old my mother took me to a doctor to figure out why I was so much smaller than the other children my age. They took some X-ray's and determined that my bones were that of a five-year-old. The doctor said it was nothing to worry about. I simply would continue to grow for a longer period of time than the other children. In the meantime, I was about two feet shorter than everybody else. "He'll grow up to be six feet tall," he assured my mother. A recurring theme throughout my life is that I would mature slower than everyone else. Not just physically though. In all aspects of life. I always had a sense of inferiority, even when I did finally grow into just shy of six feet in height.

I guess you could say that even at that young age I was maladjusted. Once a week they would take us to church for mass. I would keep the Eucharist in my mouth until we got to the school building's stairwell. As we were walking up the stairs, the Eucharist that I hadn't swallowed had turned into a white frothy goop that I could slowly release from my mouth and pretend I was having a seizure to make the other children laugh. After the laughter calmed down, they would insist I was going to hell. Back then I actually believed in hell. But I had a bone to pick with God even then. It all started with the story of Abraham in religion class. God told Abraham to go to a hilltop and kill his son. When he went to do it, God sent down an angel to stop him. "That's ridiculous!" I shouted to the teacher. "Now Stephen, God was testing his loyalty is all," she said back in a matter of fact fashion. What kind of God needs to test his followers in such a dramatic fashion? The more and more they taught us about mortal sins and edicts of that nature, the more and more I assumed I had a one-way ticket to hell.

*   *   *   *   *

The first day of high school was at yet another Catholic school called Saint Joseph by the Sea. It's the premier Catholic high school on Staten Island. I must say, it's a little unfair the pressure they put on us to get into that school because I was a certified book worm and all my idiot friends got accepted as well. Parents and teachers insisted we get our grades up to get into a good high school but, believe me, they were letting any idiot in there so long as their parents had the money to pay for it. The first day of high school was the first day I met Tony. Tony and I looked and behaved like we could be brothers. We were both short then, skinny, dark hair, brown eyes, and really handsome. To this day he swears it was me who said this but when we were introduced, he said, "This kid's short like me. I like him already!"

Our sense of humor matched up well. From that day on Tony and I were inseparable. My father was advancing in his career so we just so happened to be buying a bigger house on the same street as Tony. Tony would end up introducing me to just about every single vice I would develop. It started with alcohol. We'd take trips into the woods to drink 40's. He'd polish them off like water at such a young age. I would try to spill out half the 40 when nobody was looking so I wouldn't be labeled a pussy for not being able to finish it. Tony would often catch me spilling it out and make fun of me. On those strange days off from school like Columbus Day or Election Day we'd hang out at his house and watch Maury settle paternity disputes while he raided his parents' liquor cabinet. He'd take a few shots and fill them back up with water.

Another vice Tony introduced me to was cigarettes. May 5th 2001 my parents were going out to celebrate their non-existent Mexican heritage. I decided to celebrate as well and throw a house party against their wishes. We were sitting in my back-yard and Tony insisted I have a cigarette. "It's Cinco de Mayo, we can sit down and smoke cigarettes like gentlemen," he said. I smoked one, liked it, and had another. Under the logic that it was Cinco de Mayo, I managed to develop a lifelong habit that will probably shave ten to twenty years off my life. My mother managed to figure out that I threw a party despite our best efforts to clean up after ourselves. All throughout high school this would become a recurring theme. I think I got away with throwing a party once. We'd clean the place up top to bottom and she'd find a girl's hair in my bed or something else that seemed next to impossible for the human eye to see. Tony dubbed my mom "the CIA agent" for her efficiency at catching me.

Our sense of mischief knew no bounds. On Halloween it wasn't enough to simply throw eggs at cars and houses. We'd devise elaborate pranks. We called a pizza delivery to a random address. It took a lot of patience but we waited an entire hour in the bushes across the street from the house we chose for the delivery. The driver made his way to the door and rang the doorbell. Once the homeowner answered the door, we peppered the car, the house, the driver and the homeowner with an entire carton of eggs. We'd come up with some of the best prank phone calls as well. We'd call the parents of people we didn't like pretending to be an "Officer Donnelly" and convince them that their child had been named as an accomplice in a major crime investigation. "I'm flabbergasted! Not my Charlie!" one poor mother shouted. Her choice of the word flabbergasted had us laughing for hours.

One of my other lifelong friends I met in high school was Carmine. We did not begin as friends though. Matter of fact we despised each other. He was one of those people who did not find my humor funny at all. I wasn't big enough to play sports and the only way I knew how to get attention was through my humor. I would often overdo it in a rather annoying fashion, by trying too hard. Carmine did not take to it. One day on the bus ride home from school he threw me to the floor and pressed his foot onto my head. The grooves from the bus floor were imprinted into my face. To me, at that time, he represented everything I resented. He was part of the coolest of cool kids. I was merely an honorary member. I was allowed to live in the castle but I was simply the court jester. He, on the other hand, was a prince. Quite literally too. He was the school president, an honor student, and he was quite efficient at getting laid. He was the type of guy who slept with every candidate for prom queen. A girl pretended her grandmother died just to get out of going to the prom with me.

Two - September 11th, 2001

September 11th 2001, my innocence was stolen from me. But not for the reasons you would probably suspect. The terrorist attacks, thank God, did not claim the lives of any of my friends or family. There was a boy named Carlos who sat behind me in Mr. Portnoy's religion class. For weeks he had been offering me Vicodin. Back then I was still pretty timid when it came to drugs. I tried pot and drank a few times but I didn't really take to it like everyone else seemed to at first. I was curious to try Vicodin, just not in school. Tony had mentioned trying and loving it a few times. I wasn't sure what it would do to me and Saint Joseph by the Sea high school was pretty strict. If the dean of discipline were to see me walking through those halls looking a little loopy, he would've surely thrown the book at me. But my curiosity was piqued, mostly because Eminem wouldn't shut up about Vicodin. He was the modern-day Elvis Presley to us growing up. His first album even had an animated Vicodin pill on the disc.

The reason I decided to finally try it on September 11th was because throughout Mr. Portnoy's class, the principal was calling out about twenty names at a clip on the loudspeaker to inform those students that their parents were there to come get them. Mr. Portnoy couldn't get a word in because it was happening so frequently. After a whileI realized we weren't learning anything so I might as well try it. I turned to Carlos and had him throw me a couple of those pills.

Now in the midst of all this, we're trying to figure out what was going on. Back then our cell phones didn't have internet access and the service in that school was atrocious, so text messaging the outside world was out of the question as well. We were at the mercy of the faculty and they weren't telling us a goddamn thing. Mr. Portnoy eventually offered us some insight. "Don't believe anything you hear until you have the facts," he said. He knew something but he was holding out on us. I guess I couldn't blame him. How would you handle telling a room full of teenagers that our country, our own city, is under attack? Nobody wants that duty. Now just as the Vicodin was starting to provide me with a sense of ease and comfort that I had never experienced before, my name was called on the loudspeaker.

I walked outside to see my mother in our neighbor Diane's car because my mother doesn't drive. "You know who did this shit? Rag heads that's who the fuck did this!" Diane screamed at my mother. I tried timidly asking what was going on but I was treated as a non-entity at first. Diane and my mother were too hysterical to pay me any mind. Diane's son, who was in the backseat with me, was no help. He just shrugged his shoulders at my confused facial expression. Finally, my mother said, "Listen, I want you to know that your father is safe ok? He was nowhere near any of this ok?" I nodded my head waiting to finally hear what was going on when she finally laid it on me. It was a lot to take in.

I was fourteen years old and had no previous conception of such atrocities happening so close to home. My father's safety was all I needed to hear to relax and enjoy the euphoria I felt from the Vicodin. Plus, I got the day off from school. Hearing I would have off from school the next day as well made it even better. 9/11 was on a Tuesday but my friends and I spent that evening out and about like it was a Friday night. We went to get beer from our usual vendor, who had no problem selling to minors, but now he was getting beaten up in front of his store because of his middle eastern ethnicity. Poor guy might've been a Hindu from India as opposed to a Muslim but, on that day, it didn't matter. He was the wrong shade of brown on 9/11. If he wasn't our beer guy, punk kids like me and my friends probably would've cheered on the beating. I think that's the key to ending racism right there, just sell beer to children of another race and they'll grow up not caring about your skin color or religious adherence.

There wasn't any political correctness on that day. I'm not sure if Islamophobia was a word before that day but I certainly never heard it before then. On that day there wasn't anything wrong with Islamophobia. Matter of fact, it was encouraged. The generations before mine all spoke of the Kennedy assassination like it was a major cataclysmic event that everyone was affected by. I would imagine 9/11 was just like that but on steroids. We could see the smoke all the way from Staten Island. I was too young and drugged up to understand the magnitude of what was going on. All I knew was that I had found a pill that completely washed away my fears, anxieties, and insecurities. For the first time in my life I didn't feel maladjusted, I felt well-adjusted.

Three - High School Years

There was a short kid named Mike who lived on the same street as Tony and me. The three of us became a trio of sorts. Mike's parents had the biggest house of all of us and they were also the least strict. A lot of our friends, including myself, lost their virginity in that house. When his parents went on vacation it was like an event. We'd throw the best house parties of our adolescence there. Mike could be a little eccentric at times and we'd bump heads a lot but we were more or less inseparable in those days. We spent countless nights having little slumber parties playing Grand Theft Auto 3. Tony would steal a taxi and imitate Uncle Ralph, our favorite local cab driver who we'd have buy us beer. Now Mike, as I said, was a bit eccentric. At that time, N Sync was the hottest boy band around. Guys my age all secretly loved N Sync but none of us would actually admit it. Mike was very open about it. Most of us were too insecure about our masculinity to admit to such a guilty pleasure. Our teenaged angst just wouldn't allow it. N Sync was playing in the Meadowlands and Mike secured us tickets and a limousine. Tony, Mike, a bunch of girls, this guy Luke, and I were going to the concert in style. A couple of days before the concert, Tony and I bought suitable attire for the concert. We went to a clothing store called Image in the Staten Island mall and they had these brand-new baby blue French Connection United Kingdom t-shirts that simply said, "FCUK IT." Naturally we both had to buy one. "I'm wearing this to the N Sync concert so you better wear something else," Tony demanded. "You're off your bird if you think I'm not wearing this to the N Sync concert," I barked back at him. "It's bad enough we look and act alike, we're gonna wear the same T-shirt now?" he asked. "I don't give a fuck bro I'm rocking this to N Sync," I responded.

We all met at Mike's house for the limo. Tony aired his grievances with the shirt I chose to wear, of course, and then the pregame drinking commenced. I had dabbled briefly with some drugs and alcohol by that time but I was still quite an amateur. If I drank, I drank. If I smoked weed, I smoked weed. I didn't go mixing the two. I could barely handle one or the other. Our friend Luke was already a seasoned abuser. He was also a pot dealer and insisted I smoke weed with him. I tried to tell him I didn't want to but he twisted my arm. "Bro just throw $5 on this blunt, I can't make the girls pay and I gotta make my bill otherwise my dealer is gonna fuck me up," he said. I'm not sure how the weed game goes nowadays, seeing as how it's legal in some states and decriminalized in others. In those days it was still a lucrative enterprise for delinquent kids. Most of the kids selling it would get an ounce credited to them. Then they would sell gram sized bags and pay back their wholesale dealer. "Make my bill," was the lingo used to describe making enough money to pay off that debt. I felt badly for Luke and certainly didn't want to see him get beaten up. I reluctantly agreed to smoke some weed. By the time the limo started moving, I'd already drank an ungodly amount of vodka. A few minutes after hitting the blunt a few times, I ended up puking projectile vomit into the ice bucket. It's funny how you start an evening putting on a baby blue "FCUK IT" t-shirt, an obnoxious amount of hair gel, and an abundance of cologne with the hopeful anticipation that you'll get to make out with a girl but instead end up face down in a bucket drowning in your own puke. I spent the rest of the car ride to the Meadowlands with my face glued to that bucket.

The limo driver was appalled when he realized one of the underage kids he let drink in his limo might've given himself alcohol poisoning. My friends referred to me as Sack back then, short for Sacchi. The limo driver thought they were calling me Zack. As I lay face down in that ice bucket, unable to move from the spins, he would yell out, "Come on Zack you got to get up!" Tony kept laughing hysterically every time he referred to me as Zack and would chime in, "Yea Zack why don't you get up?" I started laughing and, in between vomit sprees, I'd plead with Tony, "Stop! Please don't make me laugh!" I managed to suck it up enough to get into the stadium. However, once we were inside, I immediately had to scurry to the bathroom and puke some more. Tony stayed with me while everyone else went to their seats. Security caught wind of me puking. They had to bring me out of the bathroom in a wheelchair. They wheeled me to this hospital of sorts within the stadium. I was terrified they were going to call my parents but they had mercy on me. They let me sleep it off for a couple of hours and even let me go enjoy the tail end of the show once I sobered up a bit. I made it back just in time to see Nelly perform with them for his remix version of the song, "Girlfriend." Nelly provided some street cred to the song so it was perfectly reasonable to admit you loved that particular N Sync song. Naturally, I danced and sang along exerting the little energy I had left.

That spring Tony and I went to the Saint Joseph by the Sea dance. This dance had an open invitation for incoming freshmen who were still in the 8th grade. One of those 8th graders was this beautiful girl named Micaela. She was adorably short with brown hair and brown eyes. Precisely my type. A friend of hers approached me and said, "My friend thinks you're cute and wants to hook up." Hooking up at that age was simply a make out session, which I was more than happy to oblige. There was no romance to this because the hook up was facilitated by a third party and I didn't know the first thing about romance at that time. We simply went into a dark corner of the gymnasium and kissed. I tried talking to her afterwards but she ran off with her friends. I figured I'd just wait for her to arrive at school in the fall.

September came around and I found Micaela graciously strutting through the hallways in her sexy Catholic school uniform. The abundance of thigh meat you get to see thanks to those uniforms is unfathomable. It makes sense that the Catholic church is flooded with pedophiles. I worked up the nerve to ask Micaela out one night but I was too socially awkward with girls to recapture the glory of that fateful moment in the gymnasium. I took her to see "My Big Fat Greek Wedding." At one point I tried pulling the old stretch and yawn trick and then slowly wrapped one of my arms around her. That was about as brazen of a move as I was willing to pull. I wanted to kiss her, but I was terrified she'd reject me and I'd have to live the rest of my high school existence in exile. In no time at all, another guy came along and stole her heart. He ended up dating her for a few years and my tender young heart was broken.

At another one of my infamous house parties, I invited these guys Gary and Jay, amongst others. Gary and Jay were a year older than me. In high school that feels like lifetimes apart. I loved hanging out with them mostly because they were in good with a door man at a place that served alcohol to underage kids. You had to at least have a fake ID which I hadn't yet been able to procure. Thanks to Gary and Jay, I was able to get in. At my house party, Jay and two girls wandered into my parents' bedroom and stole a bunch of her jewelry. Some of the pieces they stole had significant sentimental value. Jay already developed a nice drug habit so he needed it to score drugs. Word was out around school that my mother had called the police. The detective assigned to the case questioned everyone who was at the party. After the initial interrogations, my doorbell rang around 10 pm one evening. Nobody was at the door but there was a brown paper bag left on the ground filled with some of my mother's jewelry. I felt relieved for a moment until she said, "This isn't good enough, where's the rest of it?" Daphne, a friend of the two girls involved, found out who the culprits were and told me who it was. I relayed this to my mother and she said, "I want you to call this Jay and tell him to come here with the rest, otherwise he'll be arrested." I did as I was told. I was in enough trouble as it was. Jay came by, and unbeknownst to me, the detective was waiting for him. My mother didn't want to tell me he was getting arrested because she feared if she did, I might tip him off and she wouldn't get her jewelry back.

When he came by, I couldn't face him. As angry as I was at him for betraying my friendship, I didn't want to see him hauled off to jail. I stayed in the kitchen and listened to everything going on in the living room. He apologized to my mother. They spoke back and forth for a bit and then the detective came out of another room like Chris Hansen to cuff him.

I started to really experiment with harder drugs with my friends Petey and Billy. Petey was short with spikey black hair and eyes that appeared to be oriental, even though he's Italian. Billy, on the other hand, was tall and looked exactly like Edward Norton. I cliqued well with Petey at first because he was energetic like me. He had ADHD. Now because the logical remedy for ADHD is speed, Petey had an enormous supply of Ritalin that he never used. I first met Billy when he came by Petey's house to buy some from him. I had no idea Petey was sitting on a gold mine of unused drugs so I tried some myself. We all smoked a blunt in Petey's car and, once we were good and stoned, Petey had to run into his house to use the bathroom. Billy and I, strung out on Ritalin and weed, started exploring Petey's car a bit. We opened his glove box to find VHS tapes of G.I. Joe and He-Man cartoons. We sat there and laughed for about fifteen minutes at how adorable Petey was, still watching cartoons.

The real party didn't begin for me until senior year of high school. Scholastic ambition was progressively taking a back seat to my bad behavior. I was kicked out of Saint Joseph by the Sea high school for bad grades, so I finished high school at the local public school, Tottenville. Thanks to Catholic schools having a stricter curriculum, I only had to be in school until 11:30 am once I was in Tottenville high school. This opened the door for plenty of drug use. I was able to have some sense of restraint for a whilebut, with such a lack of responsibility and plenty of time on my hands, I was beginning my descent into madness. I started working as a bus boy at a place called Nonna's and every once in a while, tables would keep me there pretty late. Most of the time I was out fairly early so I would smoke pot after work with my friends until about two in the morning and just tell my parents I was working late.

The first time I let drugs come in the way of a personal relationship was with this girl Celina. I met her through a mutual friend but I knew who she was long before I met her. Brown shoulder length curly hair, a gorgeous face, and she was shorter than me which was not easy to come by in those days. No exaggeration, I considered her to be the most beautiful girl in the school. Completely out of my league. Or so I thought. A couple days after meeting her I received a phone call from her. She was neighbors with the girl I lost my virginity to.

"Oh, I'm just sitting here with Lory fighting with her because we both want you," Celina said. I couldn't believe it. I spent the first three and a half years of high school getting rejected by almost every girl I encountered and the one I coveted most was making it easy for me. We immediately started dating and it was like heaven on Earth for me at first. I'd go to her house and we'd snuggle together watching television. I got to see Janet Jackson flash her breast at the Super Bowl while spooning with Celina. I was on top of the world.

As Celina and I continued dating, she became progressively intolerant of me smoking weed. For years I would've given anything to land a girl like Celina. Now I couldn't even give up a stupid habit like smoking weed. I would try to smoke it covertly and just deny I had done it but she knew every time. The stench and the bloodshot eyes could not be contained by cologne and Visine. Not to mention I would act differently when I was high. So, she dumped me. My first real heartache. But to make matters worse Petey, of all people, ended up making out with her a week after the stake was pressed through my heart. I was devastated. I refused to talk to him for a whilebut one day he showed up with some weed and all was forgotten. This would become a recurring theme between us. He'd betray me in some way, I'd avoid him for awhile, and he'd come back to me apologetic and holding weed.

My pot intake was getting to be so expensive that there was no way I could afford it on a bus boy's salary. So, I started selling pot for one of the waiters at work. Once I started selling it, I was able to either break even or turn a profit from smoking. Selling roughly an ounce of pot per week is certainly no big feat but I was a 17-year-old kid and I felt like I was Pablo Escobar. Now because I was a promising young drug dealer, I had to be tough.

At least that's the way I perceived it. Young men always seem to measure each other's worth by how tough they are in a fight and how many girls they sleep with. The people I was hanging out with and selling weed to were jackals. If they sensed even the slightest bit of weakness, they would take advantage. Every pothead walking around always wanted you to credit them a bag and if you seemed like enough of a sucker, they just wouldn't pay you back. You had to be able to assertively use the "I gotta make my bill" excuse.

Four – College Years

Most people I knew went away to some fancy university but because I stopped caring about academics, I ended up going to Berkeley College. Berkeley College is a small school in Woodbridge, New Jersey. It's kind of like Devry University. I called it the drive thru college because it was so small and the driveway into the building was reminiscent of a fast food drive thru. It was an absolutely pathetic excuse for a college and I needed to get out of there as soon as possible. I developed a newfound love for cocaine use which rendered me paranoid because I would be up all night in my parents' house scared to death they'd come downstairs and see me bouncing off the walls. I made sure I got good grades in school just so I could transfer to a university and do drugs in peace. To add insult to injury, Petey followed me at Berkeley College for my second semester. I didn't want him to do it because I knew he would become a distraction. I wanted to do well enough to transfer but it was tricky with Petey urging me to smoke weed with him in the parking lot in between classes.

In the meantime, I was stuck at home and bussing tables at Nonna's. At work, I met a girl named Cassandra. She was a few years younger with dirty blonde hair and a sexy face. I sensed a mutual attraction and offered her a ride home. We made out for a little bit but our budding romance was cut short because I soon found out that she was already dating this guy Mitch. Mitch and I never really had a relationship. He was, however, close friends with one of my close friends. I decided to back off for the time being. He eventually found out about it though and called me to ask if something happened between Cassandra and I. I told him the truth. "Yes, I hooked up with her but I had no idea she had a boyfriend," I told him. He seemed to take it well and he also seemed to respect my honesty.

One night after work I was smoking some weed with Petey and our friend Danny. I was still selling weed so I had about an ounce stashed under the seats. Once we were stoned, Petey started annoying me as he usually did. Our argument turned into him playfully hitting me from the backseat. It was distracting my driving so I threw some friendly fire back at him. In the midst of all this horseplay, I accidentally blew a stop sign while a police car was parked there patiently waiting for someone like me. I was terrified. The car reeked of weed. The ounce was hiding within the cushion of the passenger seat. I tried making my way up the uphill ramp to the highway. They didn't come for me right away so I tried to accelerate out of there as fast as possible. Then I saw them come flying behind me in my rearview mirror with the sirens blaring. I impulsively made the poor decision of trying to run for it. The Outerbridge crossing into New Jersey was just up ahead and I thought if I could just make it into Jersey and out of their jurisdiction, I could ditch the car and then re-port it stolen. "Please bro stop the car I have a girlfriend," Petey cried from the backseat. "Bro what the fuck are you doing? Pull the car over!" chimed in Danny.

I managed to make it over the bridge and thought I was in the clear. Then a Port Authority police car came screeching in front of us and blocked the entire road. There was no way out. In the blink of an eye they were outside the car with their guns drawn. My hands immediately shot into the air. There was an older cop and a younger one with sleeves of tattoos. The older one approached my side of the car. He yelled, "I smell pot!" and then dragged me out of the car by force. When he searched my body, he squeezed my ball bag like it owed him money. He kept throwing me around the car as he tried to find the weed that he knew was in there. Seeing as how my white privilege was null and void for taking them on a high-speed chase, I needed another strategy to calm the guy down.

"Look I know I'm fucked and I'm not getting out of this but just for the sake of maybe easing this tension, my cousin is a Port Authority cop," I told them. The younger tattooed one asked, "Oh yea, who's your cousin?" I timidly said, "Tommy Brancato." To which he shouted, "No way! There's no fucking way that's your cousin!" He was upset because he really wanted to throw me a beating and take me to jail. But this guy turned out to be best friends with my cousin. Tensions certainly cooled after that and they had me sit back in my car. After a few minutes of deliberation, the older cop looked at me and said, "Hang on a second, I fucking know you." As soon as he said that I remembered him. We once had a nice long heartfelt conversation in front of Nonna's. Graduation was rapidly approaching at that time so we had a long talk about coming of age and life in general.

Eventually they called over the regular NYPD cops I originally outran. They had to get permission to cross the state line. The older cop told them I worked at Nonna's. They wrote me out four tickets and said, "We should be taking you to jail tonight but instead we're just going to hit you with these tickets. If you would've just pulled over and said you work at Nonna's we would not have given you a ticket at all." They had me call my father because if they weren't going to get a collar, they wanted to make sure I suffered some sense of consequence. Once he arrived, I was free to go.

I got paranoid about the ounce of weed. I figured my parents would comb through the car and find it. I tried to give it to Danny because I didn't trust Petey. Danny had troubles of his own with the law though so he didn't feel comfortable holding it. About a year prior, Danny and a few other kids put this guy Sal into a coma. They jumped him at the Annadale train station and smashed a glass Snapple bottle over his head. His sentencing was still pending and he didn't want to get himself into more trouble.

"I'll hang onto it," Petey eagerly insisted. I scoffed at him but I had no choice. I handed him the bag. Petey took it and smoked it all without so much as giving me a dime. I didn't talk to him for a whileafter pulling that stunt. A few months after the high-speed chase incident, I went to pay for the tickets at the courthouse. There was no record of the tickets. My cousin got them squashed for me. That really worked out for me because the gravity of the offenses would've gotten my license suspended for sure. "Don't think we're letting you joy ride in your car just because your cousin got you out of this," my mother said. But time heals all wounds and sooner or later they let me have it back.

Tony, always good for introducing me to things that aren't good for me, showed me a movie called "Fear and Loathing in Las Vegas." Thanks to this film I read the book as well and plenty of other books by Hunter S. Thompson. By then I was steadily accelerating my drug use but there was always some sense of restraint for fear that I might overdose and die. After watching that movie and seeing how much drugs those guys were doing, I realized the human body was capable of taking in a lot more than I previously thought. I also realized that Hunter S. Thompson was a writer who basically got stoned and wrote books. I didn't know you could write books about that stuff. I thought I had found my calling in life. Who knows? I applied to Hofstra University in Long Island and was accepted. I made my major print journalism because I wanted to get high, write, and get paid for it just like him.

At work, one of the older waiters, Anthony, overheard me talking about Hunter S. Thompson and my desire to one day be a writer. "You have to see One Flew Over the Cuckoo's Nest," he said. I never saw him get excited about anything before. He was usually morose and grumpy but he seemed overjoyed to tell me about this movie. One night after work, there was a showing of it at the Saint George Theatre. We smoked a few joints on the way there but couldn't find the place. Back then, there was no GPS navigation. We had to print out directions from this website MapQuest.com. We followed the directions but couldn't figure out where the theater was. Eventually I saw the movie on my own and read the book. What was truly exciting was reading about the author, Ken Kesey. From there I read all about the 60's counterculture. The hallucinogenic drug use and all the music and literature that came from that era fascinated me. I was completely spellbound by the turbulence of those times. Vietnam, the Kennedy assassination, Woodstock, Charles Manson, Timothy Leary, the Beatles, Bob Dylan, Martin Luther King Jr, Richard Nixon, the Black Panthers, and the Civil Rights Movement. It all seemed like a much better time to be alive.

Hofstra wouldn't begin for another semester. In the meantime, I was still going to Berkeley to finish my last semester. A bad magic mushroom trip led to a major life change. Petey, our friend Nick, and I decided to take mushrooms and cruise the Garden State Parkway listening to gangster rap. This was smack in the middle of the golden age of hip hop, so naturally, my delinquent friends and I were a bunch of white kids who listened to way too much rap music and were a little confused about our ethnic makeup to one degree or another. The trip turned into a nightmare. I had this epiphany that listening to too much gangster rap music and dressing like we were from the ghetto was not good for our collective consciousness. The nightmare trip turned more and more hellish and I was cramped up sitting in the backseat of Petey's Trans Am. I desperately needed a bathroom. I insisted he pull over at a rest stop. When we got there, I couldn't see straight. "Where the fuck is the bathroom?" I asked Nick. "Bro, it's right there!" he exclaimed as he pointed right behind me. I suffered a horrifying hallucination as he pointed. In the movie "The Matrix", there comes a point where Neo can see everything in the Matrix code. It's all green numbers like a binary computer code. I saw Nick the same way Neo saw the agents except the numbers that took up his shape were brown instead of green. I went into the bathroom to puke and urinate for what seemed like eternity. After that we headed home. I felt much better after throwing up so I figured I could walk into my house without my parents realizing I was in another dimension. I was wrong. They asked me a question and all that came out was gibberish. They pressed me and I came clean. At least a little bit. I simply admitted to smoking weed. They didn't need to know that a few grams of magic mushrooms had been ingested on top of it.

They had a long talk with me and went pretty easy on me. They could see I was remorseful. After their pep talk my Dad said, "Now go downstairs and play with your brother." Johnny was still just a child then. When I got to the basement, he was in his pajamas looking cute, innocent, and happy to see me. He was anxious to play a video game with me and I happily obliged. I was becoming increasingly scared that my drug use would set a bad example for my brother. A few nights prior to that, after smoking weed, I stopped at a deli to get a peach Snapple so I could alleviate the cottonmouth. I kept a picture of Johnny in my wallet. As I was paying for the Snapple, I had left the wallet on the counter with the picture of him just glaring at me. I swear to God that picture started vibrating and riddling me with guilt. He was completely unaware of the wicked world that would soon creep into his life as it had mine.

Seeing the error of my ways through that horrifying magic mushroom trip, I completely renounced rap music and started listening to classic rock. Do you have any idea how glorious it is to be a young kid taking drugs and exploring the entire catalogs of Led Zeppelin, the Doors, the Beatles, and the Rolling Stones for the first time? My friends all thought I went off the deep end. Maybe I had but I was loving every second of it. I still love all of that music but when you hear it stoned at an impressionable age for the first time it just pierces through to the depths of your soul and fires you out of a cannon. Mike and Tony were pretty heavy into classic rock already. They would ridicule me for constantly listening to rap. I finally had them educate me on what was good and what wasn't. I'd obsessively devour entire catalogs of all the best bands.

One day, the seed was planted with my little brother that I had feared so much. Petey was my barber so I went to see him to cut Johnny's and my hair. "Take a look at the stickiest of the icky," Petey said as he showed Johnny a bag of weed. "What the fuck is wrong with you?" I asked him. "What? He's going to see it sooner or later," Petey replied. Johnny's world was still video games and cartoons. I knew one day he'd encounter it but I really didn't need Petey showing him that his older brother and his friends were burnouts. I could see the look in Johnny's eyes. He was taken with it. I wanted to kill Petey. First there was him making out with Celina. Then I had him hitting me from the backseat which led to that high-speed chase. Then he smoked an ounce of my weed without paying for it. Then he shows my kid brother weed.

On another occasion, Petey brought three guys intent on beating me up to my house. Some girl cheated on my friend Brenden so I called her a slut. Her cousin Barry and his entourage demanded Petey drive them to my house. Spineless bastard that he is, he did it. He could've pretended he didn't know where I lived. Even if they already knew that Petey knew where I lived, you take the beating like a man. There's not a chance in hell I'm driving three people to beat up a friend of mine. You'd have to throw me the beating. Why I felt the need to overlook his countless offenses, I'll never know.

Once I made my transfer to Hofstra, I wouldn't have to worry about Petey for awhile. I would come home on the weekends for work but I avoided him at all costs. Danny finally got sentenced and had to spend a year and a half at some juvenile detention center upstate. He was 18 years old by then but the crime happened when he was sixteen so he lucked out. At school, my drug use escalated. I had no regard for the fact that my parents were spending a fortune on my education. All I wanted to do was copious amounts of drugs with a few friends from Staten Island going to school at C.W. Post. C.W. Post was another college fifteen minutes away from Hofstra. At that time, opioids were simply used as a way for us to come down off cocaine comfortably. Hey, we needed to get some fucking sleep here and there. We had no idea that we were taking a softer version of heroin and could potentially get addicted. None of us saw it coming or even realized it was happening until it was too late. I was becoming such a mess I couldn't even make it to class half the time. The other half I was so twisted or jittery from the night before that I'd resort to my usual class clown antics just to pass the time. A simple homework assignment would completely baffle me.

The drugs were making me increasingly irritable. In the past, I'd had some degree of patience. At work, I could take orders from my boss and not put up a fuss. One night though I took something far more personally than I should've. The owner didn't want us to throw out unused butter packets. We had to take them out of the bowl and put them back in the refrigerator. When you brought the bowl with the butter in it to the dishwasher, you usually had a million other items in your hand because you had just bussed a table. A lot of us, out of laziness, would simply throw the unused butter packets out to save time. There were always a million other things to do so I would find myself in an anxiety driven rush.

The owner saw me throw out unused butter packets so he yelled, "Now put your hands in that garbage and pull them out!" That garbage was disgusting. It was filled with about a hundred pounds of half eaten food. "Are you serious?" I asked. "Yes, I'm serious, that'll teach you to mess with my money," he replied. I felt like that was completely degrading. To expect me to put my hand in that filth as a lesson to not mess with his money pissed me off. The way I saw it was I was busting my ass for him bussing tables for $70 a night. I was too young to appreciate or understand where he was coming from. Was it the kindest way to handle the situation? Probably not. But I was throwing away something that didn't belong to me. I didn't say anything to anyone, I just walked out of there and never went back.

The one guy from C.W. Post whom I did most of my cocaine with was Jeff. I'd neglect my scholastic responsibilities to go there and sniff blow all night with him. One night, when we had a break from school, we were at a Manhattan bar near the South Street Seaport hanging out with some friends. There were a few Marines on leave hanging out at the bar and one of them told me they had cocaine for sale. Jeff and I had about $20 between us. We contemplated the prospect of snorting a small bag in one shot. We knew we'd get one line each and we'd be crawling the walls desperate for more. We made a decision based on emotion rather than logic and spent the rest of our money on a $20 bag. After snorting that bag we were, as expected, desperate for more. We used to call that overwhelming craving for more cocaine once you got started "the binge." I came up with a brilliant idea. I asked Jeff to ask the girl he was dating to give him a couple dollars. We collectively came up with $7 in singles. All I needed was a few bills. My plan was to ask for a $50 bag, hand him the $7, make a run for it, and have Jeff "accidentally" bump into whichever one of the Marines ran after me first. That way I could get a head start. Jeff figured I'd be caught and get the shit kicked out of me for sure. These guys were not only twice my size but they were fucking Marines. But he wanted that bag of coke as much as I did and he wanted to see if I could actually pull it off.

I walked up to the Marines and said, "Yo man, that bag was fire. Can I get a fifty bag?" One of them was more than willing to oblige. I made the hand off and then I made my run for it. On the way out I said to Jeff, "Here we go!" Jeff did his best to check the frontrunner but it only bought me a minor head start. One guy was hot on my tail. The street we were running on went downhill. Between the downward trajectory and my adrenaline, this guy didn't stand a chance. I sprinted as if my life depended on it because in many ways it did. If that guy would've caught me his friends were coming to back him up and throw me a savage beating. At one point, he tried to cut me off around a bus stop with a glass partition. I saw what he was trying to do and pumped the brakes on him. We locked eyes for a moment and I could see I won right then and there. He was out of gas and I had plenty to go. He wasn't chasing after me in another direction. I called Jeff and had him pick me up under the Brooklyn Bridge. The guy's friends at the bar told Jeff that not only was he a Marine, but he was also a varsity track star back in high school. When he went back into the bar he was breathing heavily saying, "That was the fastest kid alive!" Needless to say, our ride home was glorious. Snorting lines from a stolen bag was way more satisfying than the ones I paid for.

On another fateful evening, we all went to a bar called Dublin's, close to our campuses. It was the weekend so Tony came to visit us and the plan was to head home to Staten Island after.

How we drove drunk all the way to Staten Island from Long Island at that age and didn't crash is beyond me. Before the ride home though I got into a bar fight. I bumped into somebody, as you tend to do in those crowded bars, and he said, "Watch where you're going!" I responded by punching him in the face. He went down but his friend, who had a ring on, hit me just above my eyebrow where the skin is fleshy. I started gushing blood. The bouncers kicked us out and I had Tony take me home. When I looked in the mirror, I could see the bone above my eye. I went straight to Staten Island University hospital on Seguine Avenue. I had my parents meet me there because I had no idea what the protocol was for health insurance and things of that nature. I had to fill out a questionnaire in the waiting room.

One of the questions was, "Have you taken illegal drugs in the past month?" I had taken plenty. Cocaine, ecstasy, Percocet, marijuana, you name it. I was so young, naïve, and paranoid that I thought if I didn't answer that question honestly, they might give me a medicine that would react poorly with the drugs in my system and I would die. I decided to come clean and proceeded to give my parents an entire speech about how I was a full-blown drug abuser but I had seen the error of my ways and was going to stop. I ended my heartfelt speech with, "You got your son back." I meant it too. If you gave me a lie detector test, I would've passed it. They bought it and I was high again the next day.

As much as I loved doing cocaine with Jeff, I was secretly envious of him. He was pretty smooth with girls whereas I was a nincompoop. I attested it to his immense stature. He was naturally built big and strong. He had an Italian schnoz bigger than my own and looked like Triple H from the WWE with short black hair. It was all innocent jealousy until it turned into a deep envy swelling through my bloodstream. Mike was dating this girl Tatiana. Tatiana was best friends with Micaela. This was the same Micaela I met at the Saint Joseph by the Sea dance and then struck out with years prior. Micaela and her boyfriend broke up and I had a chance to get back the glory I should've had the night I took her to see, "My Big Fat Greek Wedding." My plan was railroaded by Jeff though. One night, Mike invited me to hang out on a boat that Tatiana's parents owned. It was docked at the Great Kills marina. Mike told me Micaela would be there, so naturally, I was thrilled with anticipation. I figured a little booze, a little weed, and a nice romantic double date vibe would work out perfectly in my favor. When I got there, Jeff was there too and he had his arm wrapped snugly around her. I was a fifth wheel and I left abruptly with a pit in my stomach. As I walked off the docks to my car, I noticed Jeff and Mike were parked right next to each other. They both had the same exact Ford Mustang only in different colors. They were enjoying a romantic evening while I was driving away in a Toyota to go home and masturbate. I thought that if only my parents bought me a Mustang like them then I'd be the one down there. It never occurred to me that maybe my social skills and emotional intelligence were a little underdeveloped. My whole life adults had told me I was smart. I developed an ego because of it that assumed I was right about everything and, whenever I was wrong, it was because of extenuating circumstances. It had to be the Mustang.

I eventually landed another restaurant job on Staten Island. Now that I was over the age of 18, I could be a waiter. It was an Italian chain restaurant called Carrabba's. It didn't take too long for that place to go out of business because we have authentic Italian restaurants on Staten Island. It was practically sacrilege that I was working there. While it was open, I managed to get enough staff hooked on opioids so I could get mine for free. I would walk around with a food order pad writing down how many pills each server needed and then I'd go and meet my dealer in the parking lot. I'd get a deal for buying in bulk, charge the servers full price, and snort the extra ones.

Things didn't quite pan out between Jeff and Micaela. Since I was hanging out with Mike a lot and his girlfriend Tatiana was Micaela's best friend, I was able to get a lot of face time in. Things slowly progressed and we started dating. She started smoking pot regularly which suited me just fine. I never really gave the Beatles a fair shake until we started dating. She was quite a fan so I started getting into them. We'd spend countless nights just sitting in my car, smoking pot, and listening to "Sgt. Pepper's Lonely Hearts Club Band" or "Abbey Road." It is moments like those that make youth innocent and beautiful. The problem was I wasn't all that innocent.

One night, Micaela and I were out at a bar with some friends and I was on a Percocet and Xanax cocktail. I had to keep it a secret from Micaela because although she enjoyed smoking weed,

I doubt she would've approved of my blossoming pill addiction. Every time I went outside to smoke a cigarette, I would irritate the bouncer because I was loud and obnoxious. "Look pal you got to keep it down I got neighbors," he shouted. But then I'd run into another friend I hadn't seen in some time and greet him with enthusiasm. The bouncer eventually had enough and kicked me out. I asked if I could run inside just to get my girlfriend but he wasn't having it. I defiantly charged past him with the intention of grabbing Micaela and then leaving on my own terms. He saw things differently and grabbed me by the neck just before I could reach her. He dragged me outside by my throat and threw me onto a telephone pole outside insisting that I leave. After he let go of my throat, I seized an opportunity to crack his jaw with a right hook. This bouncer was twice my size so I had enough sense to try and make a run for it after throwing that punch. Another bouncer cut me off and tackled me to the ground. They held me down until the police arrived. Micaela started crying and pleaded with them to let me go. The bouncer shook his head and said, "Honestly, I would let him go, BUT I'M FUCKING BLEEDING! I'M FUCKING BLEEDING!" I laughed at his anguish and tried to throw away my fake ID before the police arrived because it was now a felony to possess one in New York City. The bouncer caught me trying to ditch it and made sure the arresting officers got it. Luckily for me, my old religion teacher, Mr. Portnoy, had become a police officer and was at the precinct. "Sacchi just be quiet, don't give anybody any trouble, and I'll get the fake ID charge dropped," he said. "Mr. Portnoy, I'm gonna pass the fuck out, nobody's gonna hear a peep out of me," I replied. Unfortunately, the attempted assault charge stuck.

Insanity was piling up. I failed out of Hofstra after two semesters because half the time I didn't even show up and when I did, I was completely strung out. I got fired from my server job at Carrabba's because they caught me drinking on the job. Little did they know that alcohol was the last thing they should've been concerned with. To top it all off Micaela dumped me because she too had had enough. I was spiraling out of control and I was completely unaware of it at that time. I thought I was just unlucky and naively assumed everything would work itself out in the end.

I never took heartbreak well back then. It wasn't often that I had a girl's attention. I don't think I was scared of losing them so much as I was scared of being alone. One night at T.G.I. Friday's I got into an argument with her over the breakup. I wasn't mature enough to handle it and ended up spitting in her face. Then there was another instance where I coincidentally ran into her at a house party. I was in desperate need of money for cocaine so I stole one of her friend's purses. After I left the party, she called me and shouted, "Sacchi, I swear to God you better bring that fucking purse back!" I knew that nobody saw me take it; she was simply clever enough to know that it was probably me. "I swear to God Micaela I have no idea what you're talking about," I said as I snorted a line from my recently acquired bag of cocaine.

My pill addiction progressed from Vicodin and Percocet to the Rolls Royce of opioids, Oxycodone. Otherwise known by the south shore of Staten Island's mental defectives as blues. The opioid epidemic was about to begin and I was one of its very first victims. I needed at least five to get through the day but could, and would, consume plenty more if and when my funds allowed for it. Stealing purses from house parties ran its course so I would steal my mother's jewelry from time to time. One night I ran into Jay, the guy who stole my mother's jewelry years prior. He expected me to start some kind of trouble with him. I shook his hand and said, "I want you to know it's cool. I'm no better than you are." How could I stay mad at someone when I was guilty of the same exact crime? By that time, I was only mad at myself for stealing from my mother. I certainly couldn't carry a grudge with him. I got a new job at a Charlie Brown's Steakhouse on the North Shore because I was running out of jewelry to steal. She was bound to catch on sooner or later. I wasn't well received by the Charlie Brown's staff as I had been at other places. They had a lot of corporate rules that I refused to follow so I was constantly in trouble.

One night after work, Danny invited me to come meet him and a few other friends in Manhattan. He'd recently been re-leased from jail and his older brother Tyler was heavy into 9/11 conspiracy theories. A lot of celebrities were heavily involved in this whole "9/11 was an inside job" movement. One of them was a guitar player from some prominent 80's band. He invited all his conspiracy theorist buddies to come to the grand opening of his sushi restaurant in Soho. Tyler got us on the guest list. Our Albanian friend Kabib came along as well.

Kabib was a bit of a savage like me whereas Danny and Tyler weren't strung out. That time spent in jail was probably a blessing in disguise for Danny because every last one of his friends became addicted to pills when he was away. For the sake of not embarrassing Tyler, Kabib and I were on our best behavior. Around midnight Danny and Tyler wanted to call it a night. Kabib and I followed suit. Just as we were stepping into my car, I looked at Kabib and said, "Kabib, it's only midnight, we're in the middle of Manhattan, and we're on the guest list for a party that has an open bar. What the fuck are we doing going home right now?" Kabib laughed and said, "I don't know I was just following you guys." We decided to go back inside and now that Tyler was gone, we stopped behaving ourselves. We incessantly asked everyone who we thought could score drugs, if they could score drugs.

We found what we were looking for from this Vietnamese man in a suit. He told us to follow him. He had his sister with him and a middle-aged white guy with long blonde hair. The Vietnamese man extended his hand in an attempt to hail a cab. "There's no need for that, my car's right here," I told him. We all got into my car and he directed me to Queens. We ended up somewhere near Shea Stadium at a karaoke place. The Vietnamese man rented a private room which is usually used for karaoke but we were strictly there to do drugs. He ran downstairs and came back with an ice bucket full of Heinekens, ecstasy pills, and jars full of ketamine. I was like a kid on Christmas morning.

I swallowed one ecstasy pill and chopped up another one to snort it. Everybody else simply swallowed theirs. As I was snorting that ecstasy pill, I kept having the guy's sister hit me off with bumps of ketamine. Eventually she tried to cut me off. I looked up at her confused and said, "No don't stop keep em coming!" I looked to my left to see Kabib laughing hysterically. "The fuck is so funny?" I asked him. "Bro, she's worried you're gonna die!" he said. "Oh, don't worry about it I got an unprecedented tolerance. You can dump anything down the hatch," I said to put her mind at ease.

Once the ecstasy got me to the point where I wouldn't shut up, I found out that the middle-aged white guy with us was Woody Harrelson's brother Brett. I happen to be a huge Woody Harrelson fan so it was beyond a pleasure to get high on psychedelic drugs with his brother. At some point paranoia set in. "Hey it's not our birthday. Why the fuck is this guy shoveling drugs down our throats for free?" I whispered to Brett. "I don't know man but something tells me we're getting out of here alive," he assured me. I trusted Brett on this one and relaxed a little. Kabib and I went outside to smoke a cigarette and collect our thoughts. We laughed for a few minutes in complete and utter amazement at the situation we found ourselves in. I remembered that morning my mother told me that George Carlin, my favorite comedian, was going to be signing autographs at the F.Y.E. (For Your Entertainment) store in Manhattan that next morning. I suggested to Kabib that we go there. "Look if we go home, we're gonna be wide awake staring at the four walls for hours," I said. "Whatever you want to do Sacchi, you're driving," he replied. Before we left, the Vietnamese man showed us his tattoos. The entire back half of his body was covered. It was reminiscent of the serial killer in the movie "The Red Dragon."

As we said our goodbyes, Brett said, "Say hello to George for me." I felt so cool that I was given little messages to extend from a celebrity's brother to another celebrity. Kabib and I watched the sun come up on our way back into Manhattan. We were the first ones in line to see George. A store clerk insisted I had to buy a George Carlin standup comedy DVD if I wanted to meet George. I tried to talk my way out of it because I needed every dollar I had for blues. The clerk wasn't playing games though. I bought the cheapest one available, went into the bathroom to snort the last blue I had on me to calm my nerves, and waited for George's arrival. "Well you guys have certainly been party-ing all night," said George as the security guard let us through. I eagerly relayed the message from Brett to George but I could see that George had no idea what I was talking about.#

Five – B.B King's

That summer my family took a vacation to Los Angeles. This was the first time I experienced opioid withdrawal. We were gone for a week and I was too scared to sneak any on the plane. I had no idea I would even go into withdrawal. I found out the hard way when I couldn't get a wink of sleep the first couple of nights. I did manage to sneak some LSD on the plane because it's extraordinarily easy to sneak a piece of paper onto a plane. A few days into the trip I dropped some acid and went into Hollywood looking for alcohol and a good time. Sunset Boulevard is hands down the best place on the planet for a drug fueled rock and roll fanatic. I visited the Whiskey a Go Go, the Viper Room, the Key Club, and the Rainbow Bar and Grill. At the Rainbow, I got to meet Lemmy Kilmister of Motorhead. Lemmy was glued to a bar stool drinking a double jack and coke and chain-smoking Marlboro reds while playing a trivia game. He was stuck on a question that I knew the answer to. The question was, "What animal has an orgasm that lasts 30 minutes?" I shouted, "Lemmy, it's a pig!" When it was made apparent on the screen that I had steered him in the right direction, he gave me an appreciative nod. That's the most you could hope for from a grouchy rock star like Lemmy.

In the midst of my LSD fueled Hollywood adventure, I met a man who shared a penchant for opioids like me. He couldn't procure me any but we hit it off. "You should come meet me next month. I helped put together Rock -n- Roll Fantasy Camp and we're putting on a show at B.B. King's in Times Square." Rock -n- Roll Fantasy Camp is this camp where regular people get music lessons and then get to perform with household name rock stars. There wasn't anybody I liked there for the show. Paul Stanley from Kiss, and a few of the campers, were the headlining act and I fucking despise Kiss. Any band that has a no drug policy is clearly in it for the wrong reasons. Their merchandising ought to tell you that they were strictly business and not trying to produce any sort of artistic expression. They're basically a cartoon caricature of a real metal band. I prefer my rock stars to be addicted to heroin with borderline psychotic personalities and spandex. Ace Frehley was the only member of that band who truly exhibited any true sense of the rock and roll culture and he was cast out because of it.

My friend from Los Angeles introduced me to B.B. King's manager, Gerry. He looked exactly like Mike from the show Breaking Bad. I asked him for a job waiting tables and he hired me. I couldn't quit Charlie Brown's fast enough. I hated that place. They had secret shoppers who would pretend to be regular customers. They would report back to corporate if you didn't suggest an appetizer and a dessert. If I'm weeded with ten different tables I'm not suggesting a goddamn thing. "What can I get you?" is the only thing I had to say.

Now I got to work at a rock and roll nightclub and a lot of the acts were some pretty cool household names. Pat Benatar, George Thorogood, ZZ Top, and Chuck Berry have all graced that stage. When Chuck Berry played, I told him I thought Michael J. Fox did a better job..

The first night working at B.B. Kings I met a kindred spirit. Some kid named Wade was making everybody laugh and I could tell he was my cup of tea. At first, I had a sneaking suspicion I might like him but then he started singing "Touch Me" by the Doors. Then I was certain I'd like him. I tried talking to him but he blew me off. I eventually grew on him though. Turned out he was bisexual but he was a very masculine dude and slept with more women than most straight guys I knew. He was also a full-blown alcoholic so he usually would say and do some hilarious things. Another guy whom I became close with was Chase. Both of them moved to New York to try and make it as actors. So did the rest of the staff for that matter. Most of them had no shot in hell at becoming actors. Their problem was their mothers told them they were so handsome that they could become a movie star. The problem was that most of them were ugly and they lacked style and personality. Except Wade and Chase. Those guys were mavericks. On one particular evening, Woody Allen strolled into B.B. King's to see some elderly comedian named Mort Sahl who was performing. They had me serve him because I was the only waiter there who wasn't an aspiring actor. They were worried one of the other guys were going to try and slip Woody their head shot. He came with his Asian step-daughter turned wife. Maybe it's me but the vibe there creeped me out a bit. Man's still a legend in my eyes though. I still love listening to Michael Jackson so what should I care about him marrying his step daughter.

Working there was a lot of fun. If only I was smart enough to realize that my pill addiction was hindering my ability to have as much fun as I could've had. I was barely conscious half the time. One night they pulled all the tables except the booths out and opened the dance floor for a rave style DJ. There were drugs all over the place. At one point, I passed one of my tables and noticed they were sniffing lines of some powdery substance. They freaked out when I walked up to them because they thought they were in trouble. I told them, "Relax, only thing is you got to give me a line if you're going to do that at my table." They didn't hesitate to help me out. I didn't even ask them what I was snorting. I spent that entire shift asking customers what drugs they had for sale. I bought and consumed a plethora of drugs that night. When it came time for the servers to cash out, I discovered that I spent so much money on drugs that I had to borrow money from a coworker to pay the house. This waiter whom I called Seth Rogen, because he looked and acted exactly like Seth Rogen, was gracious enough to help me out.

On one occasion I got to meet a pretty awesome performer. He was a really old English guy named Terry Reid. I talked to him backstage about music and we hit it off. His singing sounded raspy like Rod Stewart. I did some homework on him when I got home. Turns out Jimmy Page of Led Zeppelin actually asked this guy to be the lead singer of Led Zeppelin before Robert Plant.

He turned Jimmy Page down because he had already committed to going on tour to open for The Rolling Stones. Apparently, Terry Reid told Jimmy Page that the only way he'd join his band was if he was compensated for missing the Stones tour and he insisted that Jimmy would have to be the one to break the bad news to Keith Richards. Needless to say, Terry didn't join but he was nice enough to point Jimmy Page in Robert Plant's direction. He never reached the same heights of stardom as Led Zeppelin but he's got a lot of respect in the Rock -n- Roll community.

One of the few rockers from the 21st century that I love is Jack White. Not too long after meeting Terry Reid, Jack White dropped his second album with his second band the Raconteurs. I was ecstatic to discover they remade "Rich Kid's Blues" on that album which was one of Terry Reid's songs.

One of the managers was a tall and fat Italian guy from Staten Island named Drew. You would think we'd get along but we were usually at each other's throats. I would constantly break his balls but my sales numbers were always high so I'd usually get away with it. The Proclaimers performed one night when Drew was the manager on duty. They were these twin brothers who sang "I'm Gonna Be (500 Miles)". When they finally did the one hit song that everybody was waiting for, I asked Drew, "Hey did you used to sing this to your hot dates back in the 80's?" One night I was working and worried about something we needed that was 86'd. 86 is restaurant lingo for we ran out of it. I offered to run to the store to get some and in a condescending tone he asked, "Why would you run to the store for that?" I was trying to be helpful and had the business' best interests in mind so it angered me that he was such a wise ass about it. "Oh, I don't know Drew. Maybe to make sure the customers are taken care of is why I would run to the store for that," I replied. Then the unexpected happened. He lunged at me and started choking me. A few of the cooks broke it up and I got spoken to by the owner and general manager. They swept the dirt under the rug because I was a phenomenal worker. I just had to kiss and make up with Drew.

I celebrated my 21st birthday while working at B.B. King's. It didn't even matter to me that I could legally drink. Aside from owning a fake ID for years, I didn't care too much for alcohol anymore. All of my money was going straight up my nose. Fortunately for me, B.B. King's was a gold mine. I made enough money legitimately but I found creative ways of squeezing extra money out. If someone on the dance floor ordered a soda, I wouldn't ring it in and collect the entirety of the money if they paid with cash. Food and alcohol had to be rung up because the bartenders and cooks made all that but the servers had a soda machine to use. Nobody ever wanted to work the Sunday night metal shows because metal heads don't spend money. I would volunteer for this shift because I would just push soda on them. After bobbing their heads around for a couple of hours, a Pepsi starts to sound quite refreshing. On Saturday nights we took the dance floor tables out and had a hip-hop DJ come in. In order to get access to a booth table you had to get bottle service. A bottle of Grey Goose or Absolut was priced at $300 with an automatic $50 gratuity. Eventually I got smart and would bring in one bottle of Grey Goose from the liquor store so I could pocket the entire $350 for myself. But someone caught wind of it and ratted me out to the boss.

They didn't fire me for my insolence right away. They really didn't want to fire me because I was great at my job. However, my erratic behavior due to pill addiction started to compound with that liquor bottle incident. Eventually they fired me and Drew got to be the messenger. "I'm sorry Steve but I was told to tell you we have to let you go," he said. He said it humbly and was professional about it but I knew deep down he was enjoying himself. I made it like I didn't care at all because I wasn't going to let that fat fuck have the satisfaction of knowing that it hurt my feelings to be fired from there.

CHAPTER

Six – The Restaurant Bandit

Once I was fired from B.B. King's, the true despair began. I was earning at least two grand a week at B.B. King's. But after being fired for my liquor bottle scheme, I was left with no income, an expensive opioid habit to maintain, and by then I was so far gone that I was practically unemployable. I found another server job at a restaurant in the Meatpacking District and managed to get fired on the very first day. The girl training me was trying to tell me the way they wanted things done there and I wasn't having it. In my mind, they were inefficient ways of getting the job done. "No, you have to put them on the tray and then take them back to the kitchen," she said when I tried bussing glasses off a table with my hands the way I was taught. "Never mind all that bullshit, this way is faster," I replied. The girl whined to the manager about my complete disregard for their rules and I was sent home before the shift even ended.

On Monday nights, everyone would gather to watch Monday Night Football at the local T.G.I.Friday's. One night I was hurting for blues. Seeing as how I no longer had a job, it wasn't looking good for me. I was starting to have withdrawals and I was desperate. My friend Eddie was selling blues at that time and he found himself a nice corner stool at the bar. I asked for one on credit but there wasn't a chance in hell he was going to give me any on the arm. Then I ran into a group of girls I went to high school with. They were happy to see me so we caught up a bit. I cracked a few jokes as I tend to do and then they paid their bill in cash and said their goodbyes. I immediately scanned the room looking for staff members. There were none in sight. The place was packed but not a soul was paying attention to me or that table. Once those girls made it out the front door, I snatched the checkbook and grabbed Eddie. "Let's run to your car," I said. "I thought you were broke," he replied with a really confused expression on his face. "Yea well things change pal," I said to ease his troubled mind as I handed him $50 for three blues. Three for $50 was the industry standard going rate back in those days. I didn't realize it in that moment, but I had just stumbled upon an ingenious way to support my pill habit without having to get a job.

I contemplated that score in my head over and over because anytime I got over on someone it brought me such joy. Spending someone else's money was always way better than spending my own. I thought about doing it again. Just waiting for a table to pay their bill and walk away. Of course, it could take a while to find someone who leaves the table with a checkbook full of cash but it was certainly an idea to consider. After pondering this for a little while, it finally dawned on me. My experience in the restaurant business certainly helped facilitate this epiphany. Instead of waiting for someone to pay and walk away from the table, I could wear dress clothes reminiscent of a maitre d' and just take the cash as soon as they put it into the checkbook. First I would wait by the bar and have a drink or two. Once I've spotted someone paying a bill in cash, I would then approach the table. With the same sort of enthusiasm that a maitre d' would have, I'd ask, "How was everything tonight folks? Good, good. Do you need any change?" Whether they said yes or no was irrelevant. Either way I would steal the check. I would feel bad if they needed change because I was looking to rip off the restaurant instead of the customers but I didn't lose any sleep over it either. The customers were so convinced I really worked there that I didn't have to take it by force. They willingly handed me their money.

Now mind you, I would wear a dress shirt, slacks, and a tie. The tie was important on multiple levels. Aside from creating the illusion that I was a staff member, it would help me conceal the checkbook on my way out. Underneath the tie, I would leave one button in my dress shirt undone. That way, once I had the checkbook in my possession, I could slip it through my tucked in shirt. Now I could walk past the real staff members gracefully on my way out because there would be nothing in my hands. To the staff I was just another average person walking out of the place. I managed to perfect this method and for six months straight it was my job. Seven days a week I was robbing restaurants. I'd hit two or three a night and support my habit through stolen checks. I would need at least $120 a day to make my nut. $100 to buy six pills and the rest was for food, cigarettes, and transportation. Some days I made more, especially on weekends, but no matter what I always hit my mark. I didn't have a car at that time so I resorted to public transportation to get around the city. After crashing two cars my parents gave up on spoiling me with a third. All five boroughs were vulnerable to this scam of mine. If I could find a friend willing to drive to New Jersey for a few bucks, I would hit restaurants there as well.

Now at first, I did it primarily on Staten Island. Eventually I had to spread out though. I would only hit corporate chain restaurants, at least for the most part, because they were big in size which gave me room to operate. Another benefit to hitting a corporate restaurant is that they'd probably call the police instead of beating me to a pulp. Which also meant that I could probably wiggle my way out of their clutches before the police even got there seeing as how I'm a slippery son of a bitch. A waiter named Tucker from Applebee's isn't exactly going to be the kind of person who's capable of keeping hold of a drug crazed Stephen Sacchi. However, a Vito from Francesca's Italian Bistro or a Rocco from Cavallini's Brick Oven Pizza will beat my head in so bad that I'd wish I could just deal with the cops. The real brilliance of hitting a chain restaurant is that there's usually at least two managers on duty and I'm dressed as one. So, if and when the unsuspecting waiter is told by the customers at the table that the manager took the check, they would have to go and find two different people scattered around a giant restaurant before they figured out they'd been played.

Once I hit all the good restaurants on Staten Island, I took my talents to Manhattan. You could find a dozen different restaurants on one city block there. The first night there I hit Planet Hollywood in Times Square and pulled a $60 check in less than five minutes. Most times, I was walking around for a whilebefore I found an unsuspecting victim. That time it was like taking candy from a baby. After that, I went two doors down to ESPN Sports Zone not realizing that both restaurants are part of the same company. I couldn't find a check to steal in there so I left. As I was coming down the escalator from the dining room floor, I saw a husky security guard in a windbreaker jacket with a secret service agent style earpiece and a microphone in his collar. He was eyeballing me and then he said into his collar, "Yea I got him." As I came off the escalator he grabbed my arm and said, "Come with me." I acted puzzled at first but I knew he was trying to seek retribution for Planet Hollywood. I behaved very submissively at first but, once the opportune moment struck, I shifted my weight one way to gain momentum then shifted it back in his direction as I pushed him off of me. I began my run for it but two more security guards came out of left field and stood in front of the exit doors looking rugged and ready to take me down. I quickly scanned the room for another way out. There was another set of doors but they had a couple sets of velvet ropes in front of them giving the impression that the doors were locked. My only shot was that those doors weren't actually locked and they just weren't being used. I crawled under the ropes and pushed the door with hope and a prayer. Sure enough, voila! On the other side of that door was a crowded 42nd street and my freedom. I disappeared into Times Square and then into the subway system. I went downtown and found another restaurant to make up for the missed opportunity in ESPN Sports Zone. After that debacle I came up with a new rule. From that point on, I would never hit two places within close proximity of each other.

All the other corporate restaurants in Times Square soon fell victim to my scam. The only place in Times Square that came remotely close to catching me was the Red Lobster on 41st street. The dining room area was on the second floor and someone must've spotted me snatching the check because they radioed down to the hostess. As I was charging down the staircase, I saw this adorable young hostess get in front of the revolving doors in a defensive stance like she was a linebacker for the NFL. At this point in time, I was probably wanted for a litany of non-violent robberies. My first instinct was to simply smack the girl out of my way because there was no chance in hell I was going to jail. Luckily for Lawrence Taylor, I decided that I was raised better than that. Instead I just clipped her and carried her through the revolving doors with me. Her hands and feet were squirming across the glass as she screamed, "What are you doing?!" Once we were on the other side, I put her down and hopped in a cab. In hindsight it probably would've been less traumatic for the girl if I would've just hit her. For a moment there she probably thought she was being kidnapped.

Stealing from restaurants wasn't the only scam I had in my bag of tricks. I was also printing counterfeit money. They weren't exactly high-quality counterfeits though. I'd make copies of an old twenty with the computer scanner in my father's office. After that I'd use an exact-o-knife to cut them out. Then I would spill black coffee on them, flick cigarette ashes on them, and leave them outside overnight. You couldn't fool a bank teller with them, but some punk kid who sold blues wasn't going to figure it out until I was long gone. Especially if you're buying them at night. One night I was hanging out with Billy. Billy was one of my favorite people to get high with. He was an absolute animal like me but his girlfriend would keep him on a tight leash. The only times I got to hang out with him was when they were on a break or if he had a good enough excuse to slip away for a night. I had been consistently buying blues from this kid they called Ry-brow. His name was Ryan and he only had one eyebrow for some reason, hence Ry-brow. "You're buying blues from Ry-brow? That's the kid I beat up with the brass knuckles," Billy said. I remembered hearing the story. Ry-brow punched Billy with brass knuckles. Billy, despite being hit with those brass knuckles, proceeded to beat up Ry-brow. The cigarette that Billy was smoking during this fight never left his mouth. Not even when he took the brass knuckled punch to the face. Or so legend has it. "I didn't realize it was him. Let's hit him with the fake bills," I told Billy. Billy drove me to his apartment. The handoff went off without a hitch but he managed to get my home address from someone and he threatened to tell my parents I used counterfeit money to satisfy my pill addiction. Not that they didn't suspect this sort of behavior already but the thought of them having to hear all that from some drug dealer with one eyebrow was the last thing I needed. So, I robbed another restaurant so I could pay back what was owed to him. Once I handed him the money he hit me in the back of the head with a hammer. I ate the hit like a champ and just gave him a sinister look dead in his eyes. He was taken aback because he was expecting me to fall down. "Just get the fuck out of here," he said timidly. I went to the hospital and got stitched up. But not before having another dealer give me a few blues.

The best score I ever came across doing the restaurant trick was with Billy. I had him drive me to the Bonefish Grill in Woodbridge, New Jersey. I walked in and saw a party of ten people paying their bill in cash. I scanned the room for a staff member but there wasn't any in sight. I grabbed the check and headed towards a side door. It didn't open right away. Panic set in as I thought the customers must've realized that I didn't work there. I looked down to see that I just wasn't pushing the handle correctly and relief came over me. Billy came screeching up to me with his Jeep and we were on our way. There was $350 in that check alone. Billy and I celebrated by buying a bunch of blues, cocaine, and booze at Big Nose Kate's, the quintessential South Shore degenerate bar to go to at that time.

There eventually came a point where I had hit all the major targets in Manhattan. No small feat, believe me. So, I started hitting the other boroughs. Mostly Brooklyn, but Queens and the Bronx got their fair share of visits from me as well. One night in Brooklyn I had to break my rule of not hitting two places within close proximity of each other. I made the mistake of picking up a check with only $40 in it. I thought there was a lot more money inside. It was late on a Monday night so by the time I took a bus to another area of Brooklyn, they would either be closed or in the process of closing. It was do or die. I had to hit another restaurant in that shopping plaza. There were about five other chain restaurants in that plaza but I decided an Olive Garden, in Brooklyn no less, deserved to be robbed because an Olive Garden existing in Brooklyn is a flat-out crime against humanity. I walked in and found a sucker in no time. As I started running through the parking lot to find a cab, a huge black man in a suit started chasing after me. At first, I thought he must have been a manager from Olive Garden. But then I saw handcuffs in his hand and realized he was an undercover police officer hoping I'd hit another restaurant after the first restaurant called them. I thought I lost him after snaking through a few rows of parked cars. I jumped into a cab and screamed at the driver, "Take me to Bay Ridge!" A second later, the cop caught up to me. He opened the door and tried to pull me out. His mistake was that he was too aggressive. He tried to forcefully throw me to the floor instead of just holding on to me. The problem with that is I'm like a cheetah with freak of nature agility. I managed to use my hands to crawl away from him, hop up on my feet, and start running again. He did his best to keep up with me but he was too out of shape. As he struggled to breathe he screamed at me, "YOU"RE GOING TO JAIL!" I just yelled back, "NO I'M NOT!" Victory was mine. I was far too elusive for him. I snaked through more rows of parked cars until I found a bush to hide in across the street from the plaza.

Then I witnessed something a bit surreal. No less than twenty blue and white police cars roared into that parking lot with their sirens blaring. I was a wanted man. The NYPD was getting so many calls about me and coming up with nothing that the one time they came close to catching me they sent all the cavalry they could. I was pretty proud of myself seeing such a parade of cop cars. The NYPD wanted me with a passion. Little did they know I'd become more of a mystery to them than DB Cooper. Once the heat died down, I looked for a safe place to hang out and wait for a cab to pick me up. I wandered into a church of all places, which amused me because I was the most nihilistic atheist that ever stepped through those doors. They were having a bible study. I can't for the life of me remember what fabricated story I fed those people but they bought it and let me hangout until my cab arrived. "Would you care to join us for Bible study?" a man with a tucked in polo shirt asked me. I politely declined of course, seeing as how I couldn't have given the slightest fuck about their interpretation of the gospel. Once the cab arrived, I thanked them for their hospitality and went on my way.

In the midst of all this, my grandmother on my mother's side was in hospice care. Every week we'd go and visit her in Woodhaven, Queens. I kept seeing corporate restaurants all around that area that I'd never even thought of hitting before. My inner dialogue tried to talk myself out of it by saying, "If you finally get caught here, up the street from where your Grandmother is dying, Mom will disown you." But that voice was drowning in a sea of other voices telling me to not only do it, but assuring me that I'd get away with it. I hit that neighborhood two or three times and thank God, I didn't get caught.

When we visited my Grandmother at that hospice, I'd nod out at this little table they had in the courtyard. "He's just tired," my mother would assure our extended family members.

Once my grandmother passed we held the wake and funeral at the same funeral home we always used when someone on my mother's side passed. It was right up the street from the hospice she stayed in and the restaurants I stole from. By then I had already met the funeral director a handful of times. As he shook my hand hello he said, "Hey I'm sorry to keep seeing you under these circumstances." I challenged that statement in a playful manner. "You're the funeral director, aren't these the circumstances you're looking for? Be honest, if there was a serial killer in the neighborhood just throwing you consistent clientele wouldn't you secretly be happy about that?" I asked.

He laughed and tried to pretend he didn't want to see that sort of tragedy happen but I begged to differ. If I owned a funeral home, I'd mail anthrax to half the houses in the neighborhood.

For the first wake I felt too guilty to go in there high. I spent the entire day in withdrawal so I couldn't muster the strength to be social with anybody. My mother, unaware that I was in withdrawal, scolded me for being anti-social. "Quit sulking and mingle with your relatives a bit. Would you please?" she said. I nodded my head and went outside for another cigarette. The next day, I decided I needed blues if I was going to get through the second wake. That day I was quite the charmer. I was comfortably maintaining conversations with everyone. I might've even fooled a few distant relatives into thinking I was a respectable human being.

At the funeral mass, all my cousins wept. I felt like a sociopath. I couldn't cry. It's not that I didn't care for or love the woman. She was awesome. She taught me how to play poker and sang Kenny Rogers' "The Gambler" while she did it. Whenever Johnny and I went to her apartment to sleepover we'd wake up to a deluxe bacon breakfast. My parents only made me bacon on special occasions. The only meat I enjoyed as a child was bacon and they would deprive me of it. Then they wondered why I was so skinny.

There was something poisonous in my soul that ran deep. If you disappeared from my world I may be upset about it a bit but I could carry on. I always felt alone anyway so why should I fret if someone died or fell out of touch. I never felt like I fit in, with my family especially. With my friends I at least had some sort of common interests but my family was on a completely different wavelength than me. Even before addiction I felt out of place. Most family occasions the guys discussed things like football. I couldn't care less about football. I could root for the home team Giants but aside from the quarterback and maybe a wide receiver or two, I couldn't tell you who else was on the team. I certainly didn't know who the offensive linemen for the Packers were. I'd always hear a cousin or an uncle say something like, "Oh the Redskins got a great cornerback this year." I'd always feel guilty like maybe I should know these things.

After the funeral I went about my usual business. It had been brought to my attention that I was on the news and they gave me a moniker, "The Restaurant Bandit." I reveled in it. They had video surveillance of me stealing a checkbook and they were asking the public to assist in my capture. Fortunately for me, I'm a pretty likeable guy. The people who aren't too fond of me aren't exactly the type of people to take the time out of their day to help in a police investigation so the news broadcast failed to help facilitate my capture. I found out about it when I was walking through Annadale. I was passing a bar in that area when an old friend of mine from high school yelled out, "Hey Sacchi, you rob any restaurants in Hoboken lately?"

My stomach immediately went into knots because I had just hit two restaurants in Hoboken a week prior and I hadn't seen that guy in years. "How the fuck do you know about that?" I asked.

He explained that his father recorded the news story because he was laughing his ass off watching me steal the check. Apparently, what was even funnier than seeing his son's old friend make the news with his thievery, was seeing the restaurant owner's frustration about the theft. First, they interviewed the two women I stole the check from and then they cut to the owner shouting, "I hope the cops don't find him because I WANT TO FIND HIM!"

A close call came at an Applebee's in Sheepshead Bay, Brooklyn. I took the check and the real manager drove up to me with a waiter in his passenger seat. He pulled up as close to me as he could get and the waiter got out of the car to chase me on foot. I sneakily took the cash out of the checkbook and then threw the checkbook away yelling, "JUST TAKE IT!" to throw him off my trail. He took the bait and went to inspect the checkbook I threw across the street. In the meantime, I started jumping through backyards. Eventually, he caught up to me again and got pretty close to catching me. I found more fences to hop over into more backyards. Once I seemed to lose him again, I found my way into a hardware store. I let the heat die down in there for about a half hour and then made my way back to Staten Island.

One day I woke up with no cash and no blues to get my day started. I had been going through withdrawals all day. The physical strength and courage to trek into another borough was out of the question. On mornings when I was broke, I could usually play on my father's gullibility and convince him into giving me $20 for "food." But that ran its course. My mother, who's not so gullible, would chastise him for giving me money. I realized there was one Applebee's on Staten Island that I hadn't hit yet. I took the train over there and searched for a check. A wrench had been thrown into my plan though. This girl I knew named Jackie was sitting at a table and immediately called me over to her table. I made small talk with her for a bit and she left. The problem was that the entire staff saw me talking to her and the real manager seemed pretty friendly with her. If I stole a check, there was a chance they could contact her and get my identity. That would lead to me being held up against the fire for an entire string of robberies. Common sense told me to go home but the opioid withdrawal was having no part of it. My body was in excruciating pain and I was sweating on a freezing winter's evening. Withdrawal in cold weather makes your bones feel like they're going to crack and your skin is screaming at you that it is uncomfortable with the temperature. The only cure is a fix.

I found a table with four college kids and took their check. They figured out what I was doing and ran after me. Eventually only one of them was still chasing me. Even with the opioid withdrawal leaving my body a shell of its usual self, I was way too fast. Adrenaline kicked in and I made my way across Hylan Boulevard and into some of the dimly lit streets of New Dorp. Once the last kid standing succumbed to a loss of breath, I headed for the train station. But before I went to get my fix, I called Jackie. I fed her some bullshit story that I stole a check from some kids who robbed my brother. I instructed her to say that she had no idea who I was if anyone from Applebee's asked. "Just say I was some random guy trying to hit on you," I insisted. I prayed to God that that plan would work because I wasn't expecting it to. This was quite a normal girl who was completely oblivious to the wretched world of drug addiction and scoundrels such as myself. A few months later I ran into her again and she said the manager from Applebee's gave her number to a detective assigned to catching me.

"I thought it was weird that I had to talk to a detective over a $100 check but I gave him the story you told me to give him," she said.

I let out a sigh of relief and thanked her.

Eventually I had to stop stealing from restaurants. I had achieved too high a level of notoriety. I started seeing staff at restaurants huddle together and ask each other, "Is that him?" On a few occasions I was chased out before I could even attempt to steal a check. "Hey buddy could I talk to you for a second?" is never something I enjoyed hearing. I'd hightail it anytime I heard that. They had run another news story on the restaurant bandit.

This time my father saw it but his level of denial was unfathomable. "Ah had to be a guy that looks just like me," I told him. The stakes were too high now. For months I was catching them all with their pants down. Now the word was out. The risk to reward ratio had to be reassessed. $100 to $200 a check against answering for all of these crimes put together did not seem worth it.

I started working odd jobs but mostly I was just stealing my mother's jewelry again to get my fix. One afternoon I took some LSD and was about to go get some blues when my mother came into my room crying. She couldn't find the jewelry her mother had left her. All this time I thought I was only stealing pieces my mother wouldn't miss. When I realized I had pawned my dead grandmother's jewelry my stomach went into knots. I tried to deny my involvement but the LSD took over and I was flooded with guilt. I came clean to her. She was hysterical crying and going off about how I had stolen jewelry from my dead grandmother. At that point I started crying too and shouted, "I'm dying Mom!" I was killing myself slowly every day and I had no idea how to pull myself out of it. I didn't even think it was possible. I completely subscribed to the notion that I was going to be a slave to a tiny blue pill until it killed me. I never even heard of recovery or sobriety. I spent that entire day tripping on LSD and going through opioid withdrawals simultaneously which is a nightmare in and of itself. My plans to get blues were sidetracked due to my mother figuring out what I had been up to. To top it all off, I had to go through the shame and humiliation of walking into jewelry stores with my parents and explaining that I needed to buy back the jewelry.

The next day I was forced to go to Seguine detox. I sat in there for six days eating cookies, nodding out on methadone, and watching old VHS tapes. Once I got out, I was back to my old tricks again. I fought the urge to steal from my parents for as long as I could but sooner or later, they caught me again. I managed to talk my way out of being forced into a detox program again. A few years prior, I'd tried quitting smoking with what's known on Staten Island as Dr. Grasso's "click in the ear." This hippie quack doctor uses some electric device to shock pressure points on your ear. According to this man that someone decided to give a degree in medicine to, there's pressure points in your ear that can be shocked to settle the pain of physical withdrawal. It didn't work for smoking but I wasn't necessarily trying to quit opioids, I just wanted my parents off my back. Not to mention a cure for the withdrawals would've been nice. I called his office to see if they offered their services for drug addiction. The receptionist said yes and I convinced my mother that Dr. Grasso was the answer to all of my problems. At the time, I was very grateful to this man because I really didn't want to sit in a detox for a week.

Now in hindsight, I hope this man gets hit by a truck. Run your scam on smokers and revel in the fact that you've actually helped a few people by tricking them into a sort of placebo effect. But do not try and give addicts and alcoholics false hope. These ear clicks did nothing for my withdrawals. He had me come in for three sessions. By the third session I was beginning to get upset. I started interrogating him a bit about this mythical device he used. "Well it's a product of Eastern medicine, Western medicine doesn't really deal with concepts like pressure points," he said. That's hippie talk that translates to, "I'm a douchebag and this thing isn't backed up by any sort of science at all."

I stayed clean for about a week. I started drinking the following Friday and was high on blues before the night was over. I ran rampant for a little while but eventually I felt it was time to straighten my act out. Not completely of course. I went and got myself a prescription for Suboxone. Suboxone is the new Methadone. Methadone gets you high whereas Suboxone simply makes you feel normal. You do get a slight buzz though and your feelings and emotions are completely numb. However, you're much more coherent and you're definitely no longer prone to falling asleep at the dinner table. The biggest benefit to Suboxone is you're not desperately seeking every dollar you can get your hands on to get high with. One pill in the morning and your withdrawals are at bay for the entire day. I would do just about every other drug in the book but because of the Suboxone, I was no longer strung out 24-7. Now I could secure employment again, in a restaurant of course, and go about my business.

Seven – A Strange Interim

I got a job working at a new restaurant in Little Italy. However, this was very short lived. After work, I had a bus boy take me to midtown to one of his dealers for some ecstasy. I popped a couple and once I was feeling pretty euphoric, I decided to have some beer. Ecstasy had me feeling like God so I felt no need to conceal my beer properly. Usually when I drank in public, I had enough sense to put the booze in a coffee cup or a giant McDonald's soda cup. A cop noticed my brown paper bag filled with beer and tried to stop me. I decided to make a run for it so he wouldn't find the rest of the ecstasy pills I'd bought. I thought I lost him but eventually I got tackled on 42nd Street by a legion of cops and arrested. I spent the night in a holding cell tripping out on ecstasy. The next day I met with a public defender who explained that I was going to be sent to Riker's Island for five days. I was mortified. Five days on Riker's Island didn't seem fair to me at all. He told me I would have an opportunity to speak with the prosecutor before the hearing and I could try to convince her that I was worthy of a lighter punishment. I put my white privilege to work. I painted a picture of me being a sweet and innocent young man who occasionally dabbled in drugs.

She bought my sob story and sentenced me to a couple of anti-drug counseling sessions and I was free to go. I wasn't released until much later in the day which proved to be problematic. I was hours late for my shift at work. I rushed downtown as fast as I could to tell them I was arrested for driving on a suspended license but they knew I was nothing but trouble and fired me. The blood-soaked shirt I had on was a dead giveaway.

Now because I switched from Oxycodone to Suboxone, I was drinking pretty heavily. A week after that arrest, relatives from my mother's side of the family, the Irish side, were over so the refrigerator was stocked with beer. I managed to get myself inebriated. I decided to go to Manhattan to bother some of my former coworkers at B.B. King's. First, I would require an 8-ball of cocaine and more alcohol. Once my dealer came by with the coke, I stuffed my waist band with as many beers as I could fit from my parents' refrigerator. Once again, I felt no need to properly conceal my booze. By the time I got to the train, I was too wasted to care.

On the train there were two metal head kids with a Metallica t-shirt and a Megadeath t-shirt on. I felt the need to explain to them that Dave Mustaine was a jerkoff and that hair bands like Motley Crue had a lot more cock and balls. I saw a documentary that showed Dave Mustaine crying actual tears while talking to Lars Ulrich about getting kicked out of Metallica. There's no crying in metal. I then went on to explain that Nikki Sixx of Motley Crue shot heroin in his dick vein. Lars Ulrich is a four-foot tall twat who sued Napster. End of discussion. As you can see, I'm very passionate about rock stars that wear spandex. I could tell that some elderly woman on the train was mortified with my choice of words and behavior. She must've phoned the police when she got off at the Annadale station because, at the Great Kills station, this bald metro cop knew exactly where to find me. I'd had a run-in with that particular metro cop once before. When my little brother turned 17 he got a license and a car. He no longer needed his student metro card. He gave it to me so I could use it to get to and from work at B.B. King's in Manhattan and save a few bucks. That was until the bald-headed cop confiscated it.

My favorite metro cop proceeded to pull me off the train and told me to sit down. I tried making my way to a bench but then he yelled, "SIT DOWN!" I guess he didn't want me to have the comfort of an actual seat so I sat on the floor as he wished. Now remember, I'm sitting on an 8-ball of coke and I had been arrested a week prior for possession of ecstasy. If this metro cop were to get the cuffs on me, he'd find the coke and I would be going to Riker's Island for an extended stay. Much to my surprise though, he went to check the train car behind the one he found me in for more delinquents I suppose. I had no intention of going to jail that night so I ran off. I didn't realize his partner was blocking the other exit though. He waved at me condescendingly as if to say, "You've got nowhere to go." He didn't understand who he was dealing with. I wasn't going down without a fight. I quickly scanned my surroundings and plotted my escape. I threw two middle fingers at the cop who thought he was a comedian and made my move. I jumped down to the tracks and crawled under the train where two cars met. As I popped out on the other side, I started running and didn't look back. Don't ask me how I didn't manage to electrocute myself on the third rail in that condition.

After running for a little while I made my way into a wooded area. In between the train tracks and a big tall fence with barbed wire at the top was about 50 yards of trees, bushes, and thorny branches. I dived into the thorny branches without any regard for my well-being. I slashed myself up pretty good. It looked like I got into a wrestling match with Wolverine. Once I was deep enough into those woods, I decided to finally look behind me. The cops didn't see me come out of the other side of the train car. They assumed I was hiding under the train. I was in the woods watching them take flashlights to the bottom of the train yelling, "Who the fuck is this guy Houdini?" For an hour they looked for me under that car. I patiently waited and watched them. I had no problem sniffing my cocaine and laughing at them for an hour. Eventually they called off their search but I wasn't out of the woods yet. I was going to hop a fence into someone's backyard until I saw a cop car with a search light looking around.

I started walking along the train tracks towards the next station but knew I had to find a way out before I reached the station because they probably had more cops waiting there for me. The tracks ran parallel to an endless sea of barbed wire fences. The thought of putting my shirt over it and eating a few more slashes to my body was beginning to look like my only option. I came across an area where the fence came down low enough so I could jump over the barbed wire. It was a long way down to the floor on the other side but it was the best I could hope for.

I made the jump and sprained my ankle a bit on the fall. Once on the other side of that fence I found myself in a fenced off parking lot with a shopping plaza that was still under construction. Inside was a black man watching the place overnight. He looked confused and concerned about my arrival at first. I thoroughly explained everything to him as best I could considering how out of breath I was. He laughed and said, "Man you running from the police? Why ain't you say so?" Never underestimate a black man's deep-seated resentment of law enforcement. Not only did he let me hang out for awhile, he passed me some cheap Georgi vodka to sip on. I called a bunch of names in my phone book but most of my friends found me rather annoying by this point and avoided me like a plague.

My friend Mark was the only one willing to pick me up and get me out of there safely. Tony first introduced me to Mark. They worked together at a restaurant called Portobello Café. Mark is the only red-haired Italian I'm aware of and he comes off as an aggressive person but he's secretly one of the kindest people I know. Mark ended up gravitating towards our group of friends. Mostly because of his penchant for drugs.

Not only did he pick me up and take me to safety but he even brought a blue for me to sniff. I may have been on Suboxone, but after all that cocaine and adrenaline, I needed to calm down. It had been at least twelve hours since I took my Suboxone dose so it didn't interfere with my Oxycodone high. If you don't wait long enough after taking a Suboxone, it doesn't work.

By the time I got home I was a disaster. Taking my father's BMW out for a drive seemed like a good idea. I stole his keys and went for a joy ride. I had nowhere to go. I was just lonely and too strung out for sleep. I came back from my joy ride after the sun rose. My extended family slept over so they all had the pleasure of waking up to witness me pull into the driveway drunk and high with my father's car. My parents were livid. They told me I wasn't welcome in the house. "I don't care where you go!" my mother screamed at me.

My loneliness felt even worse and I had no idea what to do with myself. I thought it'd be a good idea to go to Tony's house to see him. Ever since Tony and I graduated to harder drugs we didn't hang out at each other's houses like we did when we were younger. Tony's parents had no idea what he was up to at that time. The last thing he needed was me coming around inebriated. But at around 9 am that morning I came ringing the doorbell. Tony was asleep. Only his parents were awake.

They knew I was annihilated. They asked about the scars I acquired from the thorny branches. I wasn't prepared for that kind of interrogation. I couldn't tell them the actual story so my deeply disturbed brain came up with a story about stopping a rape from happening by tackling the culprit into some thorny branches. I thought if I made myself look like a hero, the seas would part for me.

"The devil's got ahold of you Stephen," said Tony's mother. Tony's mother is deeply religious. I'm not sure if there's an actual devil to attest my insanity to but there certainly was some evil entity in complete control of my mind and body. Tony's father drove me home and I pleaded with my parents to just let me inside to get some sleep. They reluctantly agreed.

I really wanted to work with Mark and Tony at Portobello. They seemed to have fun working together. I went over there to look for a job but I was completely strung out so the manager simply said, "We're actually not hiring right now." There was a lounge singer there that night singing Frank Sinatra and Tony Bennett songs. Tony, Mark, and I went outside to smoke a cigarette. "You know I prank called that singer one time," Tony said. Tony made up a character named Tony Dellarico for prank phone calls. The character, Tony Dellarico, was an aging mobster from Brooklyn with a raspy voice. When he called the lounge singer he said, "Listen I want you to do a wedding for my brother, my dear dear brother. It's gonna be one of those new age weddings. My brother's a finnochio. In plain English. What can you do? I was wondering if you'd sing at the wedding wearing one of those rainbow vests and a top hat with the American flag."

Finnochio is Italian slang for homosexual. "The guy went along at first but eventually he just started yelling who the fuck is this?" Tony added. As I was laughing, Mark took a stroll across the street to the gas station to play his lucky numbers in quick draw. He came back across the street visibly agitated. He scoffed and said, "My exact numbers came out on the draw just before I got to play. Unreal."

Halloween that year there was a party at this girl Megan's house. Mitch, Cassandra's ex-boyfriend, was there. He wanted cocaine and I was the only one at that party with a coke connection. He hated me for fooling around with Cassandra years prior even though I think I was relatively gentlemanly about it. He had our mutual friend Phil ask me to get some coke because he didn't have the spine to ask me himself. I agreed of course, knowing my dealer would hook me up and I could take a lot out of the bag for myself.

Mitch took the ride and Phil drove. I kept hearing passive aggressive snide comments from the backseat. Eventually I snapped. I turned to Mitch and asked, "Is there something you want to say to me?"

He finally told me how he really felt and it erupted into a fight. Phil was terrified of crashing. Every time Mitch tried to attack me, I would just punch him right back to the back seat. Once he realized I was getting the better of him, he decided to throw my hat out the window. Then he tried kicking me so I took his shoe off and threw that out the window. Poor bastard had to go home with one shoe.

Now around this time I was taking a lot of psychedelic drugs like LSD, mushrooms, and ecstasy. I really thought I had found the answer to all my problems. If I could just do THOSE drugs and not opioids, it would all be ok. It didn't seem like a problem that I was tripping out and trying to discuss my delusional ideas about existential philosophy and nihilism on a Tuesday night when the rest of my friends were just trying to relax with a couple of beers. A lot of grandiose ideas went flashing through my mind but none of them came to fruition. I was reading a lot of true crime books at the time, mostly on serial killers and gangsters, and had it in my head that I was going to move to Hollywood, adapt them into screenplays, and ride off into the sunset. Somehow in this drug-crazed state of consciousness I managed to sell my father on this insane idea and convinced him to send me to a small film school in Los Angeles. I don't know how he bought into that idea. Perhaps he didn't buy into it at all. Maybe he was just so sick of the tension in his house that he would've done anything to get me out of there. My mother still hadn't forgiven me for stealing her and Nana's jewelry so I was just a black hole sucking all of the light out of that house.

A few days after Thanksgiving, my mother found some ecstasy pills shaped like Bart Simpson's head. I'd bought them so I could wander the streets of Manhattan tripping out on Thanksgiving Eve. "Mom those are candy," I insisted.

She licked it and could taste that it wasn't candy. "You son of a bitch! You were gonna let me eat that!" she screamed at me.

I started laughing because I thought it would've been hilarious to see my mother high on ecstasy. She started hitting me and the argument escalated further and further. I would simply shove her off but then she grabbed a wooden stick from the closet. After a few whacks to my head, I grabbed the stick and forcefully pushed her to the floor. Her head hit the corner of a wooden bannister and a puddle of blood leaked all over the floor. I only intended on getting her off me. When I saw that I hurt her I was mortified.

"I'm going to get your grandfather!" she yelled at me. My father was out on business so she couldn't get him to reprimand me. My grandfather was living in the basement apartment then. I couldn't face him after what just happened. I may have perceived it as an accident, but my grandfather was from the World War II generation. A drug addicted kid who pushes his own mother was the lowest of the low to him whether it was an accident or not. I did my best to wipe up the blood but there was so much of it. I got out of there before my grandfather came upstairs.

When I got home that evening, my little brother Johnny tackled me and started wailing on me. He was so disgusted with me that he wanted to seek revenge for Mom.

"Get him Johnny! Hit him!" my mother shouted from upstairs. I felt horrible. I had physically hurt my own mother, subsequently ended up in a fight with my little brother, and to top it all off my mother is cheering him on like it's the goddamn WWE. Johnny was getting bigger but not big enough to take me in a fair fight yet. I shoved him off, told my parents to go fuck themselves, and went to bed.

Eight – Los Angeles

I was dead set on turning over a new leaf. My plan was to wean myself down to a small crumb of Suboxone and then be rid of Suboxone completely. I wanted to be off opioids in general once I moved to Los Angeles. The first night there I caved. At least I tried to. I was out there asking every shady character in Hollywood if they knew where I could find opioids. Finally, I gave up and headed back to the valley where my new apartment was. Once I made it back to Reseda, I met two guys who had a line on some crystal meth. I was a seasoned user of uppers but we don't really have crystal meth on Staten Island. At least as far as I knew. Crystal meth shoots you out of a canon. You will not, under any circumstances, shut your mouth for even a millisecond. Cocaine will get you pretty chatty but not like crystal meth. One of the guys who put me onto crystal meth was named Rod. He'd become part of my little band of misfits out there. He introduced me to his dealer Ethan. Ethan was a one stop shop for crystal meth and the coveted Oxycontin 80 milligrams. That pill is like the Eucharist to an opioid addict.

Within two weeks I found a few kids willing to buy both crystal meth and oxy 80's often enough so that I could get my drugs for free or at rock bottom prices. Ethan and I got along great. We respected each other. I managed to garner his respect because who wouldn't love a funny guy with a New York accent who puts money in your pocket. He had mine because he had what I needed. But his Clockwork Orange tattoo and his blatant disregard for the three strikes law certainly helped. He had two strikes against him and he still sold drugs. In California you get a life sentence after three felonies. A life sentence in prison did not deter him from continuing his criminal enterprise one bit.

I was out in Los Angeles enrolled in film school. The school was tiny and hard to take seriously. I barely made it to class. I'd either be in opioid withdrawal or sleeping off a crystal meth binge. When I did make it to class I'd make a fool of myself. The apartment I was living in was contingent on being enrolled in the film school. They didn't have a dormitory so I stayed in an apartment complex the school used for housing a couple miles away. I failed my first semester and the next semester was going to be the end of my stay in Los Angeles. I didn't want to go back home. I absolutely loved partying in Hollywood. The only part of partying in Hollywood that I didn't enjoy was that the bars closed at 2 am and public transportation was closed between midnight and 4 am. The weather in Los Angeles is beautiful though and the people out on the street at those hours are usually quite fun. I never had a problem entertaining myself for two hours waiting to catch a ride back to the valley.

Since losing the apartment was looming over my head, I managed to find a Suboxone doctor in the valley so I wouldn't have to resort to being strung out or in withdrawal all the time. I thought maybe that would help me focus and go back to class.

Any chance of that was shattered once I met Nikki. I was walking to my apartment from the bus stop and saw her from a block away sitting on a bench. She was beautiful. She was radiating some sort of mythical energy. I could feel that there was a cosmic plan at play and it involved me and her. Now because I'm so smooth, I decided to pretend to be on my phone so I could flaunt my New York accent and let her come to me. The plan worked. She wrote a cute little letter. I couldn't make out what she wrote with her chicken scratch handwriting but it didn't matter. I got the idea. We got to talking until our conversation was interrupted by some guy who pulled up to us in a BMW.

"Well I got to go but I'd much rather hang out with you," she said.

A pit developed in my stomach. After all that, she was about to disappear with this guy. "Why don't you then?" I asked in a last-minute desperate attempt to keep her around.

She proceeded to tell the guy in the BMW to fuck off and I was instantly in love. He looked at me then back at her and peeled out. I took her straight to my room and fucked her. That move she pulled with the guy in the BMW turned me on so much that I skipped past all of the small talk.

Once we finished, I realized she was a bit loopy. "You ok? You seem a little out of it," I asked her.

"I took some Xanax," she answered. Before I was smitten, now I was in love.

"You got anymore?" I asked.

"Yea, but they're back at my house if you want them. You got a car?"

"No, but I think I can get us a ride. You live far?"

"About ten minutes down Reseda Boulevard."

I knew this guy Peyton who lived next door had a car and a penchant for Xanax. He was an opera singer. Pretty good too. He'd practice whenever he was in the shower and I must say I didn't hate his singing. I knocked on his door. "Hey man, you want some Xanax?" I asked him.

"Of course"

"Ok I met this girl who has them but they're at her house. If you give us a ride she'll throw you some."

He jumped at the opportunity. On the way there Nikki told us that she had a Rolls Royce. We both looked at each other thinking she was just high and talking gibberish. But when she went inside her house, I could see that there was indeed a Rolls Royce in her driveway. Albeit an old one but, still, she wasn't kidding. "This girl is some kind of fucking anomaly," I said to my soprano singing neighbor.

She came back out and we went back to my apartment. I took the Xanax she gave me and fucked her again until I passed out.

It turned out that Nikki was a former pornographic actress. At that time, San Fernando valley was the pornography capital of the world. This was before California passed legislation forcing porno actors to wear condoms which inevitably relocated the porno industry to the Earth's asshole, South Florida. Nobody wants to see latex when they're watching porno. We spent the first few days together taking copious amounts of drugs and having sex. She would wear a lot of makeup and look pretty hot as you would imagine a former porno actress strung out on drugs would. But I must say, without makeup, she was absolutely beautiful. She was the first girl I had ever been with that asked me to choke her during sex. I was aware of this phenomenon but had never actually experienced it. I chalked it up to sexual enlightenment rather than serious psychological issues.

Forty-eight hours and a mushroom trip later we were a certified couple who professed each other's undying love for one another. We were your typical Sid & Nancy type of couple.

Nikki had an abusive alcoholic father who, according to her, used to beat her and her mother Beth. They were from Columbus, Ohio originally, but her father was living in Long Island, New York. He had been diagnosed with cancer and was reaching out to try and make peace with Nikki before he croaked. I was about to go home to visit my family for a week and after knowing her just a week, I couldn't fathom being away from her for that long.

"You think I should go see him," she asked me.

I didn't give the slightest thought as to whether it was a good idea or not. I steered her into the direction of giving him a chance. This was all a ploy so I could meet her in New York. I didn't care about her deadbeat father's problems. The plan was to meet her father for a day and then we'd hang out with my family. His name was Elliot and he seemed nice enough but definitely had an eerie vibe to him. He took us out to a Mexican restaurant in Long Island. I was terrified of my picky eating habits embarrassing me in front of Elliot but I found crabmeat enchiladas on the menu and they were absolutely delicious. The three of us pounded down drinks at dinner. Nikki kept secretly handing me pills from her collection under the table and out of Elliot's view.

After dinner we went back to his house. In an attempt to appeal to the ginzo in me, Elliot referenced the movie "My Cousin Vinny." Elliot and I enjoyed a laugh together.

Nikki having never seen the movie asked, "What am I missing here?"

At the same time, Elliot and I asked, "You never saw My Cousin Vinny?" Elliot jumped at the opportunity to put it on. We drank a little more and then laid down to watch the movie. Nikki snuggled up next to me and we started rubbing up against each other in a bit of a sensual manner. It led to me rubbing her stomach a little bit.

Elliot grabbed me and said, "I think you'd be more comfortable sitting here." I was so drunk and stoned that I didn't even realize he might not enjoy seeing me that comfortable with his daughter. Maybe I just didn't even think he really cared, considering what I'd heard about him. I didn't think I was being overly inappropriate. I didn't have my hands under her clothes and certainly not in one of the honey pots. But I still respected his wishes and apologized, attributing it to the excess alcohol. The damage was done though.

Nikki snapped at him in my defense. "Who the fuck are you to tell anybody what they can and can't do to me?" she screamed at him. I tried my best to calm them both down. There was a pain in his face that made me feel a bit sorry for him. Elliot showed me to my bedroom separate from Nikki's.

The next morning my father came to pick us up. I told Elliot I'd speak to Nikki on his behalf. He nodded his head expressing gratitude but I could tell he wasn't holding his breath.

The ride back to Staten Island was brutal. It wasn't until she was in the car with my father that I started to realize just how mentally ill she was. Not that I minded too much. I was too stoned to realize how ridiculous she was being. I paraded around town with her because I wanted all my old friends to meet my new girlfriend. I was completely oblivious to the fact that she was out of her mind. She kept falling asleep. I was half in a bag myself but, unlike my new significant other, I wasn't hugging telephone poles for a catnap. My parents drove by and saw her asleep on said telephone pole. They confronted us but I talked my way out of it as I usually do. They suspected something was off but they always wanted to believe everything was fine which allowed me to get away with quite a bit.

While home I visited my old pal Danny and he said he'd be in Las Vegas in a couple weeks to visit our friend Dylan who had moved out there with his family a few years prior.

Once Nikki and I got back to Los Angeles, I did some re-search and discovered that a Greyhound bus from Los Angeles to Las Vegas was relatively cheap. I started to get prescribed Klonopin along with my Suboxone and Nikki was getting pre-scribed a small pharmacy. Somas, Xanax, Gabapentin, Vyvanse, Adderall, and the yellow Vicodin. We sold some pills to the var-ious delinquents I befriended, bought some ecstasy and LSD to add to our already solid drug collection for the trip, and made our way to Las Vegas.

On the bus ride, Nikki and I argued for the entirety of the trip. The argument was completely drug fueled so it wasn't based on any semblance of reality. I was such a disaster that I didn't realize how embarrassed I should've been.

Danny and Dylan used to smoke weed a lot and had dabbled with stronger stuff before but those two were not strung out. I had no idea that Nikki badgering me in front of them was prob-ably an enormous burden on what should've been a nice weekend for them. To top it all off I misplaced my license so I couldn't get into any of the clubs. Basically, I just had to take abuse from Nikki in front of my friends the whole weekend watching vacationers have fun from the sidelines. At first, I was pretty passive. Then I reached my boiling point when the four of us were hanging out in Danny's hotel room at the Planet Hol-lywood Hotel.

She kept abusing me verbally as she had been all weekend until finally I put her in her place. I yelled back at her in an ag-gressive manner that completely floored her. She had no rebuttal except to spit in my face. What happened next I have no excuse for and I'm certainly not proud of. I can factually say that this is something I would never do sober. But because I was strung out, getting spit in my face in front of my friends tipped me over the edge. I smacked her across the face, dragged her by her throat across the room, spit in her face, and asked her, "How do you like getting choked now?"

She ran down the hall while I hung back in the room. After talking shit with Danny and Dylan for a little while, I ran after her. We argued some more but I calmed her down and we took a Greyhound bus back to Los Angeles. Once we got home we settled into some sense of harmony again. In a lot of ways hitting her temporarily saved the relationship. She once bragged about me hitting her to somebody. "It was just like Ginger in the movie Casino," she said. I was disgusted when I heard that. I know being half a dago from New York satisfied some kind of fantasy for her after watching "Casino," "Goodfellas", and "The Sopranos" but I never thought it would manifest itself that way. It was almost as if she was saying, "Look how much he loves me, he loves me enough to hit me."

I had her under my thumb so I decided to move in with her and her mom. I completely gave up on film school. What the fuck was I going to do? Write a screenplay? I could barely write my name half the time.

Nikki slowly became increasingly volatile. She once showed me scars on her wrists from an attempted suicide. When you're sick in the head from constant drug use, you find that sort of red flag attractive in a strange way. That was until she'd exhibit extreme depression when she was stoned. She'd constantly talk about suicide and how she had no passion or sense of pleasure in life. I felt personally attacked.

"I don't bring you any joy?" I asked.

"You do but there's something inside of me that just doesn't let me completely enjoy it," she replied.

I couldn't comprehend that. Sure I had my share of depression but I wasn't completely void of pleasure. Most of the time I rather enjoyed myself despite the extreme consequences of my actions. I would take those on the chin and trudge forward.

One night she was in a dark mood and dramatically locked herself in the bathroom. It may have just been a cry for help but I busted that door down nonetheless. Those scars demonstrated that she was willing to take it that far. Most people unknowingly slit their wrists the wrong way. Her scars showed that she did it the right way.

Whenever our own drug stash was scarce, we had this long-haired hippie kid named Tucker who was a one stop shop for everything. Uppers, downers, opioids, hallucinogens, you name it this kid had it. He'd sell just about everything out of his apartment with his girlfriend. He was the perfect drug dealer at first but eventually he would start to irritate me. On many occasions we would ask for credit and even though I always squared up my debts with him, he would give us trouble about it. Tucker was shorter than Frodo in "Lord of the Rings." After pissing me off a few times I decided I was going to rob him. I planned it out and executed the plan perfectly. I owed him a few bucks so that was going to be my purpose for going to his apartment. I also brought a flashlight, a roll of duct tape, wore a Fila velour track-suit to illuminate the intimidating New York mobster vibe, and Nikki was going to use her switchblade.

"I'm going to hit Tucker over the head with the flashlight. My only concern is his girlfriend might scream and alert their ten-ants. Once I hit him over the head you take your switchblade, press it gently on her throat and tell her not to scream," I in-structed Nikki on our way over. When we walked into the apartment to pay back what we owed, the first thing Tucker asked was, "Hey, what's with the flashlight?"

"We're staying at my apartment tonight and the power is out over there," I replied. That part was actually true. The electricity and water were shut off because I stopped going to school so I wasn't technically supposed to stay there anymore. For all in-tents and purposes, I wasn't living there anymore. But nobody had moved into the place yet. Sometimes Nikki and I would get into a fight and I'd sneak in through the window to crash there for a night until she calmed down. After we addressed the flash-light, I handed Tucker the money. Nikki sat on the couch next to his girlfriend. Since he was counting the money he was looking downward. This was all part of my plan. Seeing as how I was go-ing to rob him, he wasn't keeping a penny of that money. I just wanted him looking downward so I could catch him off guard. As he was counting the cash I swung the flashlight into the back of his skull, sending him to the floor. Nikki then did as she was told and took her switchblade to the girlfriend's throat ensuring that she wouldn't scream. Once he was on the floor I tried to close his mouth shut with the roll of duct tape.

The poor kid was crying like a baby. "You don't have to tape me up I'm going to give you what you want," he said.

I paraded him around his apartment and collected all of his drugs. Once I had all the drugs he said, "Now just get the fuck out of here." He was holding the back of his head which began leaking a fair amount of blood.

"No, no, no I want to see the stack," I replied. He had a confused facial expression. "I want the stack of cash that you and every other drug dealer has lying around," I clarified.

He crawled to the floor to reach into the bottom drawer of a cabinet and handed me a stack of cash rolled in a rubber band. "At least let me keep my weed man," he insisted. I granted him that small mercy. Nikki had a prescription for weed anyway so there was no need to keep his.

Seeing how fragile and vulnerable he was made me feel a little badly for him at first. But then I reminded myself that he was a drug dealer. That sort of thing comes with the territory. Maybe he never considered something like that would happen to him in California's San Fernando Valley. Where I'm from, you better be ready for some action if you're going to sell drugs. On the way out of the apartment I grabbed the batteries from their cell phones so they couldn't dial 911 or some friends of theirs until Nikki and I reached a safe distance.

"You guys have some bad karma coming your way," the girlfriend said to me.

I let out a diabolical laugh. "What makes you think you haven't earned some bad karma yourself? What would I be doing here? You know what I mean?" I asked her.

She was right. I certainly had some bad karma coming my way for that stunt. Thing is, I expected the cold hand of karma to collect its debts from me at any given time. I had grown accustomed to it. They were caught completely off guard.

We caught a bus to my old apartment. When we combed through the score, it felt like the movie "Wonderland" when John Holmes' friends come back with everything they took from Eddie Nash. The score included roughly a quarter pound of magic mushrooms, a quarter ounce of cocaine, a handful of ecstasy pills, a miniature pharmacy stocked with Vicodin, Valium, and Dexedrine which is like Adderall only better. Plus, the stack of cash which amounted to about $500. Not a bad day at the office. Nikki and I got stoned and had animalistic sex. After that I invited some of the delinquents I knew around the building and hooked them all up with some of our goodies. Between the adrenaline from the robbery and all the drugs I shoveled down my throat, I began losing touch with reality.

A couple days later we went to sell some pills from the score to this kid Ryan. Ryan was high on a combo of PCP and crack, the two most disgusting drugs I can think of. There aren't too many drugs I don't enjoy but PCP and crack are both on that short list. We hung out at his apartment and were acting rambunctious when there was a knock on the door. It was the building's security guard. I had my bag full of drugs with me and Ryan insisted on hiding it in the bathroom for me. We apologized for the noise and the guard left without any trouble.

I went into the bathroom to grab my stuff and saw that Ryan had thrown about an ounce of the mushrooms into the toilet. His drug induced paranoia left him believing the knock on the door was way more of a threat to us than it really was. I was pretty angry but I let it go for the moment. The next day he came by my apartment. I was hanging out in there alone to get away from Nikki for a little while. I could see that he had sobered up a bit since I last saw him.

Before I could complain or say anything about the incident he said, "Don't worry on Friday I get paid and I'll make it right with you."

Friday came and he handed me $200 which seemed more than fair for an ounce of mushrooms. Especially when that ounce was stolen in the first place.

Somehow Ryan managed to get Nikki's mom Beth's phone number. He told her Nikki and I robbed him of his $200.

Beth was furious. "Who do you two think you are Bonnie & Clyde?" she asked us. This woman provided a roof for me rent free and Ryan is telling her I robbed him.

I grabbed Nikki and we went over to his apartment. I pulled the same trick with him as I did with Tucker. I handed him some cash so he would look down and count it. Then I whacked his head with a pole I took from Nikki's shoe rack. I grabbed my money back from his hands and continued whacking him with that pole.

Then he lunged at Nikki. I panicked, threw the pole away, and started wailing on him. Ryan lived on the second floor of the apartment building. The fight made its way across the room as I continued punching him. Ryan decided to try and climb out the window. I didn't want the kid to die or end up in a wheelchair so I tried pulling him back up but it was no use. He fell down to the ground so I scurried to get out of there. I saw his wallet on the way out and figured I might as well take that too.

Ryan managed to break his leg on the fall. Word got back to me that he was hobbling around on crutches. His father called me the next day. "Look I don't care about what's going on between you guys, I just want to get my son's wallet back. His license and other documents that he needs are in there," he said. He sounded sincere enough which convinced me that he wasn't going to have the cops waiting for me. I met him at a gas station and dropped off the wallet.

"He said there was some cash in here," his father inquired after I handed it to him.

"I never saw any cash," I yelled back. Then I smirked at him to let him know that the cash went to good use. A couple days later after walking to the weed dispensary, I saw Ryan in the backseat of his friend's car. He yelled at me, "You're going to jail motherfucker! There's a warrant out for your arrest!"

I ran away laughing maniacally at him.

In July, I was scheduled to go home for a visit. My parents wanted to see me and I certainly would've loved to see them and home for a few days. Naturally, I wanted to collect as many drugs for the trip as I possibly could. Nikki went to get her prescription for the yellow Vicodin filled but we ran into a problem. The doctor got red flagged. The morning before my flight we tried going to every pharmacy in town. No pharmacy would fill our prescription. After four failed attempts, we walked into a Walgreens. The pharmacist there said it was an issue because of a little hole in the prescription sheet. Nikki's dog nibbled on it a bit but the writing on the prescription was legible. The pharmacist didn't have the spine to tell us he wouldn't fill a prescription that came from a doctor who had been red flagged. He pretended that the little hole in the document was the issue. I argued with him for a little while and, once I didn't get my way, I decided to smack a bag of potato chips off a rack on my way out and told him, "Go fuck yourself!"

Because of the heated exchange with the pharmacist, they called the police. Nikki and I were walking down Ventura Boulevard when a cop tried to stop me. I had plenty of drugs on me and was fairly certain there was a warrant out for my arrest since Ryan fell out of a window. I ran for about half a block before the cops did a dog pile on top of me. Once they lifted me to my feet to conduct a search, one police officer kicked my legs open and yelled, "Spread em!" I extended my legs a mile wide but once again he kicked my leg and yelled, "Spread em!"

"Motherfucker, I'm doing a gymnast fucking split for you right now. What more do you want from me?" I shouted back at him. He kicked my leg again which enraged me. He was standing behind me but I could see his head in my peripheral vision. I leaned forward then popped my head back into his face. Another dog pile ensued and then they took me to the station. Needless to say, I missed my flight home.

At the station, I couldn't get over how nice the cells were in Los Angeles. In New York, there's two or three guys cramped in a cell with one small bench. This cell had two cushioned bunk beds and to top it all off, I had the cell to myself. Not to mention the cell had a television set. I was quite cozy in there all things considered. As they were fingerprinting me, one cop got cute with me because I hit his buddy. "What do you think you're some kind of tough guy cause you're from New York?" he asked. "No, I think I'm a tough guy because I busted your friend's jaw for him," I yelled back. The next morning when everyone else that was arrested the previous day was taken to court, they left me behind. I asked a cop passing by, "Hey why's everyone else going to court but not me?"

"Because you're an asshole!"

"Hey it's no skin off my ass, Willy Wonka's coming on at 4," I yelled back as I pointed to the television.

The next day they finally took me to court. I received good news and some bad news. The good news was that Ryan was lying about that warrant. There was no such warrant related to his assault. He was just trying to scare me. However, there was half a dozen subway tickets I didn't pay for. You see unlike New York, where you need a metro card to get on the buses and trains, Los Angeles has an honor system. You buy a ticket but you don't swipe it for a turnstile waiting to be released upon your card's swipe. In Los Angeles, every so often a police officer would be waiting at a station to keep people honest by writing tickets to those who didn't pay the fare. I never paid the fare and would simply throw those tickets out. Regarding the initial charges of battery on a police officer and possession of a controlled substance, the judge issued a fine and community service because I had no previous charges in that area. I was supposed to go home that day which I found shocking. However, because of the unpaid tickets, I was sent to L.A. county jail.

This would be my first and last stay at a county lockup. I wish I could say I was terrified but I was so disgusted with myself that I didn't care if some gangbanger cracked my head in. I felt completely broken. By the time they started processing me and the other inmates I was in full blown opioid withdrawal. They had us all put our hands against the wall so they could search us all over again. The correctional officers were whacking anybody that moved with their billy clubs. My arms were trembling and the kid next to me was concerned I was going to catch a beating. I told him I was withdrawing from opioids and I couldn't help it. I would watch the correctional officers in the corners of my eyes. When they came my way, I would stiffen my arms the way they wanted it. These correctional officers were not playing games. I watched them throw a black kid a beating just because he looked at one of them funny. After that initial search, they put us all through a huge room where we had to take our clothes off. They had us stand around naked right next to each other holding our dicks and a bag of clothes. There we waited, dicks in hand, for them to give us our jumpsuits and take our bag of clothes. After the jumpsuits were distributed they gave us some cookies which I thought was rather festive of them. After I got my bag of cookies, I was temporarily put in a waiting room with ten other guys. There was a garbage pail in the middle of the room. Once I finished my cookies, I went to throw out the wrapper they came in. I slightly grazed some big black guy on the way over to the pail. "Say excuse me!" he snarled at me.

"What?"

"Say excuse me!"

"Oh, I'm sorry. Did I give you a little boo boo when I grazed you? Aw you poor thing."

"Oh, it's like that."

"Yea it's like that. Don't start some shit over some bullshit!"

This guy was black and twice my size. I was the minority in that room not him. He had a bunch of his homies with him but I seemed to gain their respect because they all laughed at my sarcastic remark. In there they had this thing they called politics. Politics basically is all about what gang you affiliate with. The whites had the woods, which was short for peckerwoods. I was only staying a few days. I wanted no part of their American History X Nazi bullshit. I just kept my head down for the most part. My cellmate was an older guy who was a legit Aryan brotherhood member. You could see he was for real, given all his jail-house swastika tattoos. Nice guy aside from the fact that he probably spilled the blood of somebody who wasn't white to earn those tattoos. I was in a place where I wasn't really sup-posed to associate with people outside of my own race but I couldn't help myself. Most of the interactions I had with fellow inmates were with blacks and Hispanics. I made them laugh and I related more to them than to some of those California white dudes.

One morning I was instructed to see some woman about some medical red tape. They escorted me out of my cell and brought me to her office. I was shackled to a seat next to her desk. For a moment, I was alone with her and she was the only person I'd seen in three days who wasn't a guard or an inmate. It was the first time I felt safe expressing vulnerability since I was arrested. So, I took advantage. A little teary eyed I said to her, "I'm like cancer you know. Everything I touch I destroy." That was the first honest statement I had made in years. She didn't say anything too inspirational in return but I didn't need her to. It felt cathartic just to let my guard down for a moment and have someone hear me say that.

A couple days later my parents came all the way to Los Ange-les to bail me out. They wanted to make sure I made my flight to New York this time. They tried to keep me from seeing Nikki before going home. They were furious and completely fed up with me. All I could think about was the pills Nikki had waiting for me and the fact that I wanted to get laid. I probably said I needed to see her because I "loved" her but really, I just wanted to get laid and get high. I passed on the Vicodin because I kicked opioids in jail and didn't want to develop a habit again. I took a bunch of somas along with a weed brownie. Then I fucked her as many times as I possibly could within the time frame my parents gave me.

Once we got home my parents hit me with it. They insisted I go to rehab. I refused at first. They were desperate. Rightfully so too. I was completely insane. My brain was so fried from drugs that my thinking became completely delusional. One afternoon they tricked me. They told me they were taking me to a place in Brooklyn where I could sign up for health insurance.

When we got to the place, I could tell something was up. I peaked downstairs to see a bunch of young people holding hands and praying together. It was reminiscent of a deranged cult. Some younger gentleman called my name into his office. He was in his late 20's but already had a receding hair line. He was muscular and deliberately wore a plum polo shirt one size too small. The polo was tucked into black dress slacks that were an inch or two too short. He was trying hard to look professional but his lack of dress sense made me cringe. My parents waited in the waiting room. The guy started asking me all kinds of questions about drug use. I would answer them with brutal honesty and I got quite a kick out of the savage nature of my answers. Finally, after the fifth drug related question I asked, "Hey what's with all these drug use questions?"

"Do you not know what this is?"

"I thought this was about getting signed up for health insurance."

"Well that's part of it."

Then he laid it all on me. My parents coerced me into coming to a place that signs you up for a long-term rehab with boot camp style tactics. All I heard was no sex and no cigarettes for a year and that was all I needed to lash out. "Look man, I'm sorry but my parents wasted your time, there's no way I'm going to treatment. And even if I would go to treatment, I certainly wouldn't go away for a year that's insane."

I flew out of that room and said to my parents, "Let's get the fuck out of here. You wasted this poor man's time." I stepped outside and lit a cigarette. My parents stayed behind to speak to the guy.

He explained to them that he didn't feel like his time was wasted and that I needed help. The car ride home was awkward to say the least. My poor parents were trying to get through to me for the entire duration of that car ride but I wasn't even registering the information. All I could think about was getting my next fix and in that moment it wasn't looking good. I was unemployed, broke, and swindling them was out of the question. They finally put their foot down and gave me an ultimatum. I had to either get help or get out of their house. Seeing as how I, at age 23, still very much needed their financial support, I said, "Ok but only if I could go to a regular 28-day rehab. A one-year rehab is just completely insane," I said.

They actually agreed that I might've been right about a year seeming counterproductive and were simply happy they got me to compromise.

I insisted the rehab I go to be a place that lets you smoke cigarettes. They found a place called Behavioral Health of the Palm Beaches, or BHOP as its abbreviated, in South Florida. I didn't know it yet but South Florida is an absolute cesspool for addicts. All of America shits its addict children down there based on the fantasy that a sunny beachside resort rehab is going to save their children's lives. There are some reputable treatment centers and halfway houses down there. But it's like finding a needle in a haystack now. Even if you do manage to find a good place to send your children, there's nothing to stop them from leaving AMA (Against Medical Advice), wandering the streets of South Florida, and ending up in the less than reputable places. I've seen scores of people go down there to get better and either come back way worse off or in a coffin. Girls get it the worst. When they relapse down there they end up prostituting themselves just to get a fix.

Once in Florida, I managed to skip the detox portion of treatment because it had been days since I took opioids and I didn't want to take any Suboxone. I was almost over the hump when it came to physical withdrawals. Suboxone would just negate the progress I'd already made and put me right back into withdrawal once they cut me off. So, I went straight to the treatment center. I had no idea what to expect walking in there. I must say the place was beautiful. It truly was like a resort. They even took us to the beach on the weekends. They had a volleyball court and the living quarters were exceptional. The clinical staff was phenomenal but I was an absolute menace. I questioned everything they had to say.

This man named Fred ran most of the morning groups. He looked like the mutant child of Samuel L. Jackson and a walrus. He even wore a backwards Kangol hat like Samuel L. Jackson. Another staff member who was a powerful speaker was Raheem. He was a black Muslim and was very stylish about it. He'd wear Movado watches that matched his kufi. One time I complimented him on the matching watch.

"Look man, don't ever trust a man without a watch on. HE DON'T KNOW WHAT TIME IT IS!" he enthusiastically responded.

I think his title was the spiritual coordinator. He was from Baltimore and had the best stories. One was about his friends throwing him a party before he went away to prison. They had a beautiful hooker lined up for him that he referred to as the cherry on top and she managed to squirt gonorrhea into his eye. I didn't even know such a thing was possible. "I went and saw the prison doctor thinking I got some pink eye. He said 'Raheem you don't got pink eye, you done got some gonorrhea in your eye.' I said 'in my eye?!' I called the cherry on top and said 'Sister you need to get yourself checked out because you done squirted some gonorrhea in my eye.'" I'd do a spot-on imitation of him for the other patients. Imitation really is the sincerest form of flattery because I loved Raheem. He had a sense of humor about the impressions. "I hear you talking about me," he said as he walked in on me impersonating him for the other patients.

I brought my usual brand of class clown style antics into rehab because of my poor attitude. I didn't want to be addicted to opioids anymore but everything else under the sun was just fine with me. I was there for an oil change and to get my parents off my back. The clinical staff had other ideas for me. They introduced me to a sober fellowship that wishes to remain anonymous. They insisted I quit all drugs and alcohol. They also insisted I get in touch with God. I wasn't having any part of that.

But once I found out that my counselor was having constant correspondence with my parents, I told them what they wanted to hear because I wanted them happy. I thought if I could fool the staff they would tell my parents how great of a turnaround I pulled and they would ease up. You see once I was away from Los Angeles, I was penniless. I lived scam to scam. My parents handled all my airfare and just about everything else I needed because, beyond getting high, I was absolutely useless. They knew Los Angeles was nothing but trouble for me. I wanted to convince them to get me a flight back to Los Angeles after treatment because I "missed" my girlfriend. I may have fooled the staff at the rehab but I didn't fool my parents. They got me a flight home to New York and insisted I stay there.

Once home, I figured I'd at least attempt to hang around that sober fellowship that wishes to remain anonymous. Their entire mission is to stay sober and help others get sober. Petey coincidentally started attending their meetings so I went to one with him. He was friendly with an alcoholic priest who got sober with the fellowship's help. I was a nihilistic atheist and ordinarily loved a theological debate with people who believed in God. Half my time in rehab was spent denouncing God's existence whenever they insisted I needed to have a spiritual awakening. The priest's demeanor was too kind and gentle for me to be rude though.

"Father John, this is my friend Sacchi he's just coming out of rehab," Petey said as he pointed to me.

"Hey, how are you doing?" John asked.

"I'm alright I guess. I'm a little concerned that this might not be for me though because I'm an atheist," I said. I said it politely but I was hoping he would give me some wiggle room to start a debate.

His response was calm and unexpected. "Oh, that's okay. Just don't drink and keep coming here," he said with a smile.

At the rehab all they spoke about was God and how I needed to find him to get sober. When I stood my ground on my atheism, they stood theirs. They insisted there was no way I could stay sober without some semblance of spirituality. But here was this priest, of all people, telling me not to fret about the whole God thing. He simply insisted that I kept coming back. I didn't stick around but I kept that ace in my pocket for another time.

A few weeks later, I schemed enough money to get a flight back to Los Angeles. My father, desperate for me to get a job and become a fully functioning member of society, saw an ad for security guard training. The training cost $200. I convinced him to give me the money, seeing as how it was his suggestion in the first place, and never took the class. I put together a few more dollars connecting a few dots in the street and got a flight back to Los Angeles.

Once there I regretted going back. Something felt off with Nikki. Our energies were misaligned. It felt as if the entire universe was telling me I wasn't supposed to be there anymore. I tried to make it work anyway but it didn't. We'd constantly be at each other's throats. Before I went to rehab we used to fight and then have passionate makeup sex. After rehab it became mostly just fighting. But by then I didn't care anymore. I was just going through the motions. One thing that irritated me was she'd dyed her hair blonde and had gotten breast implants when I was away. Her breasts were perfectly fine at a c cup and I'm an ass man anyway. I thought her tits looked ridiculous after those implants. I'd rather a girl be built like a 12-year-old boy than get breast implants. It's no fun to nibble on and when the nipples are pointing in strange directions it creeps me out. Any guy that enjoys fake breasts is an asshole. Fake tits are like an American made sports car. It may look sexy on the outside but if you pop the hood, that engine is filled with inferior parts, it's going to look like shit sooner or later, and it will lose its value drastically in a few years. Not to mention I loathe blonde hair.

One day we got into a fight that got out of hand. She knew I loved children and wanted children of my own one day. We were sitting on her backyard patio smoking cigarettes when she said, "I don't want to bring children into this world. I don't know how we can continue this relationship when I know having children is important to you."

I took a long drag of my cigarette so I could think carefully about my response. I knew by then that she wasn't my fairy tale bride to be but in the meantime, I didn't want to leave. "Babe, don't worry about that. I love you and I'm willing to sacrifice for you," I responded.

"You're such a bitch for compromising like that," she said.

Calling me a bitch when I made every effort to appease her enraged me. I flicked my cigarette at her in a fit of rage. I could've sworn I gave her the response she was looking for. We spent the entirety of the evening cursing and screaming at each other. We sort of made up the following morning but there was an undeniable distance between us.

I went home to New York for a funeral the next day. Both my Aunt and Uncle had passed. Their son, my cousin Tommy, had his first daughter Ava just before all of this. She was absolutely precious. It was imperative to go home and be with my family. After the funeral I was ready to take a flight back to Los Angeles.

But Nikki called me at the very last minute. "Just stay in New York, I don't want you to come back here. I sincerely hope you find everything that you're looking for," she said.

I tried to fight it but not as much as I normally would. I could've flown back that day and talked her out of it easily but I didn't. A part of me knew that I didn't belong there anymore. I was a New Yorker again. But not for long.

Nine – Back in the New York Groove

I got right back into the swing of consistent Oxycodone use once I got home. It felt good to be able to just get high in peace and not have a crazy girlfriend nagging me or looking to share. I started working at this diner called Z-One but it didn't take long to get fired. One of the owners broke the news to me but he refused to explain why I was being fired. I truly didn't understand what I did wrong. I was very careful about my drug use. I would use before and after work but never there. The manager pulled me aside and explained to me that someone saw me doing coke in the bathroom. At first, I thought I must've been sniffing an Oxycodone and it was confused for coke. But then I realized I snorted all my pills at home before coming in. I tried explaining to him, "I really wasn't doing coke. It was a Monday lunch shift. I'm not Charlie Sheen man."

He laughed and said, "I'm sorry it's out of my hands." He was kind enough to suggest I get a job at Angelina's. "You'll make a lot more money there anyway," he said.

I decided that was a splendid idea. Angelina's is a fine dining restaurant where the servers make ungodly amounts of money.

Angelina hired me right on the spot. The big test was carrying four plates as if there was food on them so they obviously couldn't be stacked. I grabbed the four plates with ease and told her, "I can carry a fifth if you want." I'm pretty smooth that way. Now I could take home roughly $300 a shift. My thirst for pills was easily quenched. Upon my arrival back home, I discovered that my little brother Johnny had developed a taste for blues as well so we'd team up and get high together. I'm sure that sounds like good old-fashioned brotherly love but in reality we'd get high, verbally abuse each other, and then physically assault one another.

One evening after scoring some Oxycodone in Annadale, I was walking towards the train station to get home and I ran into my old high school nemesis, Carmine. We said hello to each other in a friendly manner because when you're older, petty grievances from high school become insignificant. He was outside a bar on Amboy Road smoking a cigarette. "Layla is inside if you want to say hello," he said. I took him up on it. Layla also went to high school with us and Carmine explained that they were engaged.

My mind was riddled with guilt after Los Angeles. It didn't sit well with me that I had struck a girl. I told Carmine about the experience. I don't know why I decided to open up to him of all people about it but I was really glad I did. Apparently, he once lived in California for a little while and had a similar experience.

"Don't beat yourself up over that. Girls out there are fucking crazy. I'd never pull some shit like that with a girl like Layla and I'm sure you wouldn't either," he said to me.

That made me feel better. It's an unreasonable rationalization for domestic violence but it made me feel better nonetheless. I found him on Facebook that night so I could message him a thank you. Then I discovered we had the same birthday. Who would've thought?

Working at Angelina's was bringing in enough money to keep the withdrawals at bay but an opportunity arose that would make me flush with blues. My friend Jeff had a line on a dirty doctor in Queens who would prescribe a bottle of Oxycodone. All Jeff wanted for getting me in with this doctor was half the pills I received from the first visit. Problem was we needed the funds to see the doctor and fill the prescription. I was a little short but there wasn't a chance in hell I wasn't meeting that doctor. I enlisted the help of Aaron, the pill-head who lived across the street from me, and Johnny. We would get one hundred and twenty pills with sixty going to Jeff, ten to Aaron, and I had to hit Johnny off simply for being my little brother. We scrambled all day to get Aaron, the money together, the prescription from the doctor, and then to get it filled.

Getting the prescription filled was tricky because this doctor was red flagged in New York. So, we took the prescription to New Jersey where they filled it without an issue. As soon as I got my hands on the bottle I snorted two and swallowed another two. Sitting on that many pills gets to be problematic. You eventually get to a point where it's not even getting you any higher. Opioids make you constipated. Now normally, I'd have points in time where I couldn't keep up with the addiction so I'd go into withdrawal for a little while and then the constipation would cease. That's when I could finally let out a shit that I was holding in for a few days. A junkie shit feels like giving birth. A spikey log that seems to go on for about three feet will come out and leave your asshole feeling like a goddamn Fourth of July party was held there. One night I was at work and because I had that bottle of pills, I hadn't had an opportunity to shit in a very long time. I was still constipated but it desperately wanted to come out. I had to sit on the toilet bowl for about an hour trying to force this thing out. My section was getting sat and the manager started knocking on the door concerned. He wanted to send me home but I needed money. I apologized and explained that I was a little "sick" but was good to go. I snorted a few more pills and managed to survive the shift.

When I got home from work, Johnny started being a smart ass with me. "Give me a blue bro," he demanded after giving me an attitude.

"You want to be a jerkoff and now you got your hand out? I'm not giving you one until the morning now, fuck off," I said. He, in turn, jumped on top of me and we fought it out. At one point, I held my hand over his mouth until he bit my hand which made me scream. My mother yelled down, "What the hell are you guys doing down there?" We pretended we were just goofing around which put her mind at ease. In the morning, I showed him mercy but I was much tighter with the purse strings after that.

It didn't take long for that bottle of pills to vanish. We devoured them in no time at all. That doctor in Queens started to catch some heat so he started demanding X-rays for our nonexistent "back problems."

Needless to say, it was back to scoring on the street. One morning I was so desperate to get high that I couldn't even wait to get to my house. Mind you, the dealer I was meeting lived two blocks from my house. I started crushing the pills up in a folded-up piece of paper and sniffing them in broad daylight right in the middle of the street. Coincidentally, an undercover cop was driving by as I was doing this. He threw me off because he was driving a Mitsubishi Galant as opposed to their usual Chevrolet Impalas. I tried to make a run for it but another cop car was coming up right behind him. They had me cornered and at that point, I surrendered. Not that I had much choice.

Those cops were pretty cool all things considered. I begged them to let me sneak in one more cigarette and they obliged me. "You were my 100th customer," the arresting officer said with a smirk. Glad I could help him reach that accolade.

I used my phone call to tell Johnny to bring me a hoodie because I was only in a t-shirt and I knew it would get cold in those cells at night. I also gave him a bullshit story to tell my parents so they wouldn't realize I had been arrested. "Just tell them I went into the city to visit some friends and I'll be spending the night there," I said.

When Johnny dropped off the hoodie he was argumentative with the cop who arrested me.

The cop came by my cell and said, "You were a gentleman with me after we caught you so you're good with me but your brother's got a bit of an attitude. You tell him if I see him in the street I'm gunning for him."

It warmed my heart that my brother was angry with the officer for arresting his brother. We had been at each other's throats so often because of our blues addiction that I wasn't even sure if he loved me anymore. In the morning I was taken before the judge. Once I was brought through the courtroom, I saw my parents in the audience with the same disapproving stares I had seen countless times before. The sad thing is, by then I had gotten so used to it that I didn't even care anymore.

"I knew that story Johnny told me was bullshit! There was no way you went to spend the night in the city in your pajamas," my mother said to me in the car ride home.

"Can you stop at a store and get me cigarettes?" I asked.

"No! You spend the night in jail and all you're worried about is cigarettes! I'll tell you what, go and pay for your own fucking cigarettes!" she shouted back at me.

"Look Ma, I know you're pissed off right now but I sat in a cell for twenty-four hours, I really don't need a life lesson right now, I just need a fucking cigarette," I said.

After some further deliberation my father pulled over at a deli just to shut me up. I've often been accused of being annoying. Maybe so. But one of the most valuable lessons I've learned in life is that the squeaky wheel gets the grease.

Ten - Florida

After getting myself arrested for possession of Oxycodone and resisting arrest, I went back to Florida and back to that rehab BHOP. This time, I needed to spend some time in detox. I also got to see Raheem again which made me happy.

There was an older patient who got into an argument with him. I stood on the sidelines but later on that day I witnessed the older patient reading the bible to a younger patient and explaining how the bible says that Muslims like Raheem are the devil. That left a bad taste in my mouth.

"No good ever came from comparing two Gods' dick sizes," I said to him.

I was eager to tell Raheem about it. He seemed disgusted a bit with my choice of words. "Look man I appreciate where you're coming from but God doesn't need you to defend him to a fool," he said. I still wasn't sold on the God thing but that idea resonated with me for some reason. A lot of things Raheem said resonated with me. I was a mixed-up angry kid and he'd say things that made me feel a little bit gentler inside.

When I commended him for having such a knack for that he said, "That's because I speak from the heart. When you speak from the heart it goes to the heart."

The clinical staff was hell bent on having me stay at a halfway house down there after the initial 28 days of treatment. I insisted on going home to New York. I got my way and four days later I was drunk and high making a fool of myself.

Apparently, I was harassing my buddy Tony and some girl he was dating at a local bar. I had blacked out most of the night. One of the few things I can actually remember was the girl saying, "Maybe you should go back to Florida." When that memory flashed before my mind in the morning I cringed. I picked up the phone and made a call to BHOP immediately. I was hoping to go to the halfway house they offered to send me to.

After making the trip back to Florida they gave me a drug test and my urine came up positive for five different substances. They said I wasn't eligible for the halfway house with that many drugs in my system. That infuriated me because when I spoke to them on the phone, I told them what I did. Now they were going to send me back home. This was the first time I genuinely asked for help without being coerced by my parents or the law and they were sending me home. I tried to find the guy I spoke to on the phone so I could scream at him for wasting my time but he wasn't there that day.

A woman in the office felt my pain. She decided to go the extra mile and hunt down a place for me to stay. The only place that would take me in was Elite Recovery Resources. The owner was a great man named Sid operating a reputable halfway house in a town filled with people running what's called "flop houses" that corruptly exploit addicts and their insurance. One of Elite's drivers came and picked me up from the detox. When we arrived, there were three picnic tables in front of the office populated with guys wearing snapback hats with a flat brim and Jordan sneakers that had seen better days. There were a few girls with their hair in unattractive buns and they had on sweatpants from the brand Pink. I looked on in disgust as I was led into Sid's office.

"I want to make it clear that I am not in recovery. I used to drink pretty heavily but I stopped myself and I don't attend meetings," he said. He went on to explain what was expected of me while staying there. My attention span could only soak up so much of what he was saying. As he spoke I was looking around his office. There were about two dozen framed pictures of young people on his walls.

"What's with all these pictures?" I asked him.

"Those are former clients that passed away. I keep them here as a constant reminder to try harder to help people," he said.

I couldn't help but notice he had a New York accent. "Where are you from?" I asked him.

"The Bronx."

"Nice, I'm from Staten Island."

"Yea I know."

"That obvious huh?"

I would relapse every few months or so but Sid never turned me away when I came back. He'd send me to his outpatient program and implement various consequences. I know plenty of people who got an honest shot at a good life because he never gave up on us. No matter how many times we gave him a reason to believe he should give up. He let countless people stay rent free. Of course, at the end of the day it was still a business, but he definitely exuded plenty of altruism. I never stayed sober in Florida for a significant amount of time but there's no doubt in my mind that his place gave me a chance at sobriety. I'm not sure I'd be here now if it wasn't for Sid. It opened the door for sobriety to one day come into my life.

I met a lot of beautiful but doomed souls down there. I never really developed any long-lasting friendships though. You're thrown together with a bunch of sick people and the fact that I kept relapsing made it impossible to develop relationships of substance. The only significant friendship I made was with a guy named George who was a little bit older than me. He was from Long Branch, New Jersey and we just clicked. Everybody loved George. There were a lot of cliques at Elite but George seemed to be friends with just about everybody. I didn't much care for the ridiculous Louisville Slugger tattoo he had on his arm but he was a baseball fanatic so I reserved my judgement.

My second day at Elite, I received a call from BHOP. They had what's called an alumni meeting where you come and tell the people in the detox how great you're doing because of sobriety. When they invited me, they didn't realize I had been back in the detox since my initial completion. I took it as an opportunity to be a goofball because I was just in the detox. I got to speak to patients I was in there with. In a sarcastic tone I said, "Yea recovery is great. Worked fast for me but it might take you another 28 days to get to my level." 28 days is the industry standard amount of time one would spend in a rehab.

The coordinator was appalled and insisted they would pay more attention in the future to avoid situations like that from happening again.

Getting around Florida was a nuisance. My father was hesitant to give me anything but after whining like a baby enough, I was able to get him to loosen up the purse strings for a vehicle. "You're only getting a few hundred bucks so you better find something cheap," he said over the phone. I hunted down the best hunk of trash on wheels money could buy. A 1987 Chevy Astro Van. I just needed something to get me around but the bonus was I could fill that thing up with about eight people. Always on the lookout for a laugh, I spray painted Shaggin' Wagon on the hood and Grape Van on the sides. I saw a guy put Grape Van on the side of his van in the show "Workaholics." The idea is you get to have it say rape van without it actually saying rape van.

One time a cop pulled me over for speeding. As I was handing him my license and registration he asked, "Why does it say Grape Van?" I snickered and said, "If you take the G away what do you got officer?" The cop started laughing and let me off with a warning.

There was one clique from the South Jersey / Philadelphia area living at the halfway house. I hated them at first. It was mostly because they got all the girls and I couldn't figure out how to get laid down there to save my life. My disdain for them basically came from envy. Eventually I got to know them though and really came to admire them. Philly guys are cool. It's those Boston guys you got to watch out for. This one Boston guy was going on about how great Tom Brady is and the Giants were about to face him for the second time in the Super Bowl. As you know, I could care less about football. But I'll damn sure cheer on the Giants. Especially when Eli Manning was going to make a fool out of this guy's precious Messiah. Everybody down there wanted to believe they came from the better city and we'd constantly be trash talking each other's cities. Professional sports was another avenue you could go down in pursuit of these foolish city rivalries we had. They set up a TV in the volleyball court for us all to watch the game. On the last play, when Brady threw up a Hail Mary into the end zone to no avail, I rubbed it in all the Bostonians faces. I even pretended to be a Yankees fan at times, even though I grew up in a Mets household, purely for the sake of toying with Bostonians.

After my first relapse, Sid sent me to what was called the commitment house. One relapse gets you thrown into the commitment house for two weeks. You and anyone else who re-relapsed that week are thrown into a sort of time-out where you're isolated from everybody else and you go to IOP (Intensive Outpatient). IOP is basically a bunch of classes and groups to help you in your recovery. A lot of them were actually quite insightful. I would constantly torture the instructors but they knew how to humble me and get my ego back to reality. One of the classes brought out the worst in me. They took us off campus to an art studio so we could paint. There was a guy from Staten Island who'd just been thrown into the commitment house who knew my little brother. I naturally buddied up with him. We'd talk throughout the process and they kept insisting we be quiet and paint in silence. I finally found somebody from home and was excited to have someone who understood my humor. I couldn't be quiet. It was frustrating me that they insisted I sit in silence and paint. What does painting have to do with sobriety? I deliberately tried to get a rise out of them. I started painting evil paintings. One was a bunch of stick figures going through all the different forms of execution throughout history. No response from the coordinator. So, I painted another one of a stick figure stabbing another stick figure. Still no response.

Then I whispered to my Staten Island counterpart, "It's time to turn the heat up." I painted the twin towers with a plane going through one of them. I used red paint to make it appear as if a drip of blood was coming from the plane's impact. Then I added swastikas to all four corners. Then I wrote a quote from

Charles Manson and another from David Berkowitz, the "Son of Sam." Upon completing my sinister masterpiece I said to the co-ordinator, "I'm no Picasso but do you like it?" That solicited the response I was looking for.

She took me outside to reprimand me. The coordinator's name was Susan. She could be stern but she did a better job at reaching me than most. She would challenge me on my need to always use humor instead of being genuine. At first, I insisted that I was being genuine but she gradually broke me down. I genuinely had no idea how to be genuine. All I knew how to do then was be a buffoon.

When I got back to the housing area after arts & crafts, I showed my favorite tech, Declan, my masterpiece painting. He loved it. Declan had five years sober at that time and sounded exactly like Jeff Spicoli from "Fast Times at Richmont High." The next day this guy Christian went onto the laptop that was in our room and put on Creedence Clearwater Revival's "Lookin' Out My Back Door." Such a beautiful happy song. It made me feel like everything was going to be ok. I needed something simple like that to find solace in. Most of the time I was wallowing in self-pity because I was so pathetic that I had to be shuffled from program to program down in Florida instead of being wherever a normal person would be.

After my second relapse, Sid insisted I go to a 28-day rehab again. He sent me to Palm Partners, which was another rehab down there. Sid happened to be there one day, discussing business I presume, with one of their staff members and I begged him to let me back into Elite without having to stay for the full 28-day program. I wanted out of that place but Sid wasn't having it. I decided to leave anyway and found another halfway house. The problem was, this halfway house wasn't as reputable as Elite. Their hearts were in the right place. They wanted us to get sober. The clients, however, didn't necessarily want to get sober and that halfway house didn't have the resources to keep us in line. Elite drug tested us twice a week whereas this place tested you once a week if you were lucky. Or unlucky, depending on how you look at it. At first, I didn't try and get cute with them. I asked Declan to be my sponsor in the sober fellowship that wishes to remain anonymous. Now that I wasn't a client at Elite, he was legally allowed to sponsor me.

My attempt at sobriety was short lived. One of the guys at my new halfway house told me about an Urgi-Med up the street that would prescribe Xanax to me without an issue. I went in there and the doctor was this adorable little Asian man who seemed to either be oblivious or indifferent that I was clearly a drug abuser. I tried to push it as far as I could naturally. I ordered pills like I was ordering McDonald's. "I have anxiety attacks so that will require Xanax, two milligrams, twice a day. I'm in college and I have ADHD so I will require Adderall, thirty milligrams, twice a day. Also, my testicles are in some kind of pain doc, I was wondering if I could get Oxycodone, thirty milligrams, twice a day for that as well," I told him. He had no issue with the Xanax or the Adderall but the Oxycodone wasn't happening. He did, however, offer me Percocet instead. Percocet isn't as good as Oxycodone but they can certainly get the job done. He did want to inspect my balls though. He put on a latex glove and I didn't hesitate for a second. I pulled my pants down and let them hang. If I'm being honest, I probably would've let him take a gander without the glove so long as I got my bottle of sixty Percocet pills once he was done.

I left that office feeling like I hit the jackpot. The Xanax would become a problem. Because of it, I managed to blackout for a few days. I had been kicked out of my new halfway house without even realizing it. The Xanax was making me incredibly reckless. I noticed I was running out of pills in my personal stash so I was going to have to check into a rehab again sooner or later. That was until I found a credit card on the floor to keep the party going. I decided to go out to this club il Bacio on Atlantic Avenue in Delray Beach. I showed my ID to the bouncer but before I could actually go inside, I saw a credit card just sitting on the floor. I decided that it was not the night for dancing, seeing as how I managed to find a potential gold mine. I went to the nearest gas station to see if it worked. The gas pump asked for a zip code. I punched in the Delray Beach zip code and voila! It worked. At that time of the evening, just about everything was closed. The next day I went on a rampage. I woke up early so I could get down to business. I went to the Boca Raton mall and bought more gold chains than your favorite rapper. Then I immediately took it to another stand in the mall that paid cash for gold. With those funds I bought blues, cocaine, and whatever else I could get my hands on. I don't remember much from this little escapade because of the Xanax blackouts but some girl told me she saw me in the mall when I was doing this little gold chain exchange and apparently I fell over a sneaker display in front of Foot Locker.

That credit card was eventually cancelled and my little party was over. I was feeling stylish one day and decided to treat myself to some sunglasses from Sunglass Hut. The cashier looked at me funny when it declined so I got out of there fast. Once all my ill-gotten funds and pill stash completely dried up, I checked into rehab. This time I went to Ocean Mist Recovery in Pompano Beach, also known as Pompton. I didn't make many friends at this rehab. I was in a pissed off mood and I was irritating everyone. I was pissed off because I didn't want to get sober but I had nowhere else to go and everyone else there seemed to actually want sobriety. I was tired of living out of the giant suitcase I had been shuffling around and living out of since Los Angeles. I never took the clothes out of that suitcase because I was never under one roof for more than a month or so. Seemed counterproductive to unpack it all when I could just fish out what I needed. The owners of Ocean Mist were this pretty down to Earth couple who let patients stay much longer than their insurance would pay for. They offered to let me stick around for an extra thirty days but as soon as I got permission from Sid to return to Elite, I went straight there. I wanted my freedom.

I decided that I wanted to at least attempt to stay sober. However, that newfound desire for sobriety was short lived. Down in Delray Beach the sober fellowship has a clubhouse called Central House. At one of their meetings, I ran into Billy from home. Delray Beach was not big enough for the both of us to get sober. By then, I was waiting tables steadily and managed to put a few bucks together. I convinced my father to help me with some money for an apartment. He jumped at the idea because he had been paying my weekly rent at the halfway house which was $225 a week. An apartment of my own would be even cheaper. He thought I was making progress. Little did he know I was only looking to get that apartment so I could get high in peace.

I managed to secure an apartment for Billy and I in a low-income housing development. Aside from one white trash couple, we were the only white people in sight. The neighbors thought we were cops until we smoked crack in front of them. Then they all wanted to be our friends because they saw what great customers we were. It could've been a nice apartment but we didn't have any furniture or hot water. We slept on the floor and took cold showers just so we could get high all day in peace. I hit the Urgi-Med up for a collection of pills again and we were off to the races.

I had my first experience with syringes in that apartment. I was too scared to shoot heroin because I knew I would love it way too much. We would shoot cocaine and then I'd just sniff heroin or Oxycodone to come down.

The circumstances were so depraved that we were barely eating. After living like animals for a couple of weeks, I decided I was going to eat a decent meal come hell or high water. We didn't have the funds to pull off a decent meal so the plan I concocted was that we would go to the finest Italian restaurant on Atlantic Avenue and order a shit load of appetizers and an entrée. After we got our fill on the appetizers, we would book it out of there before the entrées even came out. Mussels, baked clams, fried calamari, mozzarella en corozza, and a couple Coronas. I was so hungry I feasted like a king. Everything was going according to plan until it was time to leave. Billy was so high that he went catatonic. He couldn't move a muscle. I ran for it assuming he would just suck it up and follow me. I was gravely mistaken. He sat there and explained the situation to the staff. They took a picture of his license and let him go.

After a few weeks I had enough of the insanity. I was fired from my job for coming in looking like a disaster and I was steadily running out of money and pills. One more scheme came up that kept me going for a few more days. These Haitians wanted me to buy a bunch of cell phones in my name and they'd pay me $200 to do it. I have no idea what the gag was for them, nor did I care. All I heard was $200. One could only assume it was so they could discuss crimes on those phones without fear of it being tapped or traced back to them in any way. They would give me the cash to buy the phones and I would go inside and purchase them in my name. After a few days of buying half a dozen cell phones a day, the clerk in the cell phone store said I couldn't do it anymore. We tried a few more stores to no avail. I must've been red flagged. I had a sneaking suspicion the Haitians weren't going to pay me for the day but I still had about $300 in my pocket that was supposed to be used to pay for those phones. I saw no need to remind them that I still had it sitting snugly in my pocket. When they pulled over to drop me off, the guy sitting shotgun asked for the money and the one sitting next to me in the back seat put his hand out. That $300 was my money to get high with. It was either I escape with it or go into opioid withdrawal. A sensible person would've probably suffered the withdrawals before going toe to toe with those Haitians. They were clearly gang members and South Florida Haitians are known to be homicidal maniacs. They once shot somebody in the middle of the Boynton Beach Mall. Those guys would've killed me without even thinking twice about it.

I am not a sensible person though. I threw my elbow into the face of the Haitian sitting next to me and jumped out of the car. I hopped fences into people's backyards and kept running until I got home unscathed.

Once I ran out of money, pills, and schemes to get more cash, I had enough. I told Billy, "I'm sorry bro but I got to go get clean."

He shrugged and asked, "What the fuck am I supposed to do?"

I didn't have an answer for him. There was nothing I could do to help him. "Why don't you check into this place with me?" I asked.

"I'm good man," he replied. He was going to try and hack it for himself out there.

I checked back into Ocean Mist Recovery. This stint was far more pleasant than the last time. I even took them up on their offer to keep me an extra thirty days, even though my insurance would only cover the first thirty. I don't know if it was my attitude or the new group of people but I had a lot of fun there that time.

I made a lot of friends but I did make one enemy of course. When news that this kid John from Colorado was coming, a bunch of patients who knew him were not too thrilled to hear about it. He had a reputation for being intolerable. He was a tall lanky kid and one of his eyes was completely messed up. Sure enough, he was going to be one of my roommates. One day I was walking by outside and I thought he said something to me. "What?" I asked him.

"Yea, yea, just keep walking!" he said while motioning his hand forward. He was trying to impress the guys he was talking to by acting like a tough guy with me and he picked the wrong guy to play with. It was completely uncalled for as I hadn't wronged him in any way.

"Hey pal I'll jerk off in your fucking good eye don't fuck with me!" I barked back at him. The other patients laughed and he stood silent.

He claimed he was part of the Aryan Brotherhood and was a white supremacist. I had no doubt he was a racist but Aryan Brotherhood members are known to have balls and he wasn't cold-blooded enough to even be considered for membership. John was a twat.

The next encounter I had with him was after he called one of the staff members, Nate, a nigger. Nate was one of the sweetest guys you'd ever meet. It was completely out of line and uncalled for. At night, Nate would make us all laugh with his funny stories. One of them being his discovery that Asian women do not have sideways vaginas. His friends told him they were sideways as a joke. "Man, the first time I fucked an Asian girl I pulled her pants down and said them motherfuckers was lying!" he said to a bunch of amused spectators. Now seeing as how he was a staff member, he couldn't react the way he wanted to. I decided to do it for him.

I walked up to John and started spitting on him. "Please, you could have the first shot just hit me so I can beat the shit out of you!" I screamed at him. Other patients who felt for the staff member backed me up. He ran into his room so he could pack his things and leave. I thought I would've gotten in trouble for all that but the owner laughed when he heard I started spitting on him.

After treatment, I found my way back at Elite one more time. I stuck with it for a little while but I'd had enough of Florida. My Astro van broke down and was beyond repair so I left it on the side of i95 and didn't look back. I couldn't find a job worth my time down there and I was growing more and more intolerant of my surroundings. The recovery community and subsequent relapse community turned paradise into a modern-day Sodom. The palm trees and sunshine can only distract you for a little while from the fact that there's junkies running around rampant in beaten and tattered Air Force One sneakers and Jordan basketball shorts. Even if you get sober down there, there's not much to look forward to. You're still in a fantasy land. I eventually relapsed all over again. I took a trip to Urgi-Med and started couch surfing for a little while. I finally managed to convince my family to let me come home. The Florida experiment was a confirmed failure.

Eleven - Recovery

I continued getting high once I got back to Staten Island. I met with my old pal Danny one night and felt insignificant. He was steadily moving up in the world. I was going backwards. He'd get on me about my addiction and he was absolutely right but I didn't want to hear it.

"When you're not on drugs you look like Ashton Kutcher but when you're fucked up you're a mess bro," Danny said.

I just nodded in agreement but wasn't willing to do anything about it at that moment. We used to be such close friends but age and different life choices made me feel miles apart from him even though he was sitting right next to me. Going to juvie for two years was a blessing in disguise for him. Before then he was up to the same shenanigans as the rest of us. When he was in juvie, we were graduating to opioids. It was as if the guy who was least likely to succeed became the success story.

I got high with Mike a few times but something was off there too. He was becoming increasingly reclusive. The years of drug abuse left a rift between us. I still love him to death and I'm sure that he feels the same way, but we gradually went our separate ways. He chose to clean his act up by cutting himself off completely from everything and everyone. I would inevitably choose the sober fellowship.

Johnny was still using opioids but he managed to become a certified EMT within the Fire Department of New York. I felt like Fredo from the Godfather. There I was struggling to stay sober and my little brother seemed to make something of himself while getting high. Seeing him land a career only further perpetuated my depression. I was happy for him. But why couldn't I find my place in the world? One day I simply had enough. Nothing terrible happened, I just felt guilty about continuing on with my stupidity. Especially after seeing Johnny and Danny doing so well.

I heard Mark was staying clean with the help of that sober fellowship. I reached out to him and he came by the house with his Jeep to talk. He said he was sober nine months and was loving it. "I've been getting laid more than I ever have it's great," he added. Some may say that's not a noble reason to get sober but I say whatever gets you there. I sure as hell wouldn't have minded getting laid more often.

The next day he started taking me to meetings held by the sober fellowship. I managed to actually put together some significant clean time for a change.

An entire new group of friends who were also trying to stay sober developed around me. There was Carmine, whom I hated in high school but made peace through that heartfelt talk about domestic violence. Then there was Vinny, who acted a lot like a real-life George Costanza and was balding like George too. There was Dimitri, a Russian Jew who was over six feet tall with glasses. Dimitri spoke with the same sort of rhythm and pauses in his syllables as Christopher Walken. If he was enthusiastic about what he was saying, he'd make a fist and punch his other hand for each syllable. Impersonating him became like baseball to America, it was our favorite pastime. Dimitri was in a bit of a leadership role because he had four years sober unlike the rest of us who were newly sober. Pat, another tall fellow, whom I'd known since high school and always gotten along with, had a special place in his heart for my brand of humor. I could say poop and he'd laugh. One day Pat and I were watching the zombie show The Walking Dead and I imagined a hypothetical scenario where Dimitri's little brother was on the show attempting to have the uninfected open the gate for him. In my best impression of Dimitri's brother, I said, "Let me in cuz, I didn't get bit." A month or so later Pat texted me and said, "I still randomly laugh at that."

Another new friend I made through the sober fellowship was Dom. Dom wasn't a south shore degenerate like the rest of us. He was from the Mid Island area but he was in rehab with Pat and Carmine so he gravitated towards our group. Then there was Ron. Ron had a couple years sober already but he grew up within close proximity of Carmine and Dimitri. We formed a little clique because, aside from Dom, we were all under the banner of south shore degenerates. Carmine had a year sober at one point but was fresh off an intravenous heroin use relapse. At that point in time, people who shot heroin had a certain mystique about them to me. They had crossed a line that I hadn't. The worst I had done was snort heroin and blues. Needle users ended up dead and I still very much enjoyed living.

Then there was Ron. Ron and I first met under funny circumstances. We were outside the Applebee's by the Staten Island mall with a bunch of people from the sober fellowship. I was cracking jokes and a lot of those jokes poked fun at amputees. Nobody was laughing. They all looked mortified. "These jokes usually kill, what's the problem?" I asked.

"Maybe it's because they don't find jokes about the handicapped funny!" Ron shouted at me.

"Hey sometimes you gotta crack a few eggs to make an omelet," I shouted back unaware that he himself was an amputee. He had a rare form of bone cancer when he was a kid and they had to hack his leg off. After the exchange, somebody pulled me aside and explained his situation to me. The next time I saw him I apologized for the insensitivity of my jokes.

"Bro, I don't care if you make jokes like that, I was more or less just fucking with you. But I don't know you too well yet so maybe just cool it with the amputee jokes," Ron said.

"Well I'd come up with more amputee jokes but I'm stumped," I fired back at him not being able to contain myself. We both erupted with laughter and we've been best pals ever since. His fiancée Valerie, however, was intolerable. She was like the Eva Braun of the sober fellowship. Just an absolute Nazi about the whole thing. She'd reprimand girls she sponsored over dressing promiscuously. A noble effort I'm sure but then she'd nonchalantly share about her own past promiscuity to a room full of people. "They used to call me all-the-way Val," she'd say. No man wants his fiancée divulging past sexual transgressions to a room full of friends.

Johnny's mental health was deteriorating. Some girl he was dating dumped him and he was constantly getting high. We'd go out to dinner with my parents and he'd be so high that he'd fall asleep in his food. My parents were so happy and proud that he was an EMT that they didn't want to believe he was a disaster. "Oh, he's just tired, he's working crazy hours," my mother would say to me. At first, I made no effort to bring to my parents' attention just how far down the rabbit hole he had gone. But then I stumbled upon a bunch of handwritten pages in the basement. They were disturbing to say the least. On one of them was a suicide note and a message to the girl that dumped him.

I tried confronting him at first but he just shrugged it off. "I'm fine bro, worry about yourself," he would say.

Then I laid it on my parents. I couldn't believe their reaction. "Well that was probably just a cry for help he wouldn't actually do it," my mother said. I was livid. I'm sure it was a cry for help. Either way he was still killing himself. My parents just buried their heads in the sand and hoped for the best. They were concerned that if he went to get help through a rehab, he would lose his career. I was more concerned with him losing his life. I had Dimitri come with me to try and talk some sense into him in a sort of miniature intervention capacity. My brother assured us he was fine.

Johnny may have had his head in the gutter but my life was gradually getting better. My friends and I didn't drink or do drugs but we still had fun. We'd often go out to diners after the meetings and laugh uncontrollably. One night Mark, Dimitri, and I went to a ritzy Italian food restaurant in Brooklyn after a meeting. The wait was going to be an hour so we tried to be creative. "Vito held a table for us," Dimitri said to the maitre'd.

"Oh, Vito saved you a table? Right this way," replied the maitre'd. That's the secret to getting a table to an Italian restaurant in Brooklyn. You just tell them you know Vito and you're in. They pulled a table out of the back and placed it in a spot where there wasn't ordinarily a table. We felt like Henry Hill at the Copacabana.

"Isn't it great? Having dinner like this like gentlemen? We wouldn't be doing this if we were still getting high," Mark said to me as he took a bite of his Zuppa di Pesce. I wholeheartedly agreed with him. We lived like animals for so long it was nice to have some semblance of being human again.

When Hurricane Sandy hit us, Dimitri rounded a bunch of us up to go to the New Dorp and Midland Beach area to help people clean out their flooded and destroyed homes. That was one of the first selfless deeds I had ever done. The sober fellowship has consistently stressed to me the importance of selflessness. Doing for others. I really struggle with that because admittedly,

I'm a bit more selfish than the average individual. I really couldn't understand, especially at that time, the significance of being of service to others. The whole idea is that by helping others, you get to help yourself. By helping others, you get some relief from constantly worrying about your own insignificant trials and tribulations. I stubbornly insist on clinging to my own shallow and selfish desires.

The healing process of recovery started for me when we did a big book study with Father John, the priest whom I'd met a couple years prior after my first rehab. He was Vinny's sponsor so the three of us would read the big book together. The big book is the sober fellowship's bible more or less. It describes, in detail, how the original members got sober and how we could apply their methods ourselves. Father John even performed an exorcism on me more or less. I was a complete atheist until that moment. He prayed over me and talked in tongues. I felt an undeniable sensation throughout my body that couldn't be explained rationally but was as real to me as the print on these pages.

Throughout the following years, resistance to the concept of a higher power would still creep up but now I could no longer deny it. When he spoke in tongues, I assumed he was speaking Latin. When I asked him what he was saying he just shrugged and said, "I don't know."

Pat's brother Louie was also coming around. I used to buy Oxycodone pills from him. One night a bunch of us went to Jose Tejas for dinner. Afterwards, we were all smoking cigarettes out front. Louie was riddled with guilt and shame. "I feel bad that I was selling blues. There's a lot of kids going through hell and I can't help but feel like it's cause of me," he told me.

"First off, you never held a gun to anybody's head so don't stress it. Second, three of your best customers are here now sober anyway so don't worry about it," I replied. The three customers I was referring to were Pat, Mark, and me. Mark lived right next door to Pat and Louie so naturally he bought the bulk of his blues from Louie. I could see it on Louie's face that my comforting words didn't alleviate his guilt one iota. A few days later, he disappeared.

I was at a meeting held by the sober fellowship when Pat and Mark came in late, visibly shook up. After the speaker spoke, Mark raised his hand and said, "We couldn't get in touch with Louie for a couple days so we went to his apartment to check on him. We found him dead from an overdose." Tears started to well up in Mark's eyes as he was telling us this story. I had never seen him that vulnerable before.

The next day I was hanging out at Carmine's apartment concerned that I didn't have a suit to wear for the funeral. "One of the first things an old timer said to me when I first joined the fellowship was get a suit," he said to me rather grimly. I was able to squeeze into one of my father's suits.

After we buried our friend, I finally did something I always dreamed of doing, standup comedy. I was tired of hearing people tell me I ought to be a comedian and not trying my hand at it. I put together a few funny ideas and took it to an open mic. An open mic is not what I thought it would be. I figured there'd be ordinary people in the audience. There was simply a handful of aspiring comics with little to no experience in standup packed in a small room telling poorly structured jokes to little or no laughter. It is an awkward experience to say the least. It's tough to do standup in front of a mere handful of people. Laughter is contagious. I can think of countless times where one friend of mine said something funny and I couldn't even hear what was said but everyone else started laughing and I would just laugh at the laughter. After I got off the stage thinking I was terrible, the man who was running the open mic invited me to do an actual show. At least I thought it was an actual show at first. It was a show where guys who were just getting started could bring their friends and try it out.

I invited my friends from the sober fellowship and killed it. I was on fire. In hindsight, it wasn't that good but it was great for a first try. They videotaped the show and I had them email it to Vinny who put it up on YouTube. At first, I was proud of it and even flaunted it to other friends. As time progressed and sobriety cleared more and more cobwebs in my mind, I started to cringe watching it. Sure there were funny moments but there's plenty of moments where I say to myself, "What on Earth were you thinking?" I tried to do a few more shows but I felt defeated. Perhaps standup comedy wasn't a smart career move for me.

Once I realized I wasn't going to be an overnight comedy sensation, I started working for an older member of the sober fellowship, Paulie Cabinets. He owned a business called the Cabinet Warehouse, hence the moniker Paulie Cabinets, and recently he got into the restaurant business. It was a Mexican place called Pico's. I didn't have a car then, but Dimitri was nice enough to give me a lift so I could go in and ask for a job. On the way there we made a pit stop at his grandparents' house. They mostly spoke Russian to one another but there'd be some English peppered in.

Dimitri, being the lothario that he is, was going on about his female troubles. "You should find yourself nice Russian girl," his grandmother said in broken English.

"Yea they give the best blowjobs," Dimitri said. I was mortified. I looked across the room to see Dimitri laughing. "They don't know what that is," he assured me. I looked at his grandparents' faces to make sure. Either they really were oblivious or didn't care enough to address it.

When we got to Pico's, we saw a man from the sober fellowship we call Spiritual Jason. Spiritual Jason just had lunch there and was walking back to his office up the street. We told him that I was trying to get a job so he explained to the manager that he knew me. Since he was friends with Paulie Cabinets, she hired me on the spot. I started as a waiter but Cabinets liked the work I did so much, he made me a manager. Dom was delivering food for an Italian deli up the street from Pico's. On occasion, I'd see him in a van in the morning and we'd scream "NO DOUBT!" to each other in an overly accentuated Staten Island accent. We heard some kid say it like that in a meeting held by the sober fellowship and we would imitate him constantly. When I saw a brother in early sobriety in the morning like that, I got the sense that it would be a good day.

Things stayed on a positive trajectory for me. I was steadily employed for the first time in years and not foolishly burning the money on drugs. Carmine dumped Layla and was looking for a roommate. I was 26 years old and in desperate need to get out of my parents' house. I jumped at the opportunity to move in with him. Now even though I hated him in high school, I truly came to admire him. I always thought sobriety wasn't for me. But seeing guys like Mark and Carmine get sober and stay sober, it almost gave me permission to do so. In my eyes, Carmine always seemed in total control whereas I would react immaturely to just about anything. He seemed confident whereas I either wasn't or was faking confidence.

When I was in the process of moving my stuff in we went for a ride. In the car Carmine, seeing that I was still riddled with insecurity and doubt, said to me, "You know everyone feels insecure. I feel that way too a lot." For some reason that resonated with me. Hearing that from him was comforting. As comforting as Carmine's friendship and guidance could be however, he wasn't exactly living like most sober members of the fellowship. He was still very much a drug dealer. He just wasn't using the drugs himself.

This is absolutely frowned upon by the sober fellowship. "I don't understand how you do that and not get high," I said to him in amazement.

"You see blue, I see green," he arrogantly replied. One day I was fidgeting around the apartment when I noticed a sunglasses case. I wanted to check out the glasses but when I opened the box all I found was three blues. I jumped back and immediately mentioned it to Carmine before I started to get some bright ideas.

"You know the big book promises us we will recoil from it like a hot flame," he said.

I didn't remember reading that line but it was precisely what had happened when I saw them.

I tried to get him a job with me at the restaurant but easy money spoiled him lazy. He'd only work one or two shifts and tried to get out of them whenever he could. I did, however, take immense pleasure in being in a position where he had to ask me if he could go take a cigarette break.

About a month after moving in, Carmine adopted the sweetest little dog in the world. It was definitely his dog and his responsibility though because I still couldn't manage a cold at that time, let alone a living thing. But I had the pleasure of living under the same roof as that dog. She was an adorable little Boston Terrier named Jordan. Her previous owner couldn't keep her so we inherited a fully trained and well-behaved dog who brought us endless joy. I was ecstatic because I never had a dog of my own and would always get attached to other people's dogs. Eventually, Layla and Carmine got back together. Carmine immediately put to rest any fears of me having to move out.

"Don't worry, we're taking it slow and she's going to stay at home with her parents," he said.

In order to score brownie points with Carmine, Layla bought him another Boston Terrier. Now Jordan had a companion. "What do we name her?" Carmine asked me. "Well we got Jordan, she's gotta be Pippen," I exclaimed. Carmine went for it and the rest is history. The greatest tandem of dogs was named after the greatest tandem of basketball players.

Carmine went on to adopt some more animals. Dom was always hanging by the apartment and scheming with Carmine. They concocted this idea of starting a bearded dragon breeding business. Our basement was filled with twenty tanks of bearded dragons. I loved the bearded dragons, especially this one we named after Quagmire on Family Guy. What I didn't like was that the basement smelled like a zoo. That and they ate either cockroaches or baby mice. I loathe cockroaches and the baby mice were so cute that I had trouble accepting their fate. One day I was taking a nap on the couch and, to toy with me, Carmine and Dom threw a cockroach on my leg. I dramatically got up, went to my room, slammed the door, and went back to sleep listening to the two of them giggling like little girls about it in the living room. Aside from having cockroaches thrown on me, at any given moment I could open up the freezer to find a dead bearded dragon. They would put them in the freezer as a sort of Doctor Kevorkian style euthanasia. If a bearded dragon was sick and not going to make it, they ended up in the freezer. It took forever for them to finally get two bearded dragons to mate. When God created bearded dragons he certainly didn't make it easy for them to get laid. The male has to do it doggy style but the female has to be in a really awkward position if they're going to have a romance commence. Carmine was out early one morning and asked me to check on a female who was expecting. She buried about fifty eggs in her tank. Half of the eggs didn't make it but it still seemed like a good score. Carmine and Dom would sell them through social media under the company name, Reptile Dysfunction. After seeing what an uphill battle it was to become lizard kings, they gave up on their dreams.

One kid who hung around the sober fellowship was Ray. He was pretty tight with my little brother. He was sober but he was struggling like all hell to stay that way. One night we all went to Woodrow diner after a meeting and he asked me if I prayed. The sober fellowship insists on prayer but that wasn't exactly my forte back then. I shook my head no and he in turn said, "I pray all the fucking time and I still feel out of place." He said it with an intensity and a fear in his eyes that scared me. He seemed dumbfounded that I was staying sober, seemingly effortlessly, while he was trying as hard as he could. Two days later, I saw him by the Eltingville train station sitting on the steps. I recognized his map of Italy tattoo and called his name. Upon hearing his name, he got startled and threw up projectile vomit. I knew right then and there that he relapsed. I invited him over to the apartment so Carmine and I could possibly talk some sense into him. Carmine used to babysit Ray and his brothers when they were children. We managed to convince him that going to rehab was the next logical step. The next day he went to a rehab in Georgia but inevitably he left AMA to go get high again.

He overdosed and died. I was ordinarily desensitized to people dying from overdoses but his death haunted me. The way he told me that he was praying constantly for relief from his affliction and to end up dead anyway reinforced my skepticism on the power of prayer.

Twelve - Coasting

I went on to enjoy what turned out to be my first summer completely sober since childhood. Pat's brother-in-law was a heavy marijuana trafficker and he needed guys to drive the stuff from one state to another. Carmine and I were invited to tag along for a few of these runs. He paid us $300 each just to drive from New Jersey to Connecticut or from Vermont back to New York. He had stash houses and people that he needed it delivered to all over the place. The first time I made a drop off his lawyer was there overseeing the whole thing and they had $50,000 on a table. Pat and I had to take the money back and a taste was left there for the lawyer. I had never seen that much cash before or since. Now mind you, I'm supposed to be a sober member of a spiritual fellowship. Running drugs was definitely frowned upon. But with the extra money I made, I was able to put a down payment on my first decent car in years. I leased a black Kia Optima. The day I got the car I asked Carmine to cover me at Pico's so I could enjoy it.

"I can't tonight, Layla's going on vacation tomorrow I want to see her," he said.

I was furious. "Oh, because we all know how much you care about Layla," I said condescendingly. It always disturbed me how he would treat her. Layla was beautiful and she adored him. He would cheat on her relentlessly. I couldn't understand back then why someone would do that to such a sweet girl.

"You'll be able to drive your new car anytime. I can only see her tonight," he said.

On the first couple interstate marijuana runs, I went with just Pat. But on one of them I finally met the brother-in-law. I took the ride with him and seeing as how the ride from Vermont back to New York was about four hours, we got to chatting quite a bit. He kept rambling on with justifications for his line of work. "I'm able to support my family and give them nice things because I do this. I'm able to put money in the pockets of the people I care about. Just look at how great Pat is doing," he said.

In my head I thought, "whatever helps you sleep at night buddy." In an attempt to alleviate his guilt for being an outlaw I said, "Hey man I certainly don't judge. I was arrested multiple times when I was addicted to pills." Upon hearing about my past troubles with the law, he ended up telling Pat he didn't want someone with an arrest record coming on the runs. I was upset about it but was also rather philosophical about the whole thing. Sure I'd miss the money but it wasn't exactly in my best interests to be going on drug runs.

The next run they went on, Carmine and Pat got hassled by the local cops. The weed was mailed to a house Pat's brother-in-law had in Vermont. Postal service caught wind of what was inside and had the police bring Carmine and Pat, who spent the night at the house waiting for the delivery, in for questioning. The problem for the cops was that they brought them in without letting them collect the package. They were able to just play stupid and say it must've been the wrong address. Until they picked it up themselves, there was no way to press charges unless they fessed up to it. They tried telling both of them separately that the other was snitching out the other. They both knew that was bullshit. Neither of them would rat on the other. Especially those two. They're both pretty calm individuals. Plus, that lawyer involved in the operation gets paid really good money to make sure nobody sees major trouble. Without actually handling the package, they both felt pretty safe. They were let go and one of the cops told them not to come back to their quaint little town.

A newcomer to the sober fellowship became a prominent member of our group. He already knew Ron, Carmine, and a few of the other guys. His name was Jack and he was also an Elite Recovery alumnus. He knew my buddy George so with that common ground we bonded right away. Jack was the baby of our group. He's a few years younger than the rest of us. A short stocky guy who was always smiling. We all couldn't help but love him. Eventually he asked me to get him a job at Pico's. I was reluctant at first because I didn't want to vouch for someone I barely knew and have it reflect poorly on me if he was awful. But I got him the job and he quickly became one of the best workers in there.

Mark was on his way to fulfilling his dream of following his father's footsteps into the New York Police Department. His ambitions would seemingly be railroaded by the psychological exam. The psychologist tried to push his buttons to see how he reacted. Pushing Mark's buttons is not hard to do. At times, the slightest inconvenience could get him to blow a gasket. One night, Mark and I were hanging out with Tony in Tony's parents' backyard. Tony was one of the few people from our old group of friends we were willing to hang out with since getting sober. We loved him way too much. Mark was explaining the details of his psychological examination. First, she asked him about drinking. "I used to have about two or three beers here and there," he told her. "Why'd you stop?" she asked. Not wanting to explain that he was in recovery, he went with, "I had to stop because I was beginning to get a gut." Then she pressed him about drug related summonses pertaining to marijuana that he received as a teenager. He navigated his way out of that debacle and then she asked him, "What was the saddest day of your life?" He went on to describe the day he found Pat's brother Louie dead from an overdose. "So let me get this straight, you stopped drinking because you drank so much you were getting fat, you've been caught smoking marijuana, and you have the type of friends that end up dead from drug use? Sounds to me like you're not a great candidate for the police department." This enraged Mark. Tony and I wanted to tell him it didn't sound too hopeful but we didn't have the heart to break it to him. It didn't matter though. His father retired at a pretty high rank and obviously had friends within the department. His psychological examination may or may not have been conveniently misplaced. Mark got into the police department. Despite whatever psychological issues he might have, he would go on to become a hero cop and certainly one of my heroes. Of all my friends he went on to become the first one to accomplish something I believe someone ought to be proud of. He was constantly in the local newspaper for pulling hero maneuvers. I couldn't have been happier for him. Not bad for a guy who used to sniff blues all day like they were going out of style.

September rolled around and I went on to celebrate my one-year anniversary of sobriety. I had Father John speak for the celebratory meeting. He was amazing as always. He worked as a teacher within the Catholic school system so he spoke about beating children when he was drunk which was always hilarious to me. Mark was my second speaker. I chose him because I would've never reached that milestone without him bringing me around a year prior. I should've had him speak first though because Father John is a tough act to follow. My parents then got to say a few words. It was a teary-eyed moment for me. My father said, "When I drove you to meet your friends from here one day, it was the first time I saw you happy. Genuinely happy, not the happiness you'd express when you were going to get your next fix." My mother said, "I'm proud to say I'm Stephen Sacchi's mother." That melted my heart. Johnny was there too but he was visibly stoned. He was asked to share but he kept it short and sweet. This victory was short lived though. Trouble was brewing right around the corner. Father John gave me a book called "The Power of Positive Thinking" as a gift. Inside he wrote, "Don't let the gifts of sobriety take you away from sobriety." It felt like an eerie premonition. Part of my soul felt it coming.

Thirteen - Relapse

That following autumn, Cassandra, that counter girl from Nonna's, started hanging around the sober fellowship. She had a different boyfriend named Simon at that time but I figured she had cheated before so she'd probably cheat again. Sure enough, I was able to navigate past the boyfriend with ease. Unbeknownst to me at first, Cassandra was on a different sobriety plan than the rest of us. She just wanted to stop taking Oxycodone. Everything else under the sun was on the table. She had mentioned taking ecstasy one weekend and I started to salivate like a Pavlov dog. We planned a night to take some ecstasy together under the condition that we would swear not to take any Oxycodone. I suggested she find us some Xanax for the come down instead. While planning this out, I made sure I could stay over her house that night because Carmine would've been able to see that I got high. About a week before the night we planned on taking ecstasy, Cassandra was over the apartment. Layla, who Carmine had recently patched things up with, was over as well. She was snooping around the place and noticed a box of condoms with one missing. Layla enjoyed the sensations of Fire & Ice Trojans but hadn't recalled using one from this particular box. She started crying hysterically and Carmine wasn't home to defend himself. Luckily, I had noticed the condom box by some strange bit of luck earlier that day. I told her I used it. She asked me, "What brand are the condoms?" I gave her the correct answer much to her surprise. She followed up with, "How many did you take?" I made a lucky guess and told her one. That pretty much eased her concerns.

Cassandra knew I was covering for Carmine. I think watching the emotional ramifications of infidelity gave her a bit of a guilt trip because she called it off with me that same night. She did however, agree to take ecstasy with me like we planned. After that though it would have to end.

The next morning, Carmine and I were woken up by our crazy tenant. He would often bang on his floor, our ceiling, to annoy us. We enjoyed cheap rent at that apartment but not without great cost. The man who lived above us, Dan, was old and insane. A bat-shit crazy, fat grumpy old bastard who hated us for no good reason at all. All things considered we were pretty docile for a couple of young guys thanks to sobriety. We didn't make much noise. He was especially particular about his truck. He had a motion sensor placed next to it and a camera directed at it. One time, Father John came by the apartment to pick up Carmine. Carmine's newborn niece had some complications at birth so Father John was going to give her the Anointing of the Sick sacrament. His niece, thank God, pulled through and is in good health.

After Father John and Carmine hit the road, Dan came by and yelled through the screen door, "You tell that guy if he comes near my truck again, I'm going to crack his fucking skull open!"

With a sarcastic tone I said, "Well he's a priest so I'm not going to threaten him with violence for you."

On that particular morning he was banging on his floor with something that sounded like a bowling ball. I woke up to about four or five bangs over my bedroom. Then he walked over Carmine's bedroom and banged another four or five times there. Then he came back over mine and then back over Carmine's. He repeated this routine a few more times before I finally had enough. I went outside and waved my hand over the sensor near his truck to set it off. Then I threw two middle fingers in the direction of his surveillance camera watching the truck. After that, I went back inside and waited. A moment later I heard his screen door pop open and slam shut. I ran outside and lured him to the backyard so I could hit him out of the sight of his camera. Once we were out of the camera's line of sight, I froze up. As cold of a bastard as I can be at times, I couldn't bring myself to hit an elderly man, even if he was crazy.

But then Carmine came outside throwing fists like a rabid dog. Dan proceeded to spray his eyes with a mace can. Thank God Carmine came outside like a madman because I realized the mace can was probably meant for me.

After that the gloves came off. Carmine and I just started wailing on him. By the time the mace had settled into Carmine's eyes he was hunched over Dan who was on the floor on all fours. Dan started crying, "You hit me! You fucking hit me!" I then shouted, "You know what? I'm going to hit you!" I proceeded to run towards him and delivered an upper cut to his head. We let him be after that.

Dan proceeded to call the police. That move might've worked for him if he didn't mace Carmine and come back outside of his house to greet the police with a mace can still in his hands. We spun the story in our favor to the police. We barely had to embellish the story. At one point Dan told the cops that I upper cut him. About half a dozen cops walked towards me. They wanted to see my hands. Luckily, there wasn't any bruising or blood on them. "Believe me I wanted to crack him but he's an old man what am I gonna do?" I said convincingly enough to settle their suspicions. They bought our choir boy routine hook, line, and sinker. Then they arrested Dan.

"I want to thank you for acting like an absolute boss these last couple days. You single handedly shot down Layla's suspicions, uppercut Dan, and got him thrown in jail," Carmine said to me gratefully. I was happy to be of service.

The following weekend Cassandra and I took ecstasy. We decided to go bar hopping in Manhattan because I didn't want to be out drinking and tripping around Staten Island. Members of that sober fellowship might've seen me. My plan was to keep the relapse a secret and take it to the grave. After all, I managed a business for another member of the sober fellowship. He knew exactly what kind of person I could be when I'm getting high. He would've fired me for sure. After a few hours of drinking and having perceivably deep conversations for a few hours, we went back to her house. That's when she hit me with it. "I couldn't find us Xanax but I got us an oxy to come down with," she said. At that point I didn't care. I was coming down from the ecstasy and I needed to settle my nerves. I crushed the pill up, snorted it, let yet another wave of drug-induced euphoria wash over my body, and planted the seed for a whole lot of misery to come.

We continued seeing each other. We also continued taking little excursions with ecstasy as well.

Now that I was no longer sober, I was starting to get pretty irritable. I was constantly in a dark mood. Carmine saw me struggling to pay the bills by busting my ass off at work and suggested I go back home with my parents. "I feel like you're an indentured servant around here," he said. I agreed. I was burning myself out. I told my parents it was the best thing for my recovery but it was definitely the worst thing because I was just getting started on a relapse. I just wanted to come home, live rent free, and have more money to get high with. At work, I would make Jack my emotional punching bag. It would drive him nuts because he gravitated towards the spiritual aspect of sobriety. All that spirituality was put to the test when he had to take orders from someone who was stoned all day. Not to mention he had to keep it a secret from Paulie Cabinets because he wasn't going to rat out a buddy. So, he just dealt with me unreasonably berating him every night at work.

One night after taking ecstasy with Cassandra again, I slept over her house. She had the basement to herself so we were able to sneak in through the side door. In the morning, I was awoken by footsteps coming down the stairs. I was petrified. I wasn't supposed to be there but Cassandra insisted her parents wouldn't come downstairs. Her father was a kickboxing champion and used to be a leg breaker for street guys who needed legs broken. I never was one to resort to prayer but you better believe I was praying it was her mother and not her father coming down those stairs. I pretended to be asleep and hoped for the best. Nothing was said. Once I heard footsteps going back upstairs, I woke Cassandra up and said, "Somebody came downstairs."

"What? Who?"

"I'm not sure I pretended I was asleep."

"It was probably just my mom."

She seemed to have little to no concern that we were spotted together. "I'm gonna go," I told her. "You don't have to it's fine," she replied. "I'm up anyway I'm just gonna hit the road," I said. I kissed her goodbye and got the hell out of there. It wasn't her father who came downstairs but her mother did tell him there was a young man sleeping in the same bed as Cassandra and it wasn't her boyfriend Simon. Her father sat her down and explained to her that this was basically slutty behavior that he wouldn't tolerate. She heeded his wishes and ended it with me for good this time.

By that point I was smitten with her. She had discussed leaving her boyfriend for me but that talk with her father changed everything. All in all, she wasn't the prettiest girl I dated but she was absolutely hilarious. We'd laugh like idiots together as if she was one of the guys. That was her appeal to me. She was like a best pal more than a romantic interest. Not to mention she was a soccer player. My favorite part of the female anatomy is the thigh and her thighs were almost perfect. Needless to say, I didn't take this breakup particularly well. I resorted to Oxycodone. Before it was a once in a whilerelapse. Now it was a full-time relapse.

In an attempt to get over a heartbreak that wasn't going away, I resorted to one-night stands with more girls from the sober fellowship. The first was with a stripper named Taylor. Afterwards she went on a moral high horse and told Cassandra about it. Cassandra didn't care but I didn't enjoy the information getting back to her nonetheless. I resented Taylor a little bit for that maneuver. On Taylor's's night off, we all went to the strip club she worked at. She and one of her stripper pals who also had the night off were smoking a hookah. "Hey can I try that?" I asked her. "Yea sure let me get you another hose?" she said. "Another hose? You sucked my dick!" I shouted back. It didn't even occur to me how funny of a response that was. It was simply my knee jerk reaction to the thought of her worrying my germs might contaminate her hookah hose when my cock was in her mouth the week prior. The next night at work, I was making drinks behind the bar when Jack walked over to me and said, "Another hose? YOU SUCKED MY DICK!" That was when I realized just how funny my reaction was. Jack and I would constantly be working in the restaurant when it was busy and just say to each other, "Another hose?"

Another one-night stand with a girl from the sober fellowship was with Skylar. I had given her a job at Pico's as well and, like Jack, she'd be my emotional punching bag when I was out of it and moody. She was dating this guy Bruce who was tight with Carmine and the rest of the guys. Bruce constantly made it clear that he didn't approve of me with snide comments. Needless to say, I did not hesitate to sleep with Skylar behind his back. Skylar seemed to catch feelings even though I was honest with her up front. "I'm emotionally unavailable right now. I'm still hung up on Cassandra so if we do this, it's going to be just for fun," I told her. She claimed to have no problem with that but she got upset that I didn't try to see her anymore. I couldn't understand why she even wanted to see me again. I went completely flaccid on her in the middle of sex. Unbeknownst to her, I was pretty stoned. I didn't even notice I was soft serving until she got up, grabbed my dick and said, "You're not even fucking hard!" It didn't take long for her to quit Pico's after that.

Somewhere around this time I had gotten a letter from the Department of Sanitation. This was it. In New York City, the Sanitation Department is a six-figure career, with benefits, and you get to retire with a pension after 22 years. I was finally going to have my shot at getting the house with a white picket fence. That's all I ever wanted. I wanted to get a job that I could support a family on and get my taste of the American Dream. I took the exam for the job years prior and I didn't even remember that I had taken it. My parents coerced me into taking it and I was out of it that day. Turns out I'm efficient enough to lift garbage, even in a blackout. They had a hiring freeze-out for a few years and now they were calling in people who had taken that test. It would be a little while before I got on the job but in the meantime, I had to work on getting my CDL license. The test to get the permit was incredibly difficult. Try reading a bunch of useless information about engines when you're high on blues. It took me four or five tries just to get it. On the third try, I ran into Carmine in the parking lot. He was shopping at the Burlington Coat Factory store next door to the DMV. I was sitting in my car reading information that was not being absorbed by my brain. He tried confronting me, seeing that my relapse had left me in a state of grave emotional pain. I expressed my troubles with the test. "Maybe taking the Sanitation job isn't the best idea for you in this condition," he said. "What are you nuts?" I asked. "This is the only glimmer of hope I have in my life right now. I'm going to figure this out," I added. This was a career. It was more than I could have ever hoped for at that point.

My grandfather, who had fallen ill around this time, worked for the Department of Sanitation. It brought me quite a degree of satisfaction to be able to do the job he once did. I loved him and I'm sure I was nothing but a disappointment to him. When he died, I found out I was human after all. You see, when my grandparents on my mothers' side passed, I couldn't cry. All my cousins were emotional and crying and I felt like maybe I was just an inhumane emotionless psychopath. But the night he died I was stuck at work. Brooke, the other manager at Pico's, was barking orders at me and, seeing as how my grandfather was dying, I wasn't in the mood for her attitude. Eventually, she let me leave but not without a big argument that led to me throwing a chair across the room to demonstrate I meant business. I rushed to the hospital but I was too late. He had already passed. The aids were cleaning his sheets when I arrived. "Can I just have a moment alone with him?" I asked them. "Of course, we're almost done," one of them said. I apologized to him for not spending more time with him and for not being a better person. When I got to the waiting room to regroup with the rest of my family, I broke down. As soon as I saw them, I started crying. My grandfather's name was Achilles. In Greek mythology, Achilles was a great warrior dipped in the pool of immortality. He was held by his heel and that was the only part of him that wasn't dipped into the pool. His heel was the only part of him that was vulnerable, hence Achilles tendon. That night I wished my grandfather was dipped in the pool of immortality. But he was very much human. A very sweet and loving human.

One day I expressed regret over him seeing me as the disaster that I was to my father. My father consoled me with a story that made me feel better. "Stephen, Grandpa had a special place in his heart for you. When you asked Grandma to be your Confirmation sponsor, she started going back to church after that. Grandpa believed that, thanks to you, he would get to be with her in heaven because you brought her to God," he said.

CHAPTER
_____

Fourteen – Getting Back on Track

My friends got hooked on playing poker around this time. Until then, I had very limited experience at it and merely a general understanding of the game. Once we all got hooked on playing, Vinny got me hooked on gambling in general. I had never been to Atlantic City until one afternoon he invited me to join him for a trip down there. I'll never forget the first time I walked into a poker room in a casino. I was hooked immediately. The sound of all the poker chips around the room clacking sounded like an auditory hallucination. Then the worst possible thing that could've happened, happened. I won! It was only $100 but it felt like I won a fortune. Trips to Atlantic City and Parx casino in Pennsylvania became a weekly occurrence. The one good thing that came from this newfound addiction was I got sober again for a little while. I needed money to gamble with and gambling, at least for the time being, became more important than Oxycodone. I might be the only guy on the planet that got sober through gambling. I got pretty good pretty fast and would actually win from time to time. Most of the time though, I was making donations to strangers. There were so many parameters to the game that I wasn't familiar with yet. But I played pretty tight most of the time and patiently waited to have a good hand. With a stroke of luck, I would have some pretty good paydays.

Back at work, I came clean to Paulie Cabinets about my re-lapse. I figured I'd rather him hear it from me than someone else. He didn't fire me and I assured him I was sober. But this stretch of sobriety only lasted about 90 days. I took LSD on the Fourth of July and drove down to Atlantic City to meet Vinny and his buddy Sal. Sal is hands down one of the funniest people you'll ever meet. I like to think I'm pretty funny but I honestly can't compete with that guy. I met them at the Golden Nugget. They were already in the midst of a poker tournament. I sat down at a cash game table. The LSD started kicking in around the same time I was involved in a big hand. People were throwing hundreds of dollars into the pot and I had an open-ended straight flush draw. If a four of clubs or a nine of clubs came out, I would've had a straight flush. I was terrified calling huge bets because I couldn't walk away from that draw. If my card didn't come out, I would've lost a fortune on one hand. The river card was a two of clubs. It didn't give me a straight flush but I still had an eight high flush and it was enough to win the hand. I was up almost a thousand bucks from that hand alone. I tried hiding it at first but ultimately decided to come clean to Vinny that I took some acid. I swore him to secrecy because I preferred it that Paulie Cabinets didn't find out. Vinny was pretty reliable for that sort of thing. My friends aren't bleeding hearts like most of the people you find in the sober fellowship. Most members preach rigorous honesty and would insist I come clean about a relapse.

George came home for a visit so I went to visit him down in Long Branch with Jack. We met his mother and daughter and they ordered pizza for us. I was newly sober again so I was depressed. "What's the matter bud?" George asked. He knew I wasn't myself but I didn't feel like explaining to his entire family I was depressed from a relapse so I just shrugged it off. I could've been open about it. George's mother was very down to Earth and George spoke comfortably with her about his affliction but I didn't want to burden the reunion.

I sought help from Ron as I struggled to stay sober. He was the closest friend I had with multiple years sober aside from Dimitri. I really don't know what made me turn to Ron for guidance. He had a lifelong subscription to the spiritual aspect of sobriety. I never could fully grasp those concepts but I sought his help nonetheless. He was having some emotional turmoil of his own though. He called off his engagement to Valerie and she immediately started dating this older guy Hesh. Hesh just so happened to be Ron's hero. He even had him speak at his four-year anniversary of sobriety. After attending a meeting held by the sober fellowship, Ron and I decided to go out to eat so we could discuss my inner turmoil over dinner. As we were walking into the restaurant, Valerie and Hesh were walking out. Ron chatted with him in a rather cordial manner.

"The fuck you being so nice to him for?" I asked.

"What I don't care," he replied.

"If that was me, I would've asked Hesh why he couldn't have waited five fucking minutes for the wound to heal at least," I said. I was still too immature to understand the concept of having some dignity by being polite when awkwardly running into your ex and their new significant other. In my defense though, the situation was pretty disturbing. I mean this guy was his hero. The conversation over dinner quickly shifted to his relationship with Valerie.

"You know you're supposed to be the one listening to my problems here," I told him.

That summer was filled with plenty more trips to casinos. One particular time I went with Vinny and Sal again. We started at Harrah's where I won a few hundred bucks. Then we decided to play in a tournament at Bally's. On our way there we started making a few jokes about Jesus.

Sal said, "Jesus never sinned though right?"

To which I replied, "Yea but he got really out of pocket in that market that one time."

We all laughed at Jesus' marketplace tirade. Once we arrived at Bally's for the tournament, we still had the giggles about Jesus. Especially me.

I said to the lady at the counter, "Hey you know Jesus stayed at this hotel once? Yea he put three nails on the counter and said put me up for the night." I could tell that she and the pit boss standing behind her were avid patrons of Sunday Mass because they did not like that joke at all. I sat down at the tournament and realized my phone battery was low. I had my charger with me but I needed an outlet to plug it into. I walked back to the counter and asked if they had an outlet I could use.

The pit boss snickered to himself and said, "Oh so Jesus joke guy wants to charge his phone. Let me tell you something pal you got a better chance at seeing him than charging your phone!"

After initially laughing a bit, I decided to go ahead and apologize for the joke. It's hard for me to think before speaking. As I've grown older, I learned to understand that it's really not right to make fun of someone else's religion. Just because I have my prejudices with organized religion doesn't give me the right to poke fun at something that other people hold sacred. At least not to their face in a disrespectful manner.

Later that night, we found a half black and half Asian hooker who was drop dead gorgeous. I had won about $800 so money was no object. Sal, who lost that night, tried to lowball her and his lack of funds was starting to scare her away. I was going to have her come hell or high water. I immediately took control of the situation and let her know that I had money and we came to a mutually beneficial understanding. She came back to my room and I got an overpriced blowjob. Well worth it though considering how exotic looking she was and how I paid for it with money that I won as opposed to money I labored for. My friends made fun of me for paying so much but if I could go back and do it again, I'd probably pay more.

One night I was home alone, lonely, and in a masturbatory mood. I never watched any of my ex-girlfriend Nikki's pornos. I didn't want to see someone I cared about with someone else. But enough time had passed and the emotional attachment had subsided. I figured it'd be nice exploring familiar territory. I googled her name and instead of finding pornography, I found an obituary. I sat there in shock for a few moments. Vinny started texting me and I had to tell somebody what had happened. I explained why I googled her name in the first place and he responded with, "So did you still jerk off?" Ordinarily, I live for that brand of dark humor. But even I have a limit. I felt an overwhelming sense of survivor's guilt. I couldn't help but feel that maybe if I had gotten sober, I could've helped her.

The obituary, written by her mother Beth, didn't allude to the cause of death at all. I needed answers. I knew it had to be either a suicide or an overdose. I messaged the only friend of hers I knew through Facebook. "I know you must think the worst of me because I was admittedly, a terrible boyfriend. But please, I just found out Nikki passed. I need to know what happened," I wrote.

"I set her up with my friend Bryce and they started dating. I'm really not sure what happened but my guess is it was either a suicide or an overdose. Bryce and Beth found her is all I know. They didn't exactly open up to anyone about the details and they had a private funeral it was very strange."

When she wrote that they "found her" I envisioned her lifeless corpse in a tub and felt terrible. I became completely haunted by all the could've, would've, and should've.

Fifteen - DSNY

The start date for the Department of Sanitation was rapidly approaching. The prospect of being randomly drug tested for twenty-two years to get my pension was terrifying to me. I decided I should get high for a little while with a plan to sober up just before starting the job. Coincidentally, Cassandra called me out of the blue. She was single now and looking to have some fun. I didn't hesitate to oblige. We became a regular Sid and Nancy couple all over again. I decided to extend my Oxycodone use a little longer. At the last minute, I spent three days kicking cold turkey like I had done countless times before. My third day kicking was Columbus Day. It was technically my start date for the job. My first day was a paid day off. Who was better than me? I took Cassandra and Johnny to Six Flags. Johnny, thanks to his EMT experience, knew a loophole where if he faked a leg injury, they would have to give us a handicapped pass. He walked into the special needs office with a limp and walked out of there like Keyser Soze at the end of "The Usual Suspects." We rode every major roller coaster ride twice without waiting in line. I was in severe withdrawal but the adrenaline rush from the roller coasters helped ease my pain.

The next morning was my first day on the job. I had to be at Floyd Bennett Field in Brooklyn at 6 AM for training. Seth, my old barber, also got called for the job so we rode in together. First thing he did when he got into my car was crush up and sniff a blue. "The Sanitation Department's drug tests don't test for blues. My older brother's been on the job for years and he's a total pill junkie," he assured me. I didn't need much convincing. I had endured the worst of the withdrawals but was still feeling pretty lethargic. Sniffing a blue seemed downright exquisite at that moment. I snorted it and went about my training. After work, I called Cassandra and let her know the good news. We could keep on getting high together. It was music to her ears because I was the buffoon that kept helping her get high. She rarely contributed to helping me get high. If she managed to scheme some cash together, she'd secretly keep it for herself. Towards the end of the month-long training process, I developed a bad reputation. The other guys were calling me "pills" because I was clearly on a bunch of them every morning. I was constantly nodding out. I survived that whole ordeal though and tried to straighten myself out again before arriving at my assigned garage but it was to no avail. Seth was in the garage downstairs from mine so any time I had a moment of weakness, I could just ask him for one and make the day exponentially better.

More tragedy would follow. My brother, completely strung out, managed to lose his EMT gig with the Fire Department. Out of desperation to satisfy his growing Oxycodone addiction, he made a habit of robbing Home Depot. One day they were waiting for him to strike again. Once he did, they had him arrested. If you get arrested when you work for a city agency, they immediately notify your job. Johnny was subsequently fired from an awesome career. He'd be the first Sacchi, but not the last, to have that happen. My parents urged him to go to rehab. They sent him to Ocean Mist Recovery, the same place that had helped me twice. I was happy to know that at least he would be in the hands of people who actually cared.

Cassandra was, as far as I could tell, a baby user when she first started hanging around that sober fellowship. But once we linked back together, she was progressively going further down the rabbit hole. My soul was already doomed but hers was about to be as well. One day she came over with a sad expression on her face. Her parents were forcing her to go to a rehab in Florida. I was rather accepting of the situation. As much as I loved getting high and being with her, I genuinely cared about her and would've rather seen her get well. The problem was she didn't get well. She would end up getting sucked into the seedy culture that is South Florida recovery. My brother went down there first but he kept it together for the most part. After rehab he stayed down there and got hooked up in one of those sketchy telemarketing phone rooms that sells health insurance. He really took to it and started making a killing. I could never sit still in one of those phone rooms. I liked to pretend that I had some sort of moral compass and was above resorting to making good money pulling those kinds of scams but, the truth is, I just can't sit at a phone for eight hours straight. I'd rather be broke than want to hang myself all day.

Once Cassandra left, I was stuck bearing an insufferable winter strung out and alone. The Sanitation Department is responsible for snow removal. That winter it snowed excessively. I had the lowest seniority in my garage so I was constantly getting forced to stay overtime and, if there were any undesirable jobs to do, I was stuck with it. Plowing the snow wasn't bad but getting forced to shovel snow off sidewalks was miserable. Compound that with Oxycodone addiction and it was a recipe for disaster. I was constantly giving guys an attitude with my irritability. One time I was shooting pool in the break room. I accidentally bumped into some Hispanic guy who was an ex-con. He converted to Islam whilst incarcerated. Quite a combo if you ask me. I apologized for bumping into him but he told me, "Watch where you're going!" I was aggravated, especially because I tried being cordial at first but he had to be a tough guy with me and I was in no mood. "Look man I apologized there's no need to be a cunt about it," I snapped back. After that we started getting into each other's faces and I was ready to beat him to death. He was shorter than my mother and the years clearly hadn't been kind to him. If half the garage didn't step in between us I was going to put his name on the LODI (Line of Duty Injury) board.

The first year and a half on the job is the probationary period. If you mess up in the slightest way within that time period, you get fired. The other rookies on probation all thought I should've had my head examined for almost getting into a fight. Our careers were extraordinarily vulnerable. However, my drug use was a shining example of how much I valued my career. I was too young, too stupid, and too wrapped up in my addiction and all the negative attitudes and behaviors that come along with that to let that man talk down to me.

Whenever I was lucky enough to have a day off from Sanitation, I would pick up a shift at Pico's. Not because I wanted to. I had to if I was going to stay a step ahead of my addiction. One night I was too tired to go through with it. My body was aching so I had Brooke cut me early. When I got in my car, it was facing north when I had to go south to get home. The first opportunity to make a legal U-turn wasn't going to come for a few blocks. I was so exhausted that I couldn't even fathom the idea of driving an extra two minutes, so I made an illegal U-turn at the next intersection. I also blew a red light in the process because I didn't want to be stuck waiting for the southbound traffic to pass in order to make that illegal U-turn. I got pulled over by the Metro cops. They usually handle the train stations but the audacity of my maneuver made them pull me over. I showed my Sanitation Department badge to the officer along with my license and registration. "Look officer I know that was a dumb move, but I already got a lot of points on my license for speeding and I can't afford to lose my job with the Sanitation Department. I'm still on probation. If my license gets suspended, I'm fucked," I told him.

"Look, I want to extend the courtesy because you're a city worker but you realize you not only made a U-turn where you weren't supposed to, but you blatantly burnt a red light right in front of me," he said.

"I know it was bad but I've been stuck working twelve-hour shifts because of the snow and I'm also working here at Pico's on top of that to help make ends meet. I'm just exhausted and want to get the fuck home so I can sleep. If you write this ticket, I'll lose my job with Sanitation and then I'll have to go back to college to make something of myself," I replied.

He laughed and said, "Alright I'm gonna let you off with a warning." As he was handing me back my license he paused for a moment. "You know you look kind of familiar," he said.

"Ah I just got one of those faces," I told him.

He handed me back my license and I drove off. After a few blocks it hit me. That was the same bald Metro cop that I pulled the most brazen of escapes on years prior. With a bit of luck, maybe a few days later he was eating dinner with his wife and children when it finally hit him whom he pulled over. I imagine it being a quiet dinner where all you can hear is chewing and the silverware clacking against the porcelain plates. In an attempt to break the ominous silence, the wife says, "Michael got an A on his science project." Pretending to be interested he says, "Great job buddy, I'm proud of ya!" He's not interested because he's contemplating his miserable existence. He's in law enforcement but he's not quite a real cop. Simply a Metro cop. He's like a punter on a Super Bowl Champion football team. He's on the team but he gets none of the glory nor the accolades. And then more dread enters his mind. He remembers who I was. He realizes that the one big fish he could've caught was just within his grasp. Then he flips the dining room table over and screams,

"MOTHERFUCKER! I HAD HIM!" Ketchup spills onto Michael's shirt and his wife finally musters the courage to give that divorce attorney a phone call.

Around this time, Carmine had successfully parlayed all of his money from selling blues into opening a vape store. I never admitted it to him because I love him but I was consumed with envy. I wish I had the discipline to sell blues while sober and turn that money into a legitimate business. To see his success come with such ease while I was barely hanging on to a city job drove me insane. Especially when I was spending my days off working at the restaurant and still having nothing to show for myself at the end of the week. My Oxycodone addiction saw to that but, even if I was sober, I wouldn't have been doing that much better. It's downright pathetic what the starting pay is for the Sanitation Department. It takes five and a half years to get to top pay and that might as well have been decades away. At the end of the day though, I was just a miserable ungrateful prick who was hooked on pills once again. I was looking at the glass as half empty no matter where I looked.

I was starting to get nervous about the impending pill problem. They may not have tested for blues at work but I knew I was going to get caught sooner or later. I could feel it coming. I tried going to Florida on a four-day weekend to kick cold turkey. I figured being away from home would help temptation and I could visit Johnny and Cassandra. Johnny said I could crash at his apartment when I called him. I stopped to see him at his office right after I landed. His roommates were there working as well and they saw that I was in withdrawal and were worried I

188 Stephen J. Sacchi

would steal their stuff so I could score drugs. I was livid. I had money and other things of value. I didn't need to steal their stuff if I wanted to get high. My brother may have tried to make a case for me but I was still angry with him. If the shoe was on the other foot, there's no way anybody could tell me to turn my back on my brother. But then again, I wouldn't have someone who wears a pair of Gucci loafers on an uneventful Tuesday afternoon as a roommate. These guys rip off people over the phone all day to pay for those gaudy loafers and they're worried that I'm going to steal them.

Cassandra wanted nothing to do with me either. She was on a moral high ground now that she had sixty days sober and, according to her, I was jeopardizing her sobriety. I felt completely betrayed. The two people I would do just about anything for were looking at me like I was nothing. I ended up going to hang out with Declan, my first sponsor, and George. They cheered me up a little bit. Especially Declan. When I told him what happened with Johnny and Cassandra, he said to me, "You're just getting mad because you're expecting others to behave as awesome as you would. More often than not, that is an unrealistic expectation." Putting it in those terms made me feel better. At the end of the day though, I was still in emotional turmoil. I had to stay at a Super 8 motel. It cost a pretty penny, but I had managed to secure a credit card that I was running up quite a debt with. Before that trip I was taking my dealer shopping and received a plethora of pills. It wouldn't take long for me to max out the card without any intention or means of paying it back.

Upon returning home, I managed to stay sober for a couple months. I missed Cassandra and thought that she would enjoy a visit now that I was sober and not kicking. The next three-day weekend I got, I decided to head back down to Florida. When I picked her up she was acting strange. "Just drop me off at the Dunkin Donuts on Atlantic Ave. I'm meeting one of my father's friends there I'll meet up with you later," she said. She was really going to meet some snapback hat with a flat brim wearing douchebag from Boston named Shane who had more holes than a golf course in his arms thanks to intravenous heroin use. She didn't even wait for me to drive away. Just went right up to him and kissed him. Cassandra and I were never boyfriend and girlfriend. I knew she wasn't a saint. But don't encourage me to come visit you and then ditch me for some white kid who spins his hat backwards and the pinnacle of his wardrobe is Jordan shorts. I caught her when she was alone and confronted her. "You're father's friend huh?" I asked. She didn't even say anything. She simply went crazy and started wailing on me. I already felt disrespected enough and to top it off she's slapping me for calling her out on it. If there weren't people outside, I might've knocked her out.

I decided to meet up with George and lick my wounds. Luckily, he was getting high again which was exactly what I needed. My brother, whom I'd forgiven for leaving me high and dry on my last visit, was supposed to meet me around this time. When we negotiated a rendezvous, I was planning on staying sober. By the time he finally met George and me, I let him know that the original sobriety plan had changed drastically. George and I secured some Dilaudid. George was a needle user. I still was yet to shoot up. I either snorted or swallowed it.

I was in such emotional pain from the Cassandra situation, that I decided shooting it was the logical decision. I felt terrible about involving my brother because he saw me do it and jumped right on board. I'll never forget that first experience of mainlining an opioid, especially Dilaudid. The rush from Dilaudid is even more intense than heroin is.

"It's going to feel like you're overdosing but just breathe and remember it's perfectly normal," George assured me.

I sunk into the chair and experienced an awesome euphoria that practically left me paralyzed in comfort. It was absolutely amazing. Better than sex by a long shot. You could completely kiss the idea of me getting sober goodbye after that.

Cassandra called me the following morning, somewhat apologetic. We decided to go score some dope and get high together. She claimed she had a guy. I explained to her that half the Haitian drug dealers down there were scam artists. They'll just run off and leave you with nothing. "Make sure you see the stuff before you hand them any money," I stressed to her. I was gravely concerned because it was my money she was using. She was new to South Florida but I had experienced their antics the hard way countless times when I lived down there. She assured me she had it under control but she didn't.

I emptied the bag out and said, "You see! I fucking warned you! It's rocks!" Her eyes lit up and she asked, "Crack rocks?" I shrugged. "No you fucking nincompoop! Rocks! Pebbles!" I screamed at her. I made up a bullshit story to my father as to why I needed cash deposited into my bank account and I had George get us more Dilaudid's. Afterwards, Cassandra and I went back to my hotel and had sex. Naturally, I let my guard down. I didn't even realize I would need to have my guard up. When I went to the bathroom, she snatched my Movado watch. It was the first nice watch I had ever bought. I loved that watch. She traded it for three bags of heroin. I was more upset that all she got for it was a measly three bags than the theft itself.

After that whole fiasco, I returned home and tried taking Suboxone for the sake of keeping it together on some level. I received word from various friends I had down in Florida that Cassandra was running around homeless, intravenously using heroin on a daily basis, and that kid Shane was pimping her out. When there was nowhere else to turn, she asked for my help. I got her a flight back and insisted she stay at my house for a couple days before going home. I wanted her to stay put so she could kick the habit. I let my mom know what was going on but she didn't mind. My mother loved Cassandra. One day I was at work and her father came by the house looking for her. The neighbors across the street were friendly with Cassandra's whole family and they had seen Cassandra. I wasn't home when he came by. My mother was under the impression that I was still sober for over two years. She painted me in such a positive light. Cassandra's father expressed gratitude to me but I had a guilty conscience. My heart was in the right place. I wanted to see her get sober. Especially if using meant she would subject herself to prostitution. It disgusted me to think of her doing that to herself. But who did I think I was to try and steer her in the right direction? Anytime the two of us got together, all attempts to get sober were completely off the table. She hated enduring the constant scrutiny of her family so, as soon as she found an opportunity, she jetted to Florida to be with Shane.

I was dealing with problems of my own. Most of the time I would take Suboxone strictly for the sake of saving money. Whenever I was flush with cash though I would binge on Oxycodone until I was blue in the face. One day I bought a bunch of blues before work. Then I went to meet my neighbor Aaron for some Suboxone. I can't be sure but I think he set me up to get himself out of his own troubles. I met him up the street in my car. He did a handoff through the window and, as he was passing me the Suboxone, I noticed him look behind me. Once I drove away, I peeked into my rear-view mirror to see what he was looking at and noticed an undercover police wagon behind me. I immediately swallowed the three blues I had and stashed the Suboxone in my boot. They pulled me over and searched me. There was a quarter of a Suboxone still in my middle console that I was unaware of. For that, and for that alone, they cuffed me and sank my career with the Department of Sanitation. I was in uniform and they didn't hesitate to arrest me over a miniscule amount of Suboxone. The officer acted like he caught El Chapo when he found it too.

When you work for the city, if you get arrested your job is immediately notified. Even if they weren't notified, I was still going to be fired anyway. I wasn't given my phone call in time so I was considered AWOL for my shift. That, in and of itself, was grounds for termination. The department didn't fire me immediately. I told the superintendent of my garage the truth of what was going on. Before being fired, I requested that I be sent to rehab through the Department. My health insurance was contingent on my job that I was about to lose. I had to check myself in before they fired me and my fingers were crossed that by some miracle, they would forgive my sins. They sent me to what's called the EAU department. The Sanitation Department is full of addicts and alcoholics so they had an entire office dedicated to helping its employees seek help when needed. Only difference between me and most of the other afflicted employees was they'd already been through the probationary period. They assigned a man named Brian to my case. He really had no business working with addicts and alcoholics.

He asked me, "If you're taking pills daily, why would you take this job?" As if some junkie is going to turn down a great career because it would be morally wrong to operate heavy machinery whilst getting high. I had to bite my tongue, seeing as how my job was on the line, but I wanted to ask him if he was dense in the head. He wanted to send me to a rehab in the Poconos that very day. Ron, Vinny, and I had tickets to see The Rolling Stones, that Saturday night in Buffalo. We had to go to Buffalo because they weren't playing anywhere closer on that tour for some reason. I told Brian that I couldn't afford to lose my other job on top of the one that was already in jeopardy and I couldn't get off work on Sunday so I would have to check into rehab on Monday. He bought my deception. My career was on the line and I was more concerned with seeing The Rolling Stones. My priorities were obviously in check.

Sixteen - Buffalo

Like any good junkie who's going to rehab soon, I amassed a huge collection of drugs for the road trip to see the Stones. I had it all. LSD, ecstasy, Xanax, heroin, Oxycodone, and pot. I was stocked up to see a rock band that made its mark in the 60's so I prepared accordingly. Ron and Vinny were completely sober. They basically were stuck babysitting me for the duration of the weekend. I got quite a kick out of it at the time. I'm hard enough to deal with if I'm sober. Vinny found it funny but Ron was driving so it completely tortured him. I slept for most of the ride there. The only time I woke up was to do more heroin. I'd pretend I needed to stop at a gas station for "snacks" but really, I just needed a bathroom to do drugs in without judgement from the front seat. I dropped LSD about a half hour prior to arriving at the stadium. Once there, I lit a blunt to kick start my trip. Once I was on cloud 9, I was ready to see my favorite band.

Thank God for Ron's prosthetic leg because we were able to upgrade from the nosebleed seats to the handicapped section. We were still feeling greedy though and wanted to be on the floor level. Vinny spotted a ticket usher who looked like he didn't care enough about his job and said, "If we throw that kid $100, he's going to let us in." Sure enough he did. He even gave us the proper wristbands for floor seats. The only problem was that the concert was a sold-out show. The security guards kept telling us to find our seats but we didn't have seats. Once again, the prosthetic leg came in handy. Ron asked one of the security guards if there was a handicapped section. The guard pointed to a row of seats so close to the stage it was unbelievable. I decided to go to the bathroom to snort some ecstasy because LSD and heroin wasn't enough to wet my whistle. As the line of ecstasy burnt my nostrils, I heard the opening riff to "Jumpin' Jack Flash" burst out of Keith Richards' guitar like an atom bomb. I ran out of the bathroom and back to our seats.

My friends' torture continued. I was so high that about five minutes into the song, "Sympathy for the Devil", I asked Ron, "Wait! Wait! Did Sympathy for the Devil just start or has it been on for a while?" He laughed at me and explained that I was losing my mind because the song had been on for quite some time. Much to my surprise, they did my absolute favorite two Stones songs. "Midnight Rambler" and "Can't You Hear Me Knockin'." Old and wrinkly and I'd still rather see them than anybody else. They were incredible.

After the concert we had trouble securing lodging for the evening. The Stones concert brought in a lot of out of towners so there were no vacancies anywhere. Finally, we found a motel with one room available. The clerk said, "Problem is we only have one room left with three separate beds." The three of us looked at each other confused. Was the guy being sarcastic or was he just stupid? Three separate beds for three heterosexual young men would've not only done the trick, it actually suited our needs way better than we could've expected. I was completely willing to sleep on the floor or cuddle with one of my buddies but getting my own bed worked out great. I snorted a couple bags of heroin in the bathroom and went to sleep.

The next day we did some sightseeing at Niagara Falls. There's this boat ride that takes you past one of the waterfalls called, "Maid of the Mist." I'm not sure what the cover charge was but, between the concert itself, the motel room, and everything else we spent our money on that weekend, we didn't feel like paying to get on a boat ride. However, it did pique our interest enough to sneak on. Ron, Vinny, and I are huge Andrew Dice Clay fans. We heard him go on the Opie & Anthony radio show and talk about pointing to a manager as he told store employees at the door, "It's handled. Ask that guy over there!" in an authoritative tone when he shoplifted something. They actually ended up believing him. The ticket usher was just a teenager. We made up a name. "Yea we lost our tickets but we spoke to Mike, it's handled," I said to him. "Oh, ok but do you got your tickets?" he responded. "I mean what did he just say, we lost our tickets but we spoke to Mike, it's handled!" Ron chimed in. Worked like a charm. The boat ride was not particularly impressive but because we managed to sneak on for free, we enjoyed it. You wear a poncho, get soaked, and marvel at the wonder of a waterfall.

Seventeen - Rehab in Pennsylvania

The car ride home from Buffalo began to get a little intolerable. I ran out of heroin and blues so I popped a Xanax to take the edge off of the withdrawals. Once we made it back to Staten Island, I made Ron stop at my dealer's house. I had a check from work that was going to clear in the morning and I needed a healthy dose before rehab so I insisted my dealer wake up early so I could buy more then. A driver from the rehab was supposed to come by at noon. I hopped on the train at about 9 am. By 10 am I was snorting blues like they were going out of style in my dealer's apartment. Then I received a phone call from my mother. Apparently, the driver showed up two hours early. "Well she's gonna have to wait ma!" I shouted into the phone. My mother knew exactly what I was up to. She told me that she asked the driver, "When you pick these addicts up, you come alone?" The driver, a sweet and innocent young lady, said yes. My mother then asked, "You're not worried about what might happen driving these people to and from rehab by yourself?" She assured my mother that she'd never had a problem before and that everything SHOULD be fine. She had no idea who was being unleashed upon her. Nothing could've prepared this poor girl for a completely strung out Stephen Sacchi.

I got back home around 11 am. I knew the food at this rehab would be sub-par so I wanted to get a decent breakfast. The driver was not accustomed to making pit stops on these rides but I broke her down immediately. I offered to buy her breakfast. "I'm telling you this'll be the best breakfast you ever had in your life," I insisted. For six bucks, Casale's bakery on Page Avenue gave you an elite breakfast that included eggs, bacon, toast, and their trademark breakfast potatoes with some peppers and onions. Inside I saw this older gentleman that I knew from the sober fellowship. I chewed his ear off about going into rehab. I probably ruined his breakfast because he wasn't a fan of mine to begin with. The driver kept trying to rush me out of there and I just kept telling her, "Relax! This is my friend here. I'm going away for a little while. Can I just enjoy my breakfast please? Thank you!" About an hour into the ride, I insisted I had to stop to take a piss. I really just wanted to finish the rest of the Oxycodone I bought and smoke a cigarette because I couldn't smoke in her car. I was a complete menace. The Xanax from the night before was still very much having an impact on my behavior along with the Oxycodone I had been snorting all morning. On my way inside the gas station's convenient store, I couldn't find a butt can for my cigarette so I threw it on the floor. Then I proceeded to the bathroom and finished the rest of my pills. As I was walking back out, the attendant started screaming at me about the cigarette. I inquired about the butt can. Apparently, there was one but it wasn't exactly in sight. "Well what the fuck man? I don't got a crystal ball, I didn't fucking see it!" I shouted. He continued with his tirade which really pissed me off so I lit another cigarette right inside of the store and started cursing at him. Then I flicked the cigarette at him and walked outside. He ran outside and got in my face so I started swinging at him. Fortunately for him, I was too stoned to land a punch. He retreated and yelled, "I'm calling the police!" I told him, "Go ahead!" The driver, upon realizing what kind of trouble I managed to get myself into, was mortified.

Now the best part about this whole gas station exchange was that he really did call the cops. Through the surveillance footage they managed to get the license plate number which was registered to the rehab. Cops arrived at the rehab about five minutes after I did. They couldn't touch me though because I was protected by HIPAA laws once I was inside. They had to go home empty handed. If you ever want to avoid law enforcement until things cool down, check into a rehab. The driver was reprimanded because of my stupidity. She wouldn't be the first employee there to get into trouble because of me. The guy who searched me forgot to collect my cell phone. Cell phones are strictly forbidden in rehab. They wouldn't want you calling Flacco up the road to drop something off. Once my phone ran out of battery, I turned it in and got him in trouble as well. I didn't even try to sneak it in. It was just an oversight and probably a bit of laziness on his part because I was so difficult to deal with that he just wanted to be rid of me.

Inside I was treated like the animal that I was. I was so high they were worried about how the other patients would react to seeing someone as stoned as I was. They insisted on putting me in a room by myself without a television. They seemed shocked to see somebody in my condition. "I'm sorry but isn't this a re-hab? You act like you never seen somebody high before. I'm just coming into rehab the way any self-respecting junkie would, completely annihilated with the cops after him. The fuck kind of half-assed junkies do you got coming through here anyhow?" I asked. I managed to convince them to let me hang out outside a little longer so I could smoke a few cigarettes. However, I kept nodding out and the staff member on duty had enough of me. I dragged my feet into this quarantine room they had for me. "The fuck am I supposed to do in here?" I asked him. "I don't know read the big book," he said with a bit of an attitude. "I already did," I shouted back which wasn't a lie.

I may have read the sober fellowship's sacred text before but I had no idea what it all meant back then. I could explain it all to you quite eloquently but I hadn't internalized any of it. I tried going to sleep but that was when I discovered I still had my phone. I watched all the new shows I missed the night before on my phone until the battery went dead.

On the third day I was woken up rather early by a woman who claimed to be my counselor. She insisted I come with her to her office. My body was aching from the withdrawals and I couldn't even fathom getting up to take a piss. I'd have to men-tally prepare myself to walk to the bathroom, let alone across the compound and into her office. "Fuck off," I shouted at her. Then she started to argumentatively demand that I come with her. I deliberately threw my pillow at the wall next to her. I didn't want to hit her with it but I also wanted to communicate my defiance in an aggressive manner. She left huffing and puffing and then I felt badly for mistreating her. I walked over to her office and apologized. We got to talking and when she realized I was from Staten Island and once a sober member of the sober fellowship she said, "Oh my God! I first got sober on Staten Island! David Soderberg was my sponsor!" I had always despised David Soderberg. I never had words with the man but watching him from a distance, I knew I didn't like him. He had this cult-like following and he's seen as this sobriety guru around the fellowship. Years prior, he admitted to abusing opioids that were prescribed for pain. His loyal followers came together and insisted he keep his sobriety time intact. They swept the dirt under the rug the way Christians don't like to talk about how Jesus probably slept with Mary Magdalene.

"Yea I was wondering why I didn't get along with you," I replied with a smile.

The rehab was in the Poconos so there were a lot of people from Philadelphia there. That suited me just fine, I always liked people from Philly. One thing I didn't like was they kept the guys and the girls pretty separate for the most part. I had my eyes on this hippie girl named Sara. She had dark red wavy hair, wasn't a complete ginger, and had a gigantic ass. She was wearing something with a Pink Floyd "Dark Side of the Moon" symbol on it so I wore my "Wish You Were Here" album cover t-shirt the next day and broke the ice by discussing classic rock. Some uppity nurse quickly shut all that down but I jokingly asked the nurse, "Well what if I relay the message through you?

Can I talk to her that way?" The nurse didn't appreciate my sarcasm but I got a laugh out of Sara.

My parents came by for a visit one weekend. I had them bring some food from home. Mostly cold cuts, peppers stuffed with prosciutto and provolone, and some good Italian bread so I could have a decent meal for a change. They weren't allowed to bring food but I worked my way around it. I asked who I would have to talk to in order to get permission. They told me Al. Al was some sort of upper management staff member whose voice always sounded like he was the ring announcer for a boxing fight. I kept asking him, "Can you shout 'let's get ready to rumble' for me just once?" I found out that Al's day off was Saturday and that was the day my parents were visiting. I didn't even ask Al for permission. When they tried to tell my parents that they couldn't bring the food in, I simply told them, "No it's all right. I spoke to Al, it's handled!" Once again, "it's handled" worked like a charm. Another staff member, named Donnie, was from Scranton, Pennsylvania. He looked like Rick Moranis with spikey hair and was Italian. I had a sneaking suspicion he would understand my New York guinea humor. So, I put him to the test. "Hey Donnie, you take care of that thing for me?" I asked him. "What do mean that Brooklyn thing? Yea don't worry I took care of it," he replied to my amazement.

My fun there would be very short-lived and I was kicked out for threatening a staff member who gave me an attitude. My parents were livid because they had to drive out to the Poconos to pick me up. Not to mention I had gotten thrown out of treatment with my career on the line. Much to everyone's surprise though, I didn't go home and get high. Instead, I met up with people from the sober fellowship. I definitely wasn't ready to be done with treatment though. I was completely conscious of the fact that my mind was still restless. The physical withdrawals go quick but your mind settling down takes a lot longer. Twenty-four hours after being kicked out, I received a phone call. The rehab in the Poconos had a sister rehab further into Pennsylvania. They decided to let me back into the other rehab. This place had a much more down to Earth staff. My counselor was this big Italian biker guy named Billy who understood my brand of humor. He was tall, athletic, and had a short pony tail with greasy hair. He reminded me of Steven Seagal. The first thing he said to me was, "Listen, we don't kick people out here. You start vibrating or feeling some kind of way you come talk to me before you do anything."

The first fellow patient I met was an Italian kid from the Bronx but I stayed away from him the entire stay. You would think we'd get along but he was a Neanderthal. There's some Italians where the evolutionary process just stopped. This guy was one of them. They're very stereotypical and their brains are not capable of advanced functions. I sensed this right away when he felt the need to tell me that he's from the same neighborhood as Ronnie from the show, "Jersey Shore." I was awfully proud of him, but I was losing my career due to opioid addiction. I could care less that he was an acquaintance of Ronnie from "Jersey Shore." Fuck Ronnie from "Jersey Shore" and fuck him was the way I felt about it. I had already been kicked out of one rehab. Avoiding that guy was essential to my survival there. The place was big enough to house a lot of people but there were only about a dozen of us in there. The main building had a giant room with three green couches and a television. There were two acoustic guitars and two hallways with all the patients' rooms. One for the men and one for the women. I never asked but I assumed it used to be a hotel. A separate building held a gymnasium and we were completely surrounded by woods. The ambiance of the place was quite peaceful.

The staff there was first class. Billy, my counselor, was hilarious and the techs were fantastic as well. They would run a few groups at night time and they were pretty good at it. The head tech, Joey, was stern but fair and really ran beneficial groups that got you out of your comfort zone. My stay was limited to two weeks though because I was already at that place in the Poconos for a couple weeks. This time I would leave gracefully though.

Eighteen - A Dark Run

Twenty-eight days of rehab was not enough penance to save my job. The sober fellowship is predicated on spirituality. There's lots of talk of miracles and what have you. I was always skeptical about these miracles and I highly doubted one could materialize for me but I was crossing my fingers that divine intervention would stop the Sanitation Department from giving me the boot. It didn't work out that way though. I was allowed to go back to work at first. My friend Pete who worked in the garage down-stairs saw me driving a garbage truck and exclaimed, "What a country!"

About a month after returning home from rehab, I was un-ceremoniously fired. What made it really sting was I was about to do a good deed that day. Probably the first significant selfless act of my adult life. One of the senior workers in my garage had his wife and kids stuck in the hospital because of a car accident. There was a flyer on a bulletin board explaining the situation and asking for donations of money or vacation time so he could spend your vacation days with his family as they recovered. I had an entire week of unused vacation days. The way I saw it, I got to spend a month on vacation when I went to rehab. It was considered paid sick leave. That guy deserved the time way more than I did. I called the supervisor who could transfer the vacation time for me and he said to come see him when I came in for my shift at four o' clock. I went into his office and with a heavy heart he said, "I'm sorry to tell you this but I can't give him those five days of vacation time because you've been terminated." He received an email from the higher-ups instructing him to get rid of me. He was new to our garage so he had no idea what a pain I was. "Were you expecting this to happen?" he asked. "Oh, yea I saw this coming," I replied. I handed him my badge and parking pass and that was the end of my career with the Sanitation Department. I tried to be strong, but on the way home I cried my eyes out. Here was an opportunity to have a career where I would be able to afford a normal life and I went ahead and ruined it.

I had to start working for Paulie Cabinets full time again but with a demotion because I was unreliable. I tried staying sober for a while but I was a ticking time bomb. Cassandra was homeless running around with that snapback hat with a flat brim wearing douchebag, Shane, again. This time they were ripping and running in his hometown of Boston. She got a job at Woodrow Diner and stole enough money from there to take a Greyhound to Boston. She was obsessed with a complete filth of a human. One day she tried asking Carmine and then her father for bus fare money to come home. They would send the money and she wouldn't get on the bus. Carmine and Cassandra's father told me about this so when she gave me a call, I was prepared to handle it the right way. I told her I'd come and pick her up. She said ok. Forty-five minutes later she called and said, "Wait don't come!" What was happening was she'd get into a fight with

Shane and seek help getting home. Then he'd go score a few bucks begging on the street and run back up to her like, "Babe, I'm so sorry! Let's go shoot a bag!" Then they'd kiss and make up and she'd say to hell with the bus ride home. I wasn't playing that game. I knew that if she was running around homeless, they weren't going to be too far from that bus depot. It was a leap of faith I took because she didn't have a phone. She borrowed some random stranger's to call me. I had to hope and pray that I was right about them being close to the bus depot.

After four hours on the road, all through the night, I found her. It took me about two hours of pacing around that bus depot but I found her just as I was about to give up. The two of them were begging pedestrians for spare change looking like extras from "The Walking Dead." It took me an hour of convincing her to get in the car and come home. I wasn't getting anywhere for a while because I had Shane trying to convince her to stay. Then I realized I could exploit his kryptonite. "Hey pal if I give you ten bucks to cop a bag will you fuck off?" I asked. He took the money. On the way home, Cassandra passed out. Seeing her that frail and filthy tore me to pieces. As cruel and selfish as she could be, she deserved better than that. She had treated me like a doormat countless times but I still loved her and there was no way I was going to let her be found dead in the streets of Boston alone. On the ride home I got teary eyed. Hootie & the Blowfish's "Let Her Cry" and Marshall Tucker Band's "Can't You See" provoked quite an emotional response given the nature of what was going on. She slept the whole ride home and was so still and lifeless that I felt the need to check her pulse multiple times.

As I made my presence felt back in the sober fellowship, I briefly dated a few of the girls who attended. None of them worked out. One girl I was obsessed with because she's exactly my type and has a really sexy raspy voice. Her name was Julia. I was really pissed about how that particular romance got cut short. One of her friends told her I was predatory when it came to dating. That may have been technically true but, in this situation, I was genuinely interested in pursuing a relationship and treating her like a queen. When she confronted me on this, I tried to figure out who it was that told her. She resisted telling me at first but then I said, "Ok, you give me one guess and if I guess right, you have to tell me." She nodded her head in agreement because she assumed there wasn't a chance in hell I'd guess who it was. I knew exactly who it was though. "Connor!" I exclaimed. She tried to deny it but her facial expression gave it away. "I can tell by the look on your face that it's him," I added. I decided to just take it on the chin at first and not confront him over it. I tried to convince her that he was wrong but it didn't matter. Connor's gossip sealed my fate.

I really was trying to stay sober but as time progressed, I had to escape reality. The gravity of my situation felt too severe. There was nothing on the horizon to be hopeful for, or optimistic about. One day at Pico's, I saw a friend from high school. "Hey Sacchi! I thought you were working sanitation?" he inquired. In the middle of explaining to him what an idiot I was, Brooke the manager said, "Hey Sacchi, I need you to grab a guacamole for table twelve." I wanted to kill myself right there in that moment. A few months prior to that I had a career. Now I was back at my dead-end job being instructed to get guacamole for some fat man with salsa stains on his polo shirt at table twelve. My ego found that entire scenario to be completely humiliating. I thought about jumping over the Verrazano Bridge. Then I realized I didn't have it in me to jump. What I did have was heroin. After work, I called Cassandra and the two of us went about shooting heroin together.

Cassandra was a huge fan of The Weeknd. In an attempt to score brownie points with her, I took her to see him. We picked up some ecstasy and heroin then went to Madison Square Garden to see the show. I encountered a psychosis I had never experienced before. I kept going in and out of some sort of dreamlike state and whenever I snapped out of it, I was doing something strange. At one point, I came out of it and noticed that I was petting the back of a girl's head in front of us. I looked at Cassandra terrified with a facial expression that basically said, "Please clean this mess up for me!" Cassandra calmed the girl down for me. I couldn't even hear The Weeknd. I decided to go to the bathroom. Finding it proved to be a daunting task. An even worse task was finding my way back to my seat. I kept walking through the crowd, bumping into people until security pulled me into the hallway. About five of them surrounded me asking me for my ticket. I ended up on the other side of the arena somehow. The head of security could see I was stoned out of my mind. "What drugs did you take?" he asked. I felt no need to lie to him seeing as how he was a security guard and not a police officer. "Ecstasy," I told him. "Jesus, how old are you, young man?" he asked. "Twenty-eight," I responded. He proclaimed his disapproval with my life choices. "You know it's a concert right? People do drugs at this sort of thing," I told him. He had this really high-pitched voice and he addressed all of his subordinates as soldier. As they were escorting me out of the Garden, I did a spot-on impression of him and yelled, "SOLDIER! Where is this young man's ticket?" The other security guards started laughing. I even got a bit of a chuckle out of him. As I was walking out the door I said to the head of security, "Don't take yourself so seriously man." He was a glorified rent-a-cop talking to his employees like he was in Special Ops. Once outside, I called Cassandra and told her I could entertain myself for another hour because I didn't want to ruin the show for her.

Once I got home the psychosis got even more disturbing. I don't remember doing any of it but in another dreamlike state, I rearranged the kitchen and living room. I took pots and pans and put them on the couch. Then I moved items on a table elsewhere. As I was distributing paper plates around the island countertop in the kitchen my mother came downstairs and asked, "What the fuck are you doing?" That snapped me back into some semblance of reality. I looked around and realized what I was doing and I was even more dumbfounded than her. I stuttered a bit looking for a reasonable explanation but there simply was no good reason for me to distribute a dozen paper plates at two o' clock in the morning. I just started crying. I thought my mother would freak out but she simply hugged me and said, "Come on, go to bed." She knew I was in pain and didn't want to be doing what I was doing. I just couldn't live with myself.

Back at Pico's, the resentment towards Paulie Cabinets and Brooke was building up. The loyalty I once had for them was out the window. Paulie demoted me and Brooke would constantly irritate me with her attitude. I decided I was going to rob the safe without them knowing. It had occurred to me that Paulie was not the brightest of guys. A great business man, but a bit of a simpleton. Upon this epiphany came an even greater one. The alarm code for the restaurant was his mother's birth year. I realized that he was lucky he could even remember that much, let alone an entirely different code for the safe. There wasn't a shot in hell he had another number memorized for the safe. Every night the manager puts the cash from the registers through a small slot into the safe. I may not have been a manager anymore, but I still had a key to that office. I felt pretty safe about executing this plan. I watched Paulie grab the envelopes countless times to do the payroll and he just threw them on the table and started ripping them open. He just assumed they were all there. At the opportune moment, I went inside the office, punched in the same numbers for the alarm, and voila! Open sesame! The envelopes are dated so I strategically stole an envelope from a night that my replacement was the manager on duty. The following Wednesday, I saw him do the payroll and he didn't notice the missing envelope. I decided to hit the safe again. With a score worth a little over a grand, I bought a few bundles of heroin and took the rest to the casino. I managed to parlay that money into a little bit more. All I did with my winnings was buy more heroin and give the rest right back to the casino a few nights later.

After that score started to fizzle away, I received a call from Carmine. I always tell him everything so, naturally, I told him about hitting the safe. "Paulie realized an envelope was missing and he's flipping out," he said. I assumed the jig was up and he was about to tell me that Paulie had either called the police or was expecting me to return with the money I had already blown. What seemed like an anxiety attack hit me immediately. I started breathing heavily. "What are you having a fucking heart attack over there? It's fine, he thinks the kid Miguel did it. He's making him work it off," he added. My stressed breathing went into a deep relieving exhale and then back to a reasonable pace after that. I felt terrible for Miguel. Sure he was my replacement but he was a good kid. He didn't ask to take my position. Paulie couldn't prove that it was stolen, only that it was missing and it was from one of the evenings that Miguel closed the restaurant. The guilt from that whole scenario and the fact that I was consistently using heroin intravenously forced me to seek help.

I would frequent meetings held by that sober fellowship in an attempt to crawl back into sobriety but I needed to go away to rehab. One night I went to Moore Catholic High School because they were preparing for the sober fellowship's Christmas Eve marathon. A bunch of us went outside to smoke a cigarette when these four children rode up on bicycles. Two were black and two were white. The black kids were ripping us apart with insults. I got quite a kick out of it. Even the jokes at my expense. One of them said to me, "You look like the type o' nigga that go to jail and drop the soap ON PURPOSE!" They got a few of the other guys until finally they hit this guy Brad with, "Yo son!

Your fade looks like it was done with a BUTTERKNIFE!" What happened next was rather disturbing, even for me. Brad had been sober for four years by that point and had often expressed a deep sense of spirituality. That all went out the window in an instant. He had a fiery look in his eyes and started choking the child that hurled the insult. I happened to be standing right next to him. I pulled his hand and said, "Whoa, whoa, whoa, what are you doing? He's a kid! It's a joke!" I was pretty stoned that night so everybody got a kick out of how Brad, a sober and supposedly spiritual individual, was stopped by me, an intoxicated and sinister individual, from choking a child.

Nineteen - Spokane

The inner tension was building up. I was so stoned one night that I cursed out Brooke and quit Pico's without a legitimate game plan as to what I would do for money. I decided to reach out to Sid, the owner of Elite, in Florida. My brother was doing pretty well for himself selling health insurance and I figured I'd go back to Florida under different circumstances. My buddy George had his own condo down there and needed a roommate. He was getting high again but I figured I could stay sober regardless of what he was doing. Besides, there was no way I was going to stay in a halfway house again. I wasn't going to piss in a drug test cup and come home at 9 o' clock every night. I figured I'd just ignore George and sacrifice living with a maniac for my freedom. Coincidentally, that hippie girl Sarah from the rehab in the Poconos messaged me through Facebook expressing her attraction for me. What made it such a coincidence was she just so happened to be from South Florida. So now I had a romantic liaison lined up for when I finished rehab. A minor setback was thrown into my plan though. Sid was now the owner of a rehab in Spokane, Washington. I had no health insurance at this time so he had to take me on pro bono. He just wasn't going to let me take in the sunshine in Florida. I didn't care though. I'd finish

218 Stephen J. Sacchi

my twenty-eight days in Spokane and head down to Florida after.

The day before I left, Carmine came in the clutch for me. He
spotted me a couple hundred bucks to get high one last time under the condition that I snort it instead of shoot it. That was fine
with me as I had recently given up the needle because I feared
for my survival. The heroin on the street was becoming increasingly volatile. I decided to just snort Oxycodone because at least
with those, I knew what I could handle. One bag of fentanyl
laced heroin and you could be a cadaver. Thanks to the crack-
down on doctors who prescribed opioids, the prices of
Oxycodone went up a few bucks. Junkies were switching to heroin the way normal people switch to Geico. They could save
fifteen percent or more. What law enforcement didn't realize
was that by cracking down on doctors, they were playing a game
of whack-a-mole. By trying to stop the opioid epidemic they only made it worse. Nobody was doing Oxycodone anymore. The
only reason I spent the extra cash was to ensure that I didn't
overdose. Most junkies aren't as pragmatic as myself. One day I
was walking through Woodrow Plaza and ran past some old
friends trying their luck at Quick Draw. We were discussing the
hopelessness of our existence thanks to opioids when one of
them said, "This shit is an epidermic bro!" I felt no need to tell
him the word is epidemic. I simply took solace that although I
was a junkie, I wasn't as hopeless as him.

I spent the entire evening prior to leaving for Spokane getting
high and tying up loose ends. I ran into Connor at a meeting

held by the sober fellowship. I decided to confront him. I explained to him that by him dragging my name through the dirt it subsequently ended my little romance with Julia.

"I didn't say anything to her but I don't think that's why things ended between you two," he said.

"You fucking idiot, you literally just denied it and confirmed it in the same sentence. I didn't even know that was possible until now," I told him. I didn't feel much better after letting him know how I felt. Just more bitter.

Later that night, I decided I would need a portable CD player. In rehab you're not allowed to have your phone, which is where all my music was stored, so I had to resort to primitive technology. I went to Target and coincidentally ran into Janice, another member of the sober fellowship. I explained to her my current predicament and in the interest of stimulating conversation I asked, "Hey do you know that cocksucker Connor?"

She said, "Yea why?" I proceeded to explain to her what he said to Julia. Unbeknownst to me, Connor was dating Janice at that time. Janice and I got sober around the same time only she stayed sober and I didn't. Running into her was the most beautiful of coincidences. She loves me so she let me have my revenge. We went back to her house and we posted a picture on Facebook of me kissing her on the cheek in her kitchen. This was purely for the sake of driving Connor out of his mind. When I'm crossed, I can be downright diabolical.

The next morning, I acquired some more Oxycodone pills and had Carmine give me a ride to the airport. I nodded out and he took a picture of me. I was pale as a vampire. He had a new Mercedes Benz and once I woke up, I almost threw up in it. We were on the BQE with nowhere to stop in sight. "Just get it out the window," he told me. For his sake, I sucked it up and managed to keep it together. If it were anybody else, I was making a mess of that car regardless of how nice and new it may have been.

The driver for the rehab was waiting for me in the Spokane airport. He didn't try to stop me when I went to snort the rest of my pills in the bathroom. If he would've tried being a boy scout about it, he would've had a problem. I spent four days in the detox at first. Sid recently purchased this detox along with the rehab but they were already in business long before Sid took it over. When I got there, there was an Iraq veteran who worked there that I got along with. I'd break his balls for subscribing to a different sober fellowship. There was a little kid who was a patient there who looked like Jesse Pinkman from Breaking Bad. I wasn't a fan of his. He sagged his pants down under his ass which is unacceptable to me from anyone let alone a white kid. They say don't judge a book by its cover but trust me, you can jump to conclusions when you see someone doing this. It originated in the prison system. It was a discreet way of saying you were available for sodomy. The idea of this fashion statement is to communicate that you're so badass that you've been to prison before. All I see is someone saying they'd embrace sodomy and they're very open about it.

Once I got to the actual rehab, it was a bit of a culture shock. One of the techs listened to Christian rap and was a bit of an oddball to me. He'd be driving the van and I'd tell dirty jokes to the rest of the clients. Now mind you, they separated the guys and the girls completely. This van was filled with all men. Degenerate men for that matter. I saw some girl walking out the window and said, "I'd stick my tongue so far up her asshole I'd be able to find out what she ate for breakfast." The Christian tech was not a fan of this humor. I apologized for my actions and was a bit more respectful after that.

Another culture shock was the food. They went food shopping for us on Tuesdays. I got in on a Thursday. I was at the mercy of whatever these heathens ordered for the first few days. Beyond pop tarts, it was not looking good for me. I'm a picky eater to begin with. Plus, opioid withdrawal leaves you with little to no appetite. My counselor was this big bald man with a red-haired goatee named Russell. I tried to see if I could get some real food. I asked if I could get some pasta, vodka sauce, prosciutto, fresh mozzarella, and a whole bunch of other food they'd never even heard of in Spokane. Most of the food I ordinarily eat wasn't within their budget. "Ok well how about something normal to drink? They got nothing in that fridge," I asked Russell. "What are you talking about? They got to have something in there, they don't got Tang?" he said. "Tang? What the fuck is Tang?" I asked. Tang is some sugary orange drink mix that tastes God awful. We went back to the house for a lunch break and I tried this so-called Tang. When we went back to the rehab center where they hold the groups, I went to torture Russell again. "You can't get me some fucking Pepsi or a goddamned Snapple maybe? Hell, I'll take orange juice WITH the pulp over that tang," I said. No accommodations would be made for me.

My fellow patients were pretty fun there. Spokane is a shithole town but there's some good people there. There was Carl, a really good guitar player and singer. His band was amazing. He showed me their music and I was quite in awe of the guy. If this was the 70's, he'd be a rock star for sure. Thanks to him I finally got a Pepsi. Your family is allowed to drop off little goodies there. I was the only one from the other side of the country. The rest of the guys were all locals. His parents dropped him off a case of Pepsi cans. I helped myself to one and when we got into the van to go to the rehab center, I told him, "I stole one of your Pepsi's you piece of shit." He laughed. We discovered in that moment that we were kindred spirits because we both call our friends pieces of shit as a term of endearment.

Then there was Howard who seemed to have some underlying mental health issues aside from addiction, but was absolutely adorable. He showed signs of hyper-religiosity. One of the counselors was holding a group and challenging him on his stance that his drug use wasn't that bad. At one point, she held up a picture of Jesus to inspire guilt and he immediately started crying. I never saw anything like it. Despite my prejudices with religion, I wanted to just give the kid a bear hug after that. It was that cute. One day we were in the living room of the house we all stayed in and Carl and I were discussing our woes due to addiction. I looked at Howard and rhetorically asked, "Where'd I go wrong in life Howard?"

Without hesitation he just said, "Heroin!" Carl and I laughed at the simple yet completely accurate answer.

The weekend tech, Dustin, who basically lived with us the whole weekend was amazing. He had a pretty good sense of humor. He never cringed at my ass eating jokes. Matter of fact, he encouraged them. There was an older man named Ryan who loved "Star Wars" and "The Jerky Boyz" so we got along great. Then you had this Russian kid named Clay who was scared of oral sex. We were watching Donald Trump abuse Jeb Bush in the Republican Presidential Debate when we found out he wasn't into oral sex. "You're real tough there Jeb!" Trump said to Jeb Bush. Jeb's presidential candidacy was practically his birthright and we were laughing at Trump robbing him of this. As we calmed down from the excitement on the television, I started talking about blowjobs and going down on girls. Clay made a face like he was grossed out and said, "Me and my girl-friend don't do that." I had a field day making fun of him. "So let me get this straight, when it comes to one of the absolute pinna-cles of pleasure in life, you and your girlfriend just decided, not for us?" I asked. He confirmed his stance and all the guys just unloaded on him. There were tears in our eyes from laughing so hard. My cheekbones started to hurt from laughing so much. Dustin, who was in his room doing homework, laughed so hard we heard him from the other room. He came outside to make sure what he was hearing was accurate. Clay was just young and a little innocent even though he was in a rehab. He was well

224 Stephen J. Sacchi

dressed and well groomed. He would require a few more years of depravity and feeling empty inside to really come to appreciate the catharsis that can come from oral sex.

One particular evening I went out back to smoke a cigarette. I was listening to my Creedence Clearwater Revival CD and "Proud Mary" came on. My grandmother on my mother's side that had passed, Nana, was named Mary. "Proud Mary" was considered her song. That alone was enough to get me emotional but then that first lyric, "left a good job in the city," resonated with me even further seeing as how I was devastated that I was fired from a city job. I got teary eyed. It wasn't joyful tears but they weren't tears of despair either. Crying can be good for the soul. It felt rather cleansing. I called my mother and told her about the experience. "Aw that means Nana is with you there Stephen," she said.

The rehab would take us to numerous meetings held by that sober fellowship. At one meeting, the speaker was this elderly lesbian woman. I rolled my eyes thinking I wasn't going to enjoy her story because I wrongfully assumed that I would have nothing in common with an elderly lesbian. But this woman told my story. I identified with her more than most people I've ever heard speak. One thing that resonated with me was that she would go on about embarrassing herself, blunder after blunder, and then she said, "I'd wake up the next morning, strap up my boot straps and continue doing it again." I never had boot straps to strap up but I understood exactly what she meant. I had woken up countless times after humiliating myself. Then I'd shake the events of the previous evening out of my mind and trudge forward in pursuit of further debauchery.

At another one of those meetings there was a young girl with self-mutilation scars all over her arms. She had at least fifty scars on each arm and the positioning of them were reminiscent of the movie "Cast Away" when Tom Hanks would mark down on a boulder the amount of days he was stranded on the island. The next day, Russell was holding a group at the rehab center. "You guys see that girl with those self-mutilation scars last night?" I asked the group. The guys nodded their heads. "She said she dumped her boyfriend recently. Yea she said he wasn't cutting it," I followed up with. The guys all laughed. "Now Stephen, self-mutilation is not something you should joke about," Russell responded. "Well then tell her to cut it out!" I shouted back. The guys erupted in laughter and even Russell couldn't help but let out a few giggles. I love when a joke is so foul, yet so funny, that people try to contain their laughter because they feel horrible for laughing at it yet they can't help themselves.

I think it's fair to say I was having the most fun at that rehab than any other one I'd been in before. That rehab was one of the most beneficial in terms of spiritual growth. My theory is because they completely separated the guys and the girls. That rehab in the Poconos separated us but not like they did in Spokane. I might've caught one or two glances at the girls in the hallway. Usually in rehab, there's one or two girls that are actually attractive and one or two you'd settle for given the circumstances. Opioids deplete your libido so much that you're practically sterile. When you first get sober, your libido comes back to you like a shot of adrenaline. Without the competition for those two or three girls inciting resentment towards each other amongst the guys, it allows for more camaraderie. Also, without a female audience you get to share more from the heart in the group sessions. We'd still try and one-up each other a bit but nothing like the kind of ego driven bile you'd hear when there's a girl in the room.

Sid threw another curveball at me. Apparently, I was in a program that was supposed to be for ninety days and he insisted I stay for the entirety of the program. I was supposed to move into that condo with George at the beginning of February. Even if I wasn't going to move in with George, there was no way I was staying in Spokane for ninety days. That city was one of the last places on Earth that I wanted to plant a flag. The girls in that town were amongst the ugliest I had ever seen. That may not seem relevant to the situation or pertinent at all but it absolutely felt that way to me at the time. Whenever they took us out to the YMCA for exercise or to go to the sober fellowship, I rarely saw anybody that even resembled an attractive person. The only relatively attractive one I saw seemed anorexic but had a pretty face. I had nothing to occupy my mind with aside from making fun of Clay's prudishness. That ninety-day routine would've turned into them insisting I stay for a halfway house as well. There was no point in completing ninety days. After thirty days, they have you go to what they called phase two. In phase two you go out and find a job. I was not going to interject myself into Spokane society.

The counselors tried to convince my parents that I should stay and that they ought to cancel my airfare. I'd been through so many rehabs by that point that I knew how to talk my way around those hiccups. I was like a chess player. I anticipated that move from the beginning. Russell called my mother and told her to pull the plane ticket. The next day, I managed to convince him to call her back and put her mind at ease about me leaving. I told him, "Look, I'm going home one way or the other, I'll find a way home no matter what because I'm a pretty resourceful guy. You got my mother in hysterics about me coming home now. So why don't you do her a favor and tell her you think its ok if I come home." He put up some resistance. Thanks to my experience with sobriety, I had moments where I was downright therapeutic to the other patients. Anything I said was counterproductive to the group that first week. Once I got my head in the game, I started giving them sound advice on how to maintain sobriety and live life as a sober individual. With this behavior in mind, I asked Russell, "Out of everybody you've ever seen leave early, wouldn't you say I'm amongst the top five people you'd imagine staying sober?"

"I'd say you're in my top two."

"Great! Call my mother and tell her that! Because I'm going home. The least you can do is give her peace of mind," I said. Checkmate. He picked up the phone and told my mother he had faith in my resolve. Then he handed me the phone. "She wants to talk to you," he said. I grabbed the phone. My mother was in awe of me. "How the hell did you get this guy to ease up on his stance?" she asked. I started laughing. She knew I was a master manipulator better than anyone.

Twenty - Florida Part 2

After successfully navigating through that debacle in Spokane, I flew home. I hung out for a couple days before driving down to Florida. I felt right at home when I ran into this older man, Sean, at a meeting held by the sober fellowship. He's always good for a laugh but more especially on that particular morning. One guy introduced himself as Al. Sean leaned into me and said, "You gotta watch out for that guy Al, he's a real alcoholic." With my interest piqued I asked, "Oh yea?" To which Sean said, "Yea his last name is Coholic!" After going to another one of the meetings, I ran into Connor. By then I felt bad about my actions so I decided to put his mind at ease. "Look bro I'm sorry for how I reacted. Nothing happened between me and Janice it was all just an elaborate ploy to piss you off." He apologized for what he said to Julia about me and we hugged it out. He and Janice went on to get married and have a baby together.

When I first arrived in Florida, I met Johnny at a meeting held by the sober fellowship. He came wearing his gaudy loafers and I realized he spent so much time living in Florida that his New York accent began to fade. Too much time down there had emasculated him a bit. But I was quite happy to see my brother. "You want to hang out tomorrow?" I asked him. "No, me and Lena are gonna do brunch," he replied. "Whoa, whoa, whoa wait

230 Stephen J. Sacchi

a minute. What's happened to you? You're gonna DO brunch. You either eat breakfast or you have lunch we don't DO brunch. What the fuck is that?" I told him. He just scoffed at my insults. "Listen I don't trust any of these Florida barbers with my hair. You still got your clippers?" Johnny just laughed and said, "You've been up north a long time maybe nobody went up there to tell ya, I don't cut hair anymore."

Once I made it to Florida, I realized George was in worse condition than I expected. On some nights he'd be so high that he'd throw his girlfriend a beating after arguing with her. The first and second time he did it, I ran downstairs and pulled him off of her. After that, I refused to get in between them. If the girl was too stupid to realize she should've run for the hills, I wasn't going to help someone who had no desire to help herself. The beatings got progressively worse. One time she was wearing sunglasses for a week. I'd find myself in heated debates with the two of them often. One day George was at work when his girl-friend asked me for a ride. I was exhausted and really didn't care about her personal problems. "Take a cab," I told her. "You know, we're roommates we're supposed to like look out for each other!" she replied. "Whoa, whoa, whoa let me stop you right there. When was the last time I asked you for anything except maybe some peace and quiet that I'm still yet to be afforded? Fucking never. Go take your sob story to somebody else," I told her. She huffed and puffed until finally, to shut her up, I grabbed my keys to give her a ride. On the way there, she called me a pussy for not helping her when George started to beat on her. "First couple times he did it, I was the reason you ain't a corpse.

After that, if you're too stupid to realize you should leave, well that's your problem," I told her. The audacity of her accusing me of being less of a man because I refused to play referee every single night launched me into a ferocious profanity laced tirade. She secretly called George so he could hear me screaming at her. When he came home from work that night, I was lying in bed wearing nothing but my boxers. He lunged at me and I pushed him off. "Just let me put my fucking pants on bro! You want to fight me, I'll fight you! Just let me put my fucking pants on first!" I screamed at him. In his mind, it seemed as if I just randomly decided to start cursing her out. By the time I got my pants on I could see he calmed down so I insisted we go in the backyard alone to talk. We both lit up cigarettes and I explained my position. "Bro, she's crazy. I'm lying in bed exhausted and she insists on me giving her a ride. I didn't want to but to shut her up I give her the ride. You would think she'd be grateful but she started getting on me for not stopping you from beating on her when she drives you up a wall. Called me a pussy for not stopping you. I stopped you the first two times and it really ain't my business. I can't keep getting in between you two and I don't need to be ridiculed for minding my business."

"Look man I know she's a bitch but please, for my sake, just try and be nicer to her."

"Ok man I'll do my best." We hugged it out and all was forgotten.

I tried working with my brother at first but that lasted about a week. I couldn't deal with the phones. I didn't care how much money they were making. All I wanted to do was make a few bucks to live off of, sleep with as many girls as possible, and work on my tan. At one particular meeting held by the sober fellowship, I ran into this guy Angelo from Staten Island. Angelo and I had an utter disdain for one another back at home. He once told me he was going to get pills for me. I gave him the money and he jumped through random backyards to escape with my money. It was chump change at the time but I was still pretty angry about it. We argued about it through social media and were anxious to kill one another. When we ran into each other sober in Florida though, it was nothing but love because we had to stick together. We were in a strange land and you stick with your own kind down there. Angelo always wore a backwards fitted hat to conceal his hair loss but it really wasn't necessary. He wasn't balding in a way that looked bad, it was more like a Jason Statham sort of balding. Much to my surprise, my old pal from high school, Eddie, was his step brother. Eddie was in Florida too and had just left his rehab AMA to get high. Before putting him into a halfway house, we took him out to the clubs on Atlantic Ave in Delray. Angelo, Eddie, and I desperately tried to get this group of girls to come hang out with us afterwards but we struck out. Eddie flocked straight to the fat one. "What the fuck were you doing talking to the fat ugly one?" Angelo asked Eddie. "Fat girls give the best blowjobs," he replied. Eddie spent the night with me but we got him situated at a halfway house in the morning.

Through Facebook, we discovered that another friend from high school, Dean, was also down there. In a couple weeks, I had an elite crew of Staten Island all stars. It worked out perfect because I didn't want to make new friends. Johnny would rarely hang out with us but every once in a while we'd get him to come around. Especially when he needed a haircut because the barbers down there are sub-par. Since Johnny was too much of a big shot to cut hair, we had Angelo to help keep us handsome. One day Johnny came by for a haircut wearing his loafers and at my behest, Eddie said to him, "Nice loafers! What are you going to brunch or some shit?"

I did get to see another old friend. I met a man from Baltimore at one of the meetings. "Oh, you're from Baltimore? Any chance you know Raheem?" I asked. "Raheem relapsed," he responded. I couldn't believe it. Raheem had over twenty years of sobriety the last time I was in Florida. I was able to get Raheem's number and we had a long talk on the phone. He was hurt in a car accident which led to a Vicodin prescription. After a while he sought out what he really wanted, heroin. "Yea it got bad man but you know I got ten months back now," he said. I coerced him into meeting me. He was reluctant at first because he technically wasn't supposed to meet former patients outside of work. "I'll tell you what, you come to the meeting at Crossroads at 6 AM and you can see me there," he said. I was angry that I had to wake up that early just to see him but I wasn't missing that opportunity. After the meeting I twisted his arm to come get breakfast with me. He tagged along and, to me, this was like sharing breakfast with Santa Claus. He didn't disappoint either. I started asking him about his relapse and he said, "Man it got so bad that I was looking to knock off one of them Brinks trucks." I asked him, "What's a Brinks truck?" He replied, "You know one of those armored cars. I was sitting in a parking lot shooting dope and I always carry a pistol with me. I was looking at one of those guys driving it and said to myself this guy wouldn't know what hit him."

I started dating that hippie girl Sara from the rehab in the Poconos. She lived right around the corner from Ocean Mist Recovery. I always found it strange that she went to rehab up north when she lived in the rehab capital of the world. But what did I care? She was on Suboxone maintenance. I didn't care about that either. As a sober individual I probably shouldn't have been dating someone on Suboxone but you could add that to the list of things I didn't care about. I just wanted to wrap my hands around her fat ass cheeks. Once upon a time, I was searching for the emotional connection that's supposed to come with romance. But heartache after heartache led to me becoming jaded and giving up on all that. All I knew were toxic relationships and I was still too immature to see that I shared the responsibility in that toxicity. I was slowly giving up on true intimacy. I was strictly interested in carnality. I no longer believed there was such a thing as emotional connection. At least not for me.

Sara was a little strange and was playing hard to get at first but I found my way into her heart. The only problem was I was newly sober and it was my first time getting laid so I suffered from some intense premature ejaculation. When you're coming off opioids, you're hypersensitive and it takes a little time to get some stamina back. She made me use a condom and I still finished in under a minute. She was very frustrated at that and thought I was being selfish. Maybe so. But there was no way of avoiding it. I wanted to last longer. I was just physically incapable of doing so. She dumped me after that but I didn't really care. Aside from her being a strange hippie type, which didn't really compliment my hostile nature, she also had a bush. I'd never seen one outside of a 70's playboy magazine so it creeped me out.

Angelo kept on relapsing and getting kicked out of half houses. It got to the point that his father was so frustrated with him he would come down to try and talk some sense into him. Angelo's father is a legitimate wiseguy who could strike fear into the hearts of the toughest guys I know on Staten Island. Aside from having a high rank, he was well over six feet tall, massive, and muscular. At first, I was rather timid around his father. I tend to say stupid things pretty often and he's the last person I wanted to upset. Angelo knows I love to be a relentless ball breaker and he noticed I wasn't being myself around his dad. "You know, you can break his balls, he has a sense of humor," he told me. After that I loosened up a bit. When his father came down, we had fun. Friends of his owned a cigar lounge in Boca Raton. We'd hang out there and I got to meet the alleged boss of a family from another major city outside of New York. He was rather quiet but seemed warm and friendly enough. Angelo told me, "Yea he's a nice guy but that man will shoot you in broad daylight mo!"

Angelo's father got him situated at yet another halfway house. As we were helping Angelo move his stuff in, Angelo's father said to me, "It's like a fucking summer camp in there." I laughed and replied, "Yea for degenerates!" Angelo told me about a funny exchange between the halfway house director and himself with his dad also there. "He went on a rant about how when he got sober, he had to break the mentality of thinking he was some kind of gangster," Angelo said. Then Angelo and his dad awkwardly looked at each other wondering if he was saying that because he was in the room. "I don't think he meant anything by that. How the fuck is this South Florida recovery enthusiast going to know who your father is?" I said. Angelo nodded in agreement. A couple days after he got settled in, I received a call from Angelo. "Yea, Billy is the night tech here," he said. I couldn't believe it. I hadn't heard from Billy since the last time I was living in Florida. I flew right to Angelo's halfway house and gave him the biggest hug. I assumed he was back on Staten Island or strung out somewhere. We caught up with each other in the parking lot. "Yea man I've been sober two years. I'm married now."

"You're married?"

"Yea man. So how's everybody doing? How's Tony?"

"Tony's just getting worse and worse. He's completely fucked up and the idea of recovery isn't even on his radar."

"That kid had so much potential. Now he's gonna grow up to just be a regular guy."

"Billy, you and I had potential and we're gonna grow up to just be regular guys."

"Yea but you and I are ok with that, he isn't."

Angelo insisted I sponsor him. I wasn't ready for that responsibility and I knew it. I also knew he was never going to take direction from one of those South Florida bleeding hearts. I'd torture him in the car with my brand of music but one day it seemed to relax him. He was conflicted with everything that was going on internally and the Eagles' song "Take It Easy" came on. I said to him, "Bro if you're ever vibrating and thinking about getting high just think of me singing the chorus to this." He listened closely to the chorus and said, "This is making me mad emotional mo!"

Angelo was dating some ditsy girl with a smoking body named Amanda. She had a friend named Franny whom I decided to fool around with because she had expressed attraction to me. She lived at a halfway house and I had my eyes on her roommate Dana. One night they all came by the cigar lounge and I was flirting without flirting. By that I mean I was indirectly flirting with Dana so Franny wouldn't even realize what I was doing. I was so smooth about it that Franny had no idea I was moving onto her roommate right in front of her. Johnny came by with his girlfriend Lena. As my diabolical plot was unfolding, I looked at Lena and said, "You're with the right Sacchi brother because this one is pure evil."

As I was driving them home, I made my move. I stopped at a gas station and Franny went into the store to pick up a few things. "You know Franny and I aren't boyfriend and girlfriend. What do you say you give me your number and we'll get together sometime," I said to Dana. She agreed and gave me her number. The next day I took her to my condo and we had sex. The next day we did it again, only this time, some guy who saw me pick Dana up told Franny about it. Franny called me crying saying, "I know you two are together!" When I went to drop Dana off, Franny was waiting outside crying. I felt terrible for the both of them. Dana ended up having to go to another halfway house just to escape Franny's wrath.

My buddy Dean asked, "How' was Dana in the sack? Any good?"

"You kidding? That twazole felt like a clam bake."

"I don't know bro, I think I liked Franny better."

"Whatever, I don't give a fuck. I'm out to fold as many of these girls in half as I possibly can."

Dean and Eddie ended up following Angelo's footsteps and asked me to sponsor them. Through sponsoring Dean, I found out he had become a father. I always loved children so I wanted desperately for him to get sobriety and keep it, if not for him than for his daughter. Anxious to see what she looked like, I asked him, "You got a picture of your daughter?" He pulled out his phone and said, "There's my little chubber right there." She was beautiful. Dean's halfway house had strict restrictions so he would rarely be out past sunset. He didn't want to come out for the shenanigans anyway. He had a family at home so he was seemingly determined to simply do the right thing. I could tell that he was torn up inside. He'd use humor to deflect the same way I do.

Now because working with my brother didn't work out, I went back to the restaurant business. The owner of this restaurant called Grand Tavern hired me on the spot and had his wife work up a schedule for me. "So what's your availability?"

"Anytime you need me."

"You don't live in a halfway house? I don't have to worry about you rushing back for a curfew?"

"No, I don't live in a halfway house." The restaurant was a Michigan themed sports bar with an old school ambiance. The place was littered with jerseys from Detroit sports teams. The owner was a Greek man in his forties who moved to Florida from Michigan. On the wall above one of the urinals was a plaque. Engraved was a rich history lesson about Greeks from Michigan. A bunch of Greek immigrants, before settling in Michigan, made a pit stop in Brooklyn first. There they discovered Coney Island's hotdogs. They adopted a Brooklyn staple, took it to Michigan, and now this guy was slinging hot dogs under a banner they called Coney Dogs. Some people would refer to them as Coney Island Dogs. One of my first tables was an elderly couple. The woman said, "You sound like you're from New York."

"Yea that's right."

"You're working in a Michigan restaurant. I came here for some Coney Island Dogs how am I supposed to trust that they'll be authentic if you're from New York?"

"Mam, do you know where Coney Island is?"

"No."

"Brooklyn, New York! I'm more qualified that anybody you know from Michigan. Now I can't say that these Coney Dogs deserve to be called Coney Island Dogs, but I assure you they're a close runner up to the real thing."

A few girls from another halfway house came by to eat and one of them was a sexy Puerto Rican girl named Xiara from Staten Island. The fact that we were both from Staten Island made it much easier for romance to commence. She was gorgeous and had a nice dark complexion that turned me on immensely. She was on the, "I'll just drink alcohol" program. I'd chaperone her and her other friends who were also drinking. We'd go down to Miami and I struck out with her a few times. She kept playing hard to get. One night though, she managed to secure a hotel room thanks to some guy she used to date. Her halfway house caught onto her drinking so they gave her a choice, go to detox or leave. She chose the latter since she had some guy who was willing to dish out a few bucks for a hotel room even though he wasn't even in the same state. We went up to the room and started making out. I tried pulling her pants off to no avail at first. "I'm on my period," she said. I decided to use my tried and trusted line. "I'm like Moses babe, I can part the red sea!" I exclaimed. When we were done it looked like Hannibal Lecter occupied the bed. The room came with two beds so we fell asleep on the untainted one. I definitely don't envy whoever had to clean that mess up. Making up that room required a hazmat suit. We fooled around for a couple weeks but she gave me the cold shoulder soon enough. She went from drinking to a full-on relapse and I was focused on staying sober. Naturally, we weren't on the same page so the romance was cut short.

One weekend Vinny came down for a visit. His uncle had a condo down there so naturally, we went out gambling among other things. We spent one night clubbing in Miami. Somehow, we managed to get Angelo and Eddie out of their halfway house curfews. The next night we all went to a brothel disguised as a strip club in Pompano Beach called Delilah's Dolls. I just received a nice tax return so I was spending money quite foolishly. I had a little fun with a hooker and then went to the casino with Vinny. We lost which is rare for us. Usually when the two of us get together we're each other's good luck charms. In this instance though, we gave it all to the casino.

At the Grand Tavern, I attempted to show a little ambition. The bartenders made more than the servers and I could tell the owner's wife was beginning to see my talents. "You know I've bartended before too," I told her.

"Ok, why don't you come in for training tomorrow." The next day she made one of their signature drinks and said, "Here try this."

"I can't try that."

"Why not?"

"I'm in recovery."

"When you applied here, I asked you that and you said no."

"No, you asked me if I lived in a halfway house, I don't."

"Oh, I don't like that. I don't like that you were deceitful, I don't think this is going to work out. How can you make drinks good if you can't taste them?"

"You follow the ingredients. Ray Charles couldn't see the keys on a piano and he seemed to do just fine." She laughed but ultimately, she put me back onto serving. They gave the bartender position to this girl Cindy. I was voicing my frustration to her when she was training and reiterated my Ray Charles line. "That's totally different, making drinks and playing piano are not the same thing."

"Look it's a metaphor, what do you think you're splitting the fucking atom back there? You follow the ingredients and measurements, put a little love into it, and call it a fucking day! You know what I mean?"

"I don't like the way you're talking to me right now." I often forget my hostile Staten Island nature can be perceived the wrong way by someone from Florida. I assured her I held no animosity towards her but her sensitivity irritated me. She tried her best to befriend me after that but I knew she was too soft to handle me. I was talking to another server about a customer I wanted to murder and Cindy tried to playfully chime in, "I can help you."

"Help me what?"

"Help you get rid of the body."

"Cindy, let me explain something to you. I used to work sanitation in New York City. What makes you think I need you to help me dispose of a body?"

Angelo ended things with Amanda and started dating this girl Diana from Staten Island. The three of us were hanging out one day when Angelo had to be home for his halfway house curfew. "Hey I'm going out with Frank tonight you want to come?" she asked me. Frank was very close friends with Carmine back in the day. He had a reputation for being an absolute savage. He completely lived up to the expectations I had of him. He was on a Vivitrol shot so he tried to just drink that night after about sixty days sober. Vivitrol makes it so you can't get high off of opioids for about a month or so. They have one for alcohol now but Frank wasn't on that one. He drank to celebrate some money he had won at the Hard Rock casino.

"You only won $30 Frank!" Diana said. "That's still a come up right there," responded Frank. As soon as his Vivitrol shot dissipated a few weeks later, he started getting high again.

My merry band of misfits began to fall apart. We were all hanging out at the pool one day when Angelo began talking about throwing in the towel on sobriety. I was secretly losing hope myself but I was trying to be strong. I tried talking some

244 Stephen J. Sacchi

sense into Angelo hoping it would not only get through to him, but hopefully I'd internalize what I was saying myself.

"I don't give a fuck mo. I'm tired of feeling this way," he said. It didn't take long for Angelo to relapse again. I was to follow suit myself. Eddie was reclusive so he was barely hanging out with us anymore and our other friend Dean went back home. A couple days after Dean took his flight back, another friend from Staten Island, Sean, emerged.

One day Sean asked me to pick him up from some town forty-five minutes north of where we lived. He was hanging out with family and drank that day. "Sacchi, I'm just letting you know now that I'm going to get high tonight," he said. I felt no need to be on a high horse and talk him out of it. We got to talking and he mentioned that he didn't like Dilaudid. Sean never shot up before.

"You just don't like it because you don't do it right," I said. "Sniffing it doesn't really get you too high but if you shoot it it's amazing," I added.

"Well what's it like when you shoot it?" he asked.

When he asked me that I got a bad case of euphoric recall. I started describing it and then I asked, "Can you get some?"

He was hesitant at first. "You sure you want to do this I don't want to be the reason you fall off," he said.

"I'm a big boy I make my own decisions. Can you get it?" I responded.

"Yea I can get it," he answered and that was it. We were off to the races.

It was a disaster right from the start. He wanted to buy crack but instead was given drywall crumbles disguised as crack. Eventually we got real crack, Dilaudid, and some heroin. We went to my condo so I could shoot up and then went back out into the night for more shenanigans. He got ripped off a couple more times and then went home to Staten Island the next morning. Once he was gone, I was left with the urge to keep getting high but had nobody to play with.

I ended up reaching out to Frank. "You got any girls we can chill with?" he asked.

"I wouldn't subject girls to me in this condition. I'm still trying to operate with some sense of a moral compass."

"We're shooting dope out here kid, there's no room for a moral compass."

I wished I shared his sentiment but in no time at all I was such a disaster I couldn't even look at girls. Frank and I would score together but he would terrify me. Whenever he got high, he would start howling like a wolf was being attacked by a vicious parasite.

One morning he roared into my driveway like a bat out of hell at 6 am. His girlfriend threw him out and he had a giant Ziploc bag filled with crack and heroin. We shot up and he starting making his howling noises and slurring his speech. Then he demanded I drive his car to the store so he could get a Mountain Dew. As we got into the car he said, "Please, I'm begging you dog, don't drive fast it's down the block."

"Yea we're only going up the street."

"I know it's just I get nervous."

"You're in good hands."

"I don't know about that."

Then he let out another howl and yelled, "You know?"

"Yea."

"I'm a mess every time you see me."

"This is definitely the worst I've seen you."

"This?"

"Yep."

"All right! All right! I'm breaking records!"

We both laughed then pulled into the 7/11 parking lot. "I'm gonna get a fucking Mountain Dew bro. Nothing's better than an ice-cold Mountain Dew bro," he insisted as we were walking into the store.

"I'm not a Mountain Dew man," I told him.

"What? You're out your mind kid. I'm gonna put you onto the Code Red right now."

"It's not like I haven't had it before, I just don't like it."

He grabbed his Mountain Dew Code Red and as he was paying the cashier, he let out an enthusiastic whistle and said, "Mountain Dew bro, dynamite!" Until that day, I never seen anybody that passionate about heroin and Mountain Dew. He was a kid in a candy store.

We made our way back to my condo when Frank asked if he could take a nap. As we were walking upstairs to my bedroom, he said, "Let's see the room!" He seemed like he was anticipating something nice but I lived like an animal.

"It's just a bed and some clothes, I haven't gotten around to any interior decorating." I said as I turned the light on. He noticed a pack of condoms on the floor and asked, "What the fuck is condoms?"

"Well if you're gonna fuck girls from halfway houses, you really should use them."

"Well what you do is you don't fuck 'em. Just blowjobs."

"Yea, I'm not really one to use condoms but with these girls down here in Florida, I'm cautious."

"I go by the honor system. If you don't got nothing, me either. Just like in the Boy Scouts."

After that morning I was weary of meeting up with Frank again. He was on a death crusade so he terrified me. Billy, who was more my speed, called me a couple days later looking to borrow money because he too had relapsed. "Why the hell didn't you call me sooner, you mean to tell me we could've been getting high together this whole time?" I asked. "I figured you were still sober," he replied. We got high together for a couple weeks. His wife had a kid from another guy and the wife was getting high with us. I remember feeling terrible for the child but what could I do about it? One day I had errands to run so I left some money with his wife instructing her to have Billy pick something up for us later. He kept it all for himself and disappeared on me.

After getting high for a couple weeks, I quit my job. I woke up one morning with the worst kind of withdrawals so I decided to not show up and not call. Place was one of the worst restaurants I'd ever worked in. There wasn't much money to make and you have to run your own food and bus your own tables. Even without having to tip out bus boys and runners, I was still making garbage. Not to mention I hated the owner's wife for not letting me work behind the bar.

One night I had nobody to help me shoot up. Billy ghosted me and Frank terrified me. I could never shoot up on my own. I was too squeamish when it came to the part where you draw the syringe back to see if blood comes into it. That's how you know you hit a vein. For some reason I could never master that part. On some occasions, when I had to shoot up alone, I would skip that part. I basically threw up a Hail Mary hoping that I actually hit a vein. I usually did hit it though because I had really good visible veins. One night I purchased some really good heroin down in Overtown, Miami along with some cocaine for a speed-ball. I wanted to make sure I shot it up properly.

I heard Xiara was getting high again. She was at one of those fake halfway houses that lets you get high there, so long as you pay the rent. She was living there with her new boyfriend. I called her and said, "Listen if you shoot me up, I'll share some of what I got with you."

"Ok but we have to be quick. My boyfriend's asleep I don't want him to know I'm gone."

Once she was in the car, I took her by my house because I was incredibly paranoid and felt safer shooting up in my drive-way. After she shot me up, she said, "Ok hurry up I need to get back there."

"Wait, don't you want to do yours?"

"Just give it to me when we get there."

I jumped back onto i-95 and did my best to rush back. I kept nodding out behind the wheel which was freaking her out. She started cursing at me for perceivably putting her in danger. As I approached her place, she had her hand out. "You ain't getting shit! You think you could talk to me like that? When you were sucking my dick, you could get away with that, but I ain't giving you shit if that's the way you're gonna talk to me!" I shouted at her. She immediately started throwing punches at me. I curled into a defensive position and let her get it out of her system a bit until I got fed up. I then grabbed both of her wrists to subdue her and yelled, "Either you get the fuck out of my car right now or I'm driving to the Everglades and leaving you in a fucking swamp without a cell phone!" She got out of the car empty handed after that.

At first, I was trying to hide that I relapsed from George. I was a little embarrassed because when I was sober and he was acting like a psycho, I was often quite judgmental of him. Eventually, swallowing my pride and informing him seemed like the logical thing to do. I needed somebody to help me shoot up anyway. One night after we shot up, we went to the backyard patio and lit a couple of cigarettes. "You ever just wish a relapse would finally kill you?" I asked him.

"It'd be easier that way," he replied.

We both had significant clean time before but neither of us ever achieved everlasting happiness or a sense of peace. We were too stupid to realize then that life is definitely worth living if we could just learn how to get out of our own way.

Twenty-One - Rosita's

I decided to come clean to my parents about relapsing in hopes that they'd let me come back home. They wanted nothing to do with me but my friend Jack from Staten Island was willing to let me sleep on his couch until I figured things out. Ron and Vinny picked me up from the airport when I came home. I was only clean a couple of days so the withdrawals were in full swing. Sitting in coach on an airplane in opioid withdrawal is undoubtedly the most uncomfortable situation I could think of. Sitting in traffic on the Belt Parkway, I began telling Ron and Vinny all of my misadventures in Florida. When the subject of Frank came up, Ron said, "It's an insult to the dead that he's still alive."

Before shacking up with Jack, I spent the weekend with Vinny at his family's beach house in New Jersey. It was there that I discovered the cure for opioid withdrawals. It is not Suboxone or Methadone. The answer is jet skis. I never rode one before but Vinny and I took his father's out for a spin. All of the aches and pains were completely taken away once I hit the throttle.

Reality sunk in quickly back on Staten Island. I was using an air mattress to sleep in Jack's tiny apartment. I went back to the sober fellowship and I was able to get a job with one of its members. We were working in a phone room, but this time I at least got a base pay as opposed to strictly commission. I lasted two weeks. They were pushing business loans. I couldn't hack it. The owner and his manager were murdered a few months later. He hired a lot of ex-cons and one of his former employees was angry that he never received a payment he thought he was entitled to. He came by one day and shot them both. That was the second time I just missed a murder at a job. One time I worked at this restaurant and the owner had a knack for sleeping with other men's wives. Not just any men's wives, wiseguys' wives. One of them sought retribution and shot him ten minutes after I left work. The next morning, I was supposed to go to work and I was really hung over. My father woke me up and said, "Stephen I don't think you got work today. Your boss was murdered last night!" Instead of expressing concern I just said, "Nice!" Then I went back to sleep.

Carmine relapsed around the same time as me and was getting sober again a couple weeks behind me. Like me, he went beast mode through the withdrawals. No detox. No rehab. Just went to meetings held by that sober fellowship. One day we went to Woodrow Diner before one of the meetings. His buddy Bruce, who's girlfriend cheated on him with me when she was working at Pico's, had died from an overdose a year prior to then. At the diner, he ran into Bruce's aunt. When you're in withdrawal you get overly emotional. After speaking with her he started to get teary eyed. Carmine would much rather be void of all emotion. Any time I acted up based on emotion he'd ridicule me for it. It disgusted him. As we got into his car after the diner he said, "I got to get it together I'm crying. I can't let people see me like this." I started laughing and said, "You know, I hope they have a fire speaker at the meeting." His cries turned into laughter. "If the speaker has me crying, I swear to Christ I'll walk the fuck out of there!" he added.

His marriage to Layla was rapidly approaching. I believe that factored into his decision to get sober again. He had gotten cold feet so many times but this time it was Layla who called it off at the very last minute. Any closer to the day he would've been left at the altar. The caterer and other services were already paid for. Carmine was livid. In a lot of ways though, I think he was relieved. Their relationship was rocky to say the least. A marriage might've been the worst thing that could've happened. He'd get over it quite quickly though.

There was a newcomer girl named Lauren hanging around the meetings who was quite beautiful. She was showing up with some kid who I assumed was her boyfriend. Turns out that guy wasn't her boyfriend. He was just some loser who was obsessed with her and she had zero interest in him. Carmine managed to scoop her up and jumped right into a relationship with her. I didn't understand why he put himself through the trouble though. Her father would take her to meetings and wait outside for her. He initially had to pull stealth missions to get her alone. When it came time to meet her parents he was put under intense scrutiny. The mother got all the dirt she needed on him from somebody who knew him. She knew about the cheating on Layla, she knew he used to be a drug dealer, and she knew that he had relapsed countless times. He told me he just used his trademark brutal honesty when he was held up to this scrutiny.

He managed to win them over. "I don't know how the fuck you do that," I said to him. "After everything we've been through. I feel like we can handle situations like that gracefully," he told me. I really liked the sound of that. I wish I shared his sentiment. I had no idea how to handle anything gracefully.

Since I quit that phone room gig, I had to look for work again and fast. Living on Jack's couch wasn't cutting it. I decided to go back to the only thing I knew, waiting tables at restaurants. But I couldn't bring myself to do it on Staten Island. The idea of someone I knew seeing me at age 29, soon to be 30, still waiting tables was out of the question. My self-esteem was hanging by a thread as it was. I decided to head to New Jersey where I wouldn't be seen by people I knew. At first, I drove down to the Freehold Mall. I was so depressed I talked myself out of asking for a job at any the restaurants there. Then I drove north up highway 9 towards Staten Island. About ten to fifteen minutes up the road, I saw a really big Mexican restaurant called Rosita's. I missed the turn but I pulled over about a block or so away. I tried to use the same pessimism I had at the Freehold Mall to talk myself out of walking in but I swear I felt the universe calling me in there like a magnet. Something was telling me to walk inside. Then I started to experience a sense of optimism. I realized I had managed a Mexican restaurant before, so getting a waiter job there ought to be a piece of cake.

When I walked inside, I realized right away that I had made the right decision. In less than a minute I saw three female staff members and every one of them was drop dead gorgeous. I filled out an application and asked to speak to a manager. The manager was busy but I got her name, Flo, from the hostess. I decided I would try and speak to her directly on another day. I didn't have to though. A day or so later I received a phone call instructing me to come in for an interview. The interview was with this bald man named Charlie who I thought was another manager but he turned out to be one of the owners. Navigating through this interview was a bit tricky because he seemed a bit quirky and socially awkward. I like to think I have a knack for being deceitful when I need to be. However, this guy was asking me questions where I couldn't help being honest. Honesty for a guy like me on a job interview is never a good thing. "So, I see you used to manage a restaurant. Tell me, what's the one thing that employees do that irritate you the most?"

"I guess laziness. Not holding up their end."

"Mine's cell phone use. How do you feel about cell phone use?"

"I guess that doesn't really bother me so long as the customers can't see them doing it."

"It's one of my pet peeves. I don't want anybody playing with their phones in the restaurant at all."

I was worried my lack of caring about cell phone use might dissuade him but he gave me the job. Charlie, I would learn, tries really hard to be stern but deep down he's a great guy. One of the best bosses I ever had, if not the best. His two partners, Colin and Walter, were great too. Colin and Walter tended to watch the other restaurants they owned for the most part. I learned pretty quickly not to work lunch shifts because that's when Charlie was lurking around.

As much as I hated that I had to work as a waiter in a restaurant as I was rapidly approaching age thirty, I absolutely love the restaurant business. I love everything about it. I love the breed of jaded and broken people it employs. I love the smell of bleach from the mopped floors. I love the aromas of all the different foods being cooked. I even love the putrid smell of spilled alcohol on the bar that hasn't been properly cleaned. I love most of the customers that come in. I love kicking it with the Mexicans working in the kitchen. I love the camaraderie you feel with your co-workers because you get the sense that you've been on a battlefield together on a busy night. I love it all. Not to mention that this restaurant had a bunch of female staff members that I absolutely had to get my hands on. They all responded favorably to my Staten Island accent. My accent is pretty thick to begin with but I definitely would embellish the pronunciation of certain words for a little flare. I found it amazing that the accent actually helped me in the romance department just a half hour drive into Jersey. It always helped when I was on vacation but seeing it work this close to home was a treat.

My first night training was with this girl Sarah. Sarah had blonde hair which isn't exactly my forte but I put the charm on nonetheless. It's not enough to just be charming to the intended target. In a situation where you plan on running through an entire staff of beautiful girls, you want all of them to speak highly of you. They could speak negatively too in some cases. Nothing works better than some girl warning another to watch out for you because, "He's an asshole." Any publicity is good publicity, just get them talking about you.

A half hour drive into Jersey wasn't far enough to escape running into people I knew apparently. It happened a lot more often than I expected. Fortunately for me, the restaurant was huge and I'd usually manage to dodge a bullet. They'd be seated in one area of the restaurant and I'd stay in mine. If I had to pass their area I would do it stealthily or go the long way around them. I'd love to say that I was above all this and didn't care what people thought of me but I found it to be completely humiliating. The worst was when Charlie was there. He'd make sure you checked into the restaurant on Facebook. I would show him I did it and then immediately run into the bathroom and delete the post. I didn't want my friends on Facebook knowing not only where I worked but that I was such an enthusiastic employee that I'd advertise it. Eventually, I found a way to post something on Facebook with an option that made it so nobody could actually see it but myself. I would show Charlie my phone and without a proper investigation, it all appeared as if I had actually shared it with the world.

I initially had my eye on a bartender named Allison. But before I could get to her, I sensed a vibe from this hostess Fiona. A few friends of mine from Staten Island were in the Freehold area one night and I mentioned to her that I was happy because I'd get to meet them at a nearby diner after work.

"Oh, I want to go! I love diners!" she said with an enthusiasm that suggested she wanted to hang out with me. Nobody is THAT passionate about diners. My friends ended up back on Staten Island way before I finished work but she said she was up for going with just me. I decided to merely plant a seed and not make a move right then and there. The following Monday night though, it was on. She came to Staten Island with me after work and we met the gang at Denino's. After that, I took her to Carmine's apartment and he gave us a little privacy. Fiona was a sweet girl and drop dead gorgeous but I had wandering eyes. I wanted to end the fling softly so I could move on to the next target but I didn't have to stress it. Her father died from smoking and she insisted I quit if I wanted to keep dating her. I told her I had no desire to quit and she ended it before I had to.

One Saturday night a girl was working whom I never saw before. Her name was Lydia. She only worked Saturdays because she had some internship at Ralph Lauren in Manhattan. I planted the seed and spoke to her a little bit. She had a boyfriend but that never stopped me before. I preferred girls with boyfriends. Truth is I'm terrified of rejection. It's easier to handle rejection when a girl has a boyfriend because you could just attest the rejection to the boyfriend and not take it personally. Once the shift was over, the entire staff, including her, was at the bar drinking. I felt pretty solid in my sobriety at that time but a part of me was sad. They looked like they were having fun and didn't have a care in the world. I knew I was different from them but I desperately wanted to be normal like them. I didn't want to be this weird guy who doesn't drink because he's worried he might do heroin. I cashed out and got out of there as fast as I could. The ride home was miserable. All I could think about was the wondrous evening they were certainly going to have and how mine was simply over. To make myself feel better I reminded myself that all the money I made that night I would get to keep instead of spending it on stupidity. But deep down, I would've rather spent it on stupidity.

One night the entire staff was hanging out at Rosita's sister restaurant, The Standard. I heard Lydia was going so I made sure I was there. She ate up everything I said. She had to leave early though because she had work at that internship in the morning. Her mother came to pick her up and, a few moments after she left, I received a text from her saying, "You're literally the best kind of person." Only natural she'd feel that way. After Lydia left, I set my sights on the bartender Allison. I had to walk over to 7/11 to get cigarettes and she needed something as well so we walked over together. She kept making self-deprecating statements. Saying things that alluded to her not thinking she was attractive. I charmingly corrected her and she replied, "You're not so bad looking yourself." At that point I offered my designated driving services. She took the ride but insisted that having a boyfriend would prevent her from succumbing to my charm. I ignored this road block and drove straight through it. Once I got her to her destination, she let me kiss her.

The following Tuesday night after work, I managed to get Allison to my house. After a couple months sober, my parents were gracious enough to let me move back in. Living with my parents again was humiliating but living on Jack's couch was just awful. Allison was on her period but I convinced her to give me a blowjob. The next day, I continued working on Lydia. I pretended that I happened to be in Manhattan and was wondering if she needed a ride back to civilization. She took me up on it and I was able to put some more charm on. As I was dropping her off I said, "I can't help but feel like there's something between us, what do you say I take you out sometime?"

She giggled and said, "You're not wrong but I have a boyfriend so I got to figure that out and get back to you."

The next night I had Allison come by and she blew me again because she was still on her period. At one point she said, "I'm not looking for anything serious." I tried to act as if I wasn't completely thrilled to hear that. Neither was I. The following Friday as I was leaving work, Allison texted me that she was in Atlantic City and had a room for the night. Gambling and sex were my idea of an ideal Friday night. But she wasn't answering her phone because she lost service in whatever hotel she was in so I never got to meet her.

The following evening was Saturday, so Lydia was working again. I was in a tight spot here because I assumed it would take me much longer to get Lydia to cheat on her boyfriend. Apparently, she dumped him earlier that week. That night at work the back and forth between us was escalating fast. She'd playfully shove me and we'd crack jokes together. The vibrations between us was electric. Julio, a server and friend of Lydia's since high school, pulled me aside and said, "She wants you bro." The entire staff was going to a place called Moore's after work in

Freehold. Moore's is the kind of place you suspect that Bruce Springsteen was talking about in the song "Glory Days." I was worried how I was going to juggle this Allison and Lydia situation. I thought a solution presented itself but I was mistaken. I overheard someone invite Allison to Moore's to which she said, "I can't go, my father is an alcoholic and he drinks there." I was elated.

I drove Lydia over to Moore's and made out with her in the parking lot. I decided to come clean to her about Allison. I made it clear to her though that it was her I really wanted. Allison was merely for sport. Lydia was more my type. She didn't seem to mind that I had been fooling around with Allison. She really had no grounds to complain anyway. Forty-eight hours prior she was still in a relationship. All seemed to be well until we went inside to meet everyone else.

Upon arriving inside, my mood went from being quite satisfied with myself to complete and utter dismay. Allison said she wasn't coming, but there she was sitting at the bar drinking and giving me dirty looks. She wasn't quite sure if I was up to no good with Lydia just yet, but she was definitely suspicious of me. I was cringing in my seat hoping it wouldn't all explode in my face. But sure enough, it did. It didn't take long either. Allison walked over to me and asked, "Can you drive Julio home later?"

Lydia, in a very catty fashion, barked at her, "He's taking me home and Julio lives on the way so yea." I got to admit, part of me was aroused by Lydia marking her territory. Another part of me was mortified that I was caught with my hand in the cookie jar.

Allison stormed out of there so I ran after her. I tried to make an excuse for myself by reminding her, "Hey you said yourself that you weren't looking for anything serious." She pouted and yelled back, "You don't deserve to be with anyone!" I felt terrible but I started laughing once she turned her back. She was absolutely right. I knew I was completely maladjusted and decided to stop struggling to be normal. I felt in my element being a monster.

I managed to put together about three months of sobriety. Every Saturday morning Carmine, his new girlfriend Lauren, and I would go to a meeting held by that sober fellowship. This girl we called Horses, because she gave horse riding lessons, came up to us and offered us what was called recovery coach training. She got these scholarships to provide the training for free. Recovery coach meant we'd be working in recovery-based places like a detox, rehab, or an outpatient program.

"We only got around ninety days sober though," I said to her.

"Oh, that doesn't matter just so long as you're sober," replied Horses.

The classes were a lot of fun. They were held at this new outpatient facility called Teddy's Reason. Teddy was the name of the owner's son who died of an overdose. I wasn't sure what the training was leading to but I took the classes with a bunch of members of the sober fellowship.

Angelo eventually came home from Florida to answer for some pending arrest warrants. Before turning himself in, I took him and Dean to a meeting held by the sober fellowship. My little Florida group had a bit of a reunion, not counting Eddie. Eddie stayed in Florida for a while. Dean relapsed but claimed he wanted to get back into sobriety. I picked him and Angelo up for a meeting but Dean was so stoned he fell asleep during the meeting. Angelo, as far as I could tell, was sober. First, I dropped off Dean. Then I dropped Angelo off at his mother's house. He was going to Riker's Island in the morning to answer for those warrants. "Good luck tomorrow. Don't sweat it bro, you'll be out of there before you know it," I told him. "I love you mo," he replied. "I love you too," I responded.

A few days later he was found dead in his cell from an overdose. The shock didn't hit me initially. I went to see Eddie, and the rest of the family for that matter, at their house. Eddie was crying and gave me a big hug. I tried to be as consoling as I possibly could but what did I know? I had and still have no idea what to say or do to be comforting to someone in that situation. If you're in a bad mood I could try and make you laugh. In a situation as grim as that I got nothing funny to say to cheer you up. I just tried to be there for him as best I could.

Angelo's death didn't really hit me until I was driving to work a couple weeks after he passed. The Eagles' "Take It Easy" came on the radio and I started to get teary eyed. Then it really hit me. I recalled listening to that song with Angelo. The fact that he died in a place like Riker's Island disturbed me. Nobody deserves that. Underneath it all, once I got to really know him, I found out he was a really good kid. We had a lot more in common than I initially thought. I couldn't help but feel like I let him down. I wanted to be able to guide him in his recovery but I couldn't even maintain my own. I didn't realize at the time that I was not fit to be helping anyone. Least of all my friends.

One Saturday an older woman who worked at Rosita's, Lucy, was throwing a house party. After four months of sobriety I decided to throw it all out the window and do some cocaine with Lydia and Julio. I figured I was in New Jersey so none of my friends from the sober fellowship would find out. Julio and I went on a little excursion to get the stuff and that first line washed over my soul with a wave of euphoria. That wave of euphoria was followed very abruptly by panic, fear, and anxiety. I felt reclusive and paranoid the entirety of the evening. Simple conversation was a hassle. Lydia tried to console me but I was in a pit of despair. Riddled with guilt, I even tried to apologize to Allison but my jaw was rocking so bad that I was simply a stuttering fool. I got to know this waiter Jordan at the party pretty well though. He dropped a line from the movie "Paid In Full" that made me laugh and a friendship blossomed from there.

I started gradually using Oxycodone again but not enough to develop a full-fledged habit just yet. "Star Wars: Rogue One" was about to hit theatres so I rounded up all of my fellow "Star Wars" geek friends. I knew Petey loved "Star Wars" and, despite everyone's complete and utter disdain for him, not to mention my own prejudices, I decided to invite him. You had to order the tickets on a credit card and I was not in possession of one. I had my father order it and told him I'd pay him once I collected the money. I assumed it'd be a non-issue and that all my friends should be able to afford a fifteen-dollar ticket. The night of the movie, Petey came to me with a sob story as to why he couldn't pay me and promised he would pay me back. I had heard this song and dance from him for years. I invited him against my better judgement. He was strung out on heroin but I don't care what your bad habits are. If you're a "Star Wars" fan over the age of thirty and can't scrounge together fifteen dollars for a ticket, there's something seriously wrong with you. I told him I had to give the spot to someone else but there was nobody else.

I sat next to an empty seat on principle. He texted me about three or four paragraph long rants about how I was a lousy friend. I cut him out of my life completely after that. He was always a selfish person and a lousy friend, himself. The audacity of him to accuse me of being a bad friend sealed his fate. I always forgave him and turned the other cheek but that was the last straw.

Two days later my 30th birthday fell on a Saturday. I ended up working my birthday so I could finally sleep with Lydia. Aside from the timing being right, her parents were out of town so we had her house to ourselves after work. She made me use a condom which I hated but reluctantly agreed to. I could sense that Lydia was starting to feel bad about leaving her boyfriend. I wasn't exactly making a great case for myself considering I started getting high again. When you're constantly high you're not exactly an attractive individual. I tried to keep my drug use to a minimum but it never really pans out that way.

The following evening, I met up with Lydia, her little brother, a bunch of her brother's friends, and a few other Rosita's staff members. They were drinking at this place called the Court Jester. After they had their fill, they were all going to Lydia's house. I assumed I was invited. Apparently, I wasn't. I took two trips to drive them all home so they wouldn't have to pay for an Uber. Erin, a waitress from Rosita's, was allowed to go because she was a girl and the other guys were allowed because they were her neighbors.

"So let me get this straight? You invited me out, had me drive you all here, and now you're telling me to fuck off?" I asked her.

"Zane wouldn't be allowed to come in," she said. Zane was the boyfriend she had just dumped.

"My name ain't Zane now is it?" I replied.

She reluctantly let me join the festivities but I should've just gone home. They had a pool table in the house and I schooled her little brother in a game of eight ball. I underestimated him at first. He was up to the eight ball and I still had four balls left on the table. Once he missed the eight ball, I sank the four balls one after the other and then the eight ball. There was some trash talking back and forth throughout the game so I gloated when I won. About ten minutes later, he ran upstairs and came back with a baseball bat screaming, "Get the fuck out of my house!" I threw my hands up in the air to communicate surrender and went quietly. I assumed he was just young and a really sore loser but Lydia later explained to me that he was under the impression that I was hurting her. I was pretty high that night but I don't know what could've given him that impression. I may have spoken to her in an argumentative tone but I wasn't behaving like Ike Turner.

The next day I went to do my Christmas shopping at Freehold mall before work. I coincidentally ran into Lydia in Macy's and the exchange was just flat out awkward. She made it clear later that day that it wasn't going to work out between us. A week or so later, she was back with her boyfriend Zane. One night a bunch of people from Rosita's hung out at Moore's. I wasn't expected to come so Lydia brought Zane with her. My presence created an undeniable tension but I'm not sure if he understood what was going on. I'd like to think that my sinister smile and Lydia's visible anxiety made it very awkward for the both of them. I truly loved ruining and putting stress on other people's relationships. Mostly because I could never seem to have a healthy one of my own. Bringing others down to my level of loneliness brought me joy.

Word got to Marie, the owner of Teddy's Reason, that I was getting high. "Did you relapse?" Marie asked me over the phone. I denied it of course. I needed another source of income aside from waiting tables. "Nah, I just haven't been able to make as many meetings as usual so people probably assumed that I've fallen back into my old ways," I told her. She bought my deception. I decided to get my act together because I really did not want to lose a job opportunity. I took a couple days off at the restaurant and successfully kicked another blues habit cold turkey.

At work, I started sensing a vibe from another bartender, Sofia. Sofia was drop dead gorgeous and she was dating some personal trainer I liked to call Ricky Martin. I called him that because he had some blonde streaks dyed into his hair like they used to do in the 90's. Initially, I thought my usual charm wouldn't work going against a guy like that. But Sofia would do things like grab my ass cheeks as she walked by which made me start thinking otherwise. I'd make her laugh with Sylvester Stallone impressions from "Rocky" and by passing her notes while she was busy behind the bar that said, "Send Nudes." We'd hang out at work pretty often and she'd entertain my advances a little bit but ultimately, she would just play hard to get. I'd constantly ask her to hang out with me sometime and she'd say, "It'd be inappropriate if I hung out alone with you."

Late January, Rosita's and its sister restaurants had their annual Christmas party at the Freehold Hotel. I used the opportunity to try working on Sofia. At the end of the night, I was a perfect candidate to drive Sofia home because I was sober. She was going to take an Uber at first but since I wasn't drinking, she let me take her home. I remember thinking I should be a gentleman and not try anything funny because she was drunk and I didn't want to take advantage. But upon arriving at her house, she stayed in the car and spoke to me for a little while. Then she began acting a little promiscuous. She started simulating fellatio on my fingers and wasn't stopping me when I started to rub her thighs a bit. I tried kissing her but she wouldn't let it go that far.

After that initial relapse, I was able to keep my act together for about a month or so. I completed the recovery coach training and was waiting to be put to work. I soon decided that I was going to try and just drink alcohol. My new job might give me a drug test, but they probably wouldn't have been looking for alcohol. Besides, the recovery coach gig was rooted on Staten Island. I had an entirely separate life going on in New Jersey. Word of my sins would never reach there. The first night I picked up a drink I met Lydia and a few other girls from Rosita's out at some bar in Middletown. For the time being, Lydia and I were on cordial terms even though we were no longer dating. I hadn't tried to just drink in years. Usually it went along with another substance like bacon and eggs. After a few drinks, I felt an overwhelming sense of joy as if just sticking to alcohol was the answer to all my problems. I loved the way it felt. The girls were calling it an early night so I decided to meet Jack, who had recently decided to stick to just drinking himself. He was having some female issues of his own so he had me driving to meet him all over town. As I was driving on his street, he texted me, "Sorry bro I'm just gonna go to bed." As I was reading this text, drunk and enraged by his indecisiveness, I managed to plow into a parked SUV. It was three in the morning so I scanned my surroundings and sped out of there once I assessed that I hadn't been seen. I called Jack and explained what had happened. My car was demolished but I could still drive it so I was laughing about it.

The next morning Jack called. "Bro I think you hit Ron's grandmother's truck bro!" he said.

I was appalled. I couldn't believe it but Jack insisted he was serious. He saw her talking to a police officer. My heart dropped. I had a pit in my stomach the entire day thinking of how I would explain to Ron that I hit his grandmother's truck. At first, I thought Jack might've been messing around with me but then I realized he wasn't clever enough to think of a prank like that. Later that night, around 9 o' clock, I was just staring at my phone. I finally worked up the nerve to make the call.

"Hey Ron, did somebody hit your grandmother's truck last night?" I asked.

There was a pause, then he slowly said, "Yea, why?"

I let out a deep breath. "Well, it was me," I timidly stated.

I thought he'd be furious but he was relieved. As it turned out, her insurance didn't cover random collisions while the car was parked. Needless to say, my decision to come clean really saved them from a lot more pain and suffering. My insurance would end up higher but at least I did the right thing by my friend.

I temporarily gave up on this strictly drinking fantasy. Seeing as how I managed to not only total my car, but Ron's grandmother's car as well, it seemed like the right decision to make. Not to mention I was going to soon be starting a job based on sobriety. The first job I got as a recovery coach was offering outpatient services to people arrested on minor drug possession charges. Basically, they could get their charges dropped if they reported to the outpatient. If there wasn't anybody who fit the criteria arrested during my shift, I stayed home all night and got paid $60. If I did get a call, I would meet the prospect at whichever precinct they were arrested at and then I'd get paid $120. I'd tell them what we were offering and I'd give them a Narcan kit. Narcan reverses the effects of an opioid overdose. The powers that be insisted we get as many of those out onto the streets as they are legitimate life savers. Narcan would soon be needed to ensure my own survival. Eventually, Marie opened up a detox in Brooklyn.

Luckily detoxes are open 24 hours a day. They worked around my restaurant schedule and gave me three overnight shifts. I was even allowed to take a little snooze at work. Now that I was working two jobs, I could afford getting out of my parents' house again.

Twenty-Two Best Summer Ever

Despite working in the recovery field, I managed to find myself drinking again. What got me started was this girl Margaret from Rosita's. We started dating and she gave me the, "You're not drinking?" routine. The first time I had only three blue moons. It escalated to the point that she was concerned almost immediately. I'm an alcoholic as much as I am a drug addict because I tend to drink alcohol faster than I would drink water. When I wasn't drinking with her, I was drinking with my two friends from work Jordan and Lucy's son Tom. We called Tom, "Dreamy Eyes" because his eyes are simply majestic.

Somewhere around that time, Frank came home for a visit. He had about ninety days clean. Even though I was drinking, I went with him and Carmine to a meeting held by that sober fellowship. But before that, Frank infuriated Carmine's girlfriend Lauren. He didn't even do anything wrong. It was simply his aura that was enough for her to say to Carmine that she didn't want him hanging around. "I feel like he's the type of guy that'll rob you and help you look for it. He just seems like a scumbag," Lauren said.

"Yea but he's OUR scumbag," I replied. Frank sensed the hostility from Lauren. At the meeting, he exchanged passive aggressive comments with her. Carmine wrote Frank off after that. Frank, in a fit of rage, went back to Florida. A few days later, he overdosed and ended up paralyzed from the waist down. Doctors said he'd be in a wheelchair for the rest of his life.

I took Margaret out on our first real date and I made quite an impression on her. I took her to the new Denino's in Manhattan and then to the Comedy Cellar for a comedy show. There we put down a couple pitchers of Blue Moon. The comedians put on a great show. Afterwards we spent the night at her house because her parents weren't home.

A few nights later, I visited Vinny in Long Branch, New Jersey. Long Branch is a beach town fairly close to Rosita's and all the bars I was frequenting. He was living with his new stripper girlfriend Anna who lived out there. He asked me to be his roommate, and as it turned out, he started drinking too. This all felt as if I hit the lottery. Now I could finally get out of my parents' house again. I was planning on drinking down at the shore all summer long anyway. Now I didn't have to worry about driving drunk all the way back to Staten Island. His only concern was my notoriety for sleeping with guys' girlfriends. I put his mind at ease. I wanted to tell him that I hate blondes so I found his girlfriend repulsive but I didn't want to be cruel. After all, I was about to share a roof with them both.

Drinking was slowly deteriorating my mental health but I couldn't see it. Margaret was starting to get fed up with me but I didn't care. I wanted my freedom anyway. I'd just discovered alcohol again and all I wanted to do was get drunk and talk to girls. The friction between us started when we were all drinking at The Standard and I started flirting with a gorgeous older woman. Margaret saw the exchange and expressed her anger but I pointed out that there was no title on our relationship. Besides, she was moving to Colorado to go back to college soon. It's not like we were going to live happily ever after. She broke it off once she saw my true colors.

I decided I needed to make more money to support my blossoming alcoholism so I took a job delivering for this health food delivery service the owners of Rosita's and a personal trainer were trying to put together. On Sundays I would deliver the food all over North Jersey and they'd give me $150 for each shift. Then I had the detox that I was unethically working at while in the grips of active alcoholism. Plus three shifts at Rosita's. I also would occasionally be on call to offer outpatient to people who had been arrested on minor drug charges. There was a long stretch of time where I was never getting a call though. One night I was supposed to be on call. I ordinarily would stay at my parents' house because being on call required me to be within a half hour's distance of all the Staten Island police precincts. Since I was rarely getting a call, I found myself drinking at a bar in Jersey assuming I wouldn't be needed. Not only did I receive a call, but it was at the 122 precinct. The 122 is on the North Shore which was the farthest precinct from where I was. It would take a normal person an hour to get there. I flew on the Garden State Parkway drunk and managed to make it in forty-five minutes. How the cops at the precinct didn't suspect I was drunk is beyond me. There were four guys arrested. Three were white and one was black. "If you guys go to outpatient these charges completely disappear so you should definitely do it. Especially you, since you're black," I said. Thank God the black guy had a sense of humor. One can never be too sure how people are going to react to a joke like that these days but it went over well.

I was becoming increasingly unhinged and I would constantly be in an irritable mood at whatever job I was working. I knew I was acting erratic but I managed to gain leverage at both jobs. The three overnight shifts at the detox were tough shifts to get covered so I felt pretty safe there. Most of the staff and all of the bosses worked the day shifts so I was always out of sight and out of mind anyway. Delivering for the health food service really cemented my employment in the restaurant. Charlie was desperate to get it off the ground and the personal trainer who came up with the recipes absolutely adored me. I may come into work hungover and irritable, but aside from that I get everything done that's expected of me.

At work I started to really get to know Charlie the owner. We were discussing someone who was a heroin addict and Charlie rhetorically asked, "Do people like that get better?"

Against my better judgement, I opened up about my past afflictions.

"I did," I said.

"What did you used to do?" he asked.

I made a hand gesture that looked like I was pressing a needle into my arms. The conversation went from the servers' station to the office and got deep from there. Apparently, his sister was a heroin addict. I mentioned that the one thing I want and always wanted, was a family and children of my own.

"Only problem is I know I have this thing inside me. I haven't touched heroin in over a year but I'm terrified of bringing a kid into this world and slipping up again," I told him.

He comforted my concerns in a way that was reminiscent of an elder member of the sober fellowship. "Before I became a father, I could be selfish and foolish but if you're anything like me, it'll change you. Once you have a child it's no longer about you, it's about them," he said.

I never even thought about it that way. In that moment I realized if I can accomplish my goal of becoming a father, I would never fail my child. I love kids too much. The only problem was I had no means of starting a family. I could barely pay my rent and as much as I felt like Don Juan going after any girl with a pulse, I knew nothing about relationships and commitment. The only thing I was really committed to was drinking.

Drinking progressed into doing cocaine occasionally. That led to snorting blues here and there and by August, I was shooting heroin again. I was pretty careful to not develop a solid heroin habit. I would space out the use and maintain my drinking habit to pass the time in between. I didn't want to become physically dependent on heroin again. Then Frank came home. He was in a wheelchair but that wasn't stopping us from intravenous heroin

278   Stephen J. Sacchi

use. I was surprised to see Frank had a sense of humor about being in a wheelchair. One day we were strolling into a CVS to buy syringes when a lady was trying to walk in ahead of us. "Whoa hang on! I've got the right of way here," he shouted at her.

One night we were waiting for some girl he knew to get out of work so she could score heroin for us. In the interim, we bought blues to hold us over from some guy who I actually knew from the sober fellowship's meetings on Staten Island. We made conversation after the purchase and as I was shooting a blue, I mentioned that I was working at a detox even though I had relapsed. After sharing this information, I let out a sinister laugh. I had to laugh at the tragic irony of my double life. What else could I do? He later texted Frank that he didn't find it funny. "That shit ain't cool, working at a detox while he's getting high," he texted Frank. The Oxycodone salesman had a moral standing on people who relapsed working in the recovery field.

Once the girl got out of work, we secured the heroin. Frank shot two bags and started doing his wolf howl. I immediately decided that I would only shoot one bag instead of two. If Frank was howling like a wolf from two bags, I would've surely died from shooting two. One bag was more than enough to do it though. I gradually started slipping into an overdose. For some reason, I ended up crawling out of the driver's seat of my car. Thank God for that because it saved me from getting a DUI. The girl got in the driver's seat in a panic so she would receive that honor. This all happened in front of a few houses and one of them called the police because that girl started screaming when

Frank and I fell out. When the cops came, I was overdosing on the curb with a needle still in my arm. The police took me to the hospital and I was given Narcan. I immediately spewed out projectile vomit into a trash can.

Once I was brought back to life, I noticed I was handcuffed to the bed with a cop sitting next to it. I showed this man no hostility at all. I expressed gratitude to him because I was fully aware of the fact that he probably saved my life. Sure I was under arrest and probably going to suffer some consequences but all of that I could handle. The officer said to one of the nurses, which prompted me to say - "Officer, back off! That's my future ex-wife you're talking to." Another nurse had a sourpuss face around me though. "I'm sorry. Do I offend you or something?" I asked. "Ugh, no. It's just, I hate to see people like you hurting yourselves and you don't look like a junkie." I laughed and said, "That's because I'm a fucking stud. Junkies come in all different shapes and sizes." It must've been very confusing to see me like that because I was only using heroin for a couple weeks. I was dressed pretty dapper and not looking as rugged as a junkie who had been using it for an extended period of time. Most junkies who overdose have a nice tint of filth on them. I looked like a GQ magazine model.

Much to my surprise, I would not be spending the night in jail as I expected. New Jersey had this new thing called bail reform. Under bail reform, you're free to go home that night. You simply have to appear before a judge at a later date. When we got to the station, Frank and the girl were already on their way out. The cops told me I had to have someone pick me up. Ron was my first try. He wasn't having it. There was no way he was putting his prosthetic leg on and coming to Jersey. Vinny, who was now back with Anna and living with us again, put up some resistance at first. He didn't want to pick me up because he felt it would just be enabling me.

I thought I could avoid having my family find out about this little escapade. However, the court in Jamestown sent something in the mail to my parents' house. Frank's father was in the courtroom and I couldn't bear to look the man in the eye. I knew damn well I should not have been shooting heroin with his son who became paralyzed from shooting heroin in the first place. He spared me the shame of confronting me. After that, I kicked heroin again cold turkey.

Twenty-Three - Back to School

I thought with the summer coming to a close my insanity would too but I was just getting warmed up. Vinny and Anna broke up again but I once again felt the need to stay where I was, despite the awkward living situation. I was living in a college town and I didn't even realize it. Tuesday nights and Thursday nights, we'd drink until the bars closed. They were all packed with college kids. I loved every minute of it.

I was eventually taken off probation with the state of New Jersey earlier than expected. After passing two of their drug tests I was off the hook. At first, I reached out to Cassandra to see if she could get heroin. She claimed she had nobody to call so I decided to go to Asbury Park and get it myself from a sketchy part of town. I asked Cassandra if she wanted to get high with me and she agreed, of course. I ended up crashing my car into a telephone pole on the way there and breaking my hand. I pulled out of there and made my way onto the Garden State Parkway. Cassandra was waiting for me by my parents' house and once I got there, she simply had her hand out. I handed her a few bags and she started heading towards her car. After that, I finally accepted what I always knew about her deep down. She never cared about me or my feelings for her, she only cared about what I could do for her.

My car was totaled in the accident. The insurance gave me close to the same amount I paid for the car. I was able to put a down payment on a brand-new Hyundai accent. This was one of those blessings in disguise because I hated the car I got after totaling my Kia. The one issue I did have was I couldn't work in the restaurant until my hand healed. Charlie was nice enough to give me a mercy shift. I was delivering for the health food company he was trying to build with that personal trainer on Sundays. Now he was giving me Wednesdays as well. I was pretty grateful for this because Charlie wasn't stupid. He knew damn well I didn't swerve into a telephone pole avoiding a deer.

Spring time came around and I would come up just a bit shy of death once again. I was drinking with my Jersey friends when I got a random phone call from Tony. Opportunities to hang out with him were scarce so I drove to his new apartment in Brooklyn to see him. Once I got there, I developed quite a craving for some heroin. We drove into Manhattan to meet his connection. The dealer was concerned as to whether or not I'd be shooting it because it was strong stuff. "I've mainlined in the past but tonight I'm just gonna sniff it because I haven't done heroin in awhile," I told him to put his mind at ease.

After snorting one bag I started to fall out. Tony saw it coming before I did and insisted I pull over. At first, I ignored him because he's a hypochondriac and always assumes the worst. But after another block or so I felt woozy. I thought maybe I ought to let him drive. I don't remember pulling the car over at all. In what felt like the blink of an eye, I woke up with a police officer's hand on my head holding me down yelling, "Everything's all right man!" I suspected that everything was not all right and he was just saying that to keep me calm. I could hear Tony crying in the background, "Oh my God he's gonna be so mad at me for calling you guys." To ease his mind I said, "Don't worry Tony I'm not mad at you." I was terrified, yet in a place of deep spiritual contentment. I thought that I must've crashed into someone, which is why the police were there and I was clearly going to prison. But in that moment, after a near death experience, I felt absolutely ready to accept the consequences of my actions and not harbor any ill will towards Tony for calling the police. It turned out that I had successfully pulled the car over to safety somehow. The cops came to hit me with Narcan because I overdosed. They had to use two doses to wake me up. Tony thought I'd be mad at him but he saved my life that night. You see, Tony was unaware of the Good Samaritan laws and thought we were going to jail. To encourage people to save the lives of overdosing heroin addicts, they came up with the Good Samaritan laws. If you call the police to report an overdose, no legal action can be taken against you or the overdose victim. Tony was scrambling to stash the remaining drugs somewhere when he could've just kept it in his pocket. We were free to go once I came to.

Once the police officer took his hand off my head, I got up like a man possessed. The police had me get into an ambulance to get checked out at the hospital. Once we got to the hospital I was starting to sharpen back up again. After they took my vital signs, I decided I wasn't waiting in a waiting room to be told I was fine. I knew I'd be fine so I went walking to my car. Tony, being the hypochondriac that he is, said, "You're just gonna leave? Don't you think you should let them take a look at you to be safe?"

"I'm fine bro I gotta get out of here. I got work in the morning. I just want to get some sleep."

We started walking to my car when I realized my entire body was covered in dirt. "What the fuck is all this?" I asked.

"I had to drag you out of the car so you wouldn't get a DUI. Before I called the cops, I tried smacking you and giving you CPR."

"Jesus Christ!"

"Yea, I had to put my lips against yours. You're lucky I love you it was gross."

Once we made it to my car, I discovered that he must've stolen $300 I had in my glove box. That sense of spirituality you get when you're fresh off a near death experience had faded by that point. I was furious. He tried to blame the police that saved me because, according to Tony, they had to move my car. I walked right up to the precinct hoping he'd fess up to it but he didn't. I made a fool of myself, I'm sure, by asking those cops if they took it but I figured it was worth a shot. You never know, the cops may have taken it. The officer suggested I count my blessings seeing as how I almost died. If it was Tony, he did save my life by making the call and the police administered the Narcan so I can't really be mad at either of them. If they took a little gratuity so be it. What could I do about it anyhow? $300 was a small price to pay for my life.

After I dropped off Tony and I was alone in my car, I put on Pearl Jam's "Alive" and screamed the chorus line, "I'm still alive" from the top of my lungs to celebrate my survival.

A few days later I was lying in bed when I received a phone call from my mother. She was crying. "A police officer called me. He said you overdosed with Tony!" she wept into the phone. My stomach went into knots. At first, I denied it and demanded a phone number to reach the officer who called her.

"Why the fuck would you call my mother with this? I'm 31 years old and I live on my own. What would possess you to scare my mother?" I inquired.

After voicing my frustration, he said, "Look man, I'm just trying to get this stuff off the street so we don't have to Narcan other people."

That floored me. The part of me that was still human appreciated where he was coming from. He wanted information on the dealer but I really didn't have any to give him. The dealer was Tony's connect and I wasn't going to solicit Tony's help so he could get the guy. Tony would've gotten angry with me if I even asked.

Twenty-Four - Kerry

A week after my brush with death, I was working a Taco Tuesday. Just as my shift was about to begin, I saw a girl with the most beautiful face and the most beautiful head of curly dark hair I had ever seen walk across the dining room. She was wearing all black dress clothes. She sat down with Flo, the manager, for a job interview. Time completely stopped when I saw her walk across the room. She was the most enchanting girl I had ever come across before or since. Once again, I felt the universe telling me that this was someone special walking into my life. A cosmic plan was unfolding before my eyes. Her name was Kerry. It was undoubtedly love at first sight for me.

I went over to Flo to get signed into work and said, "Sorry to interrupt but I gotta get out there, I got fucking mouths to feed."

She peaked back at me and laughed. I knew I had her right there at that moment. Later that night, Flo asked me to work one of my days off as a favor. "Under one condition, you let me train that new girl," I said. She agreed without much resistance. "You just did a deal with the devil and probably ruined this poor girl's life as a result Flo," I told her as I was on my way out of the office.

The following Monday, Flo threw a curveball at me. She originally said that another server would be training her Monday night and I would handle it Tuesday night. But on Monday she had me train her instead which caught me completely off guard.

"I thought you'd be happy," Flo said.

"I'm coming off an overnight from my other job, I'm exhausted, and I wasn't expecting to do this tonight. I'm not mentally prepared but daddy's gonna improvise don't even worry about it," I replied. I managed to spend the entire shift making Kerry laugh at all my little anecdotes. "You smoke?" I asked her.

"Yes"

"Here come with me."

"I don't want to sneak out for a cigarette my first night working."

"Listen, ordinarily I wouldn't do it if I was you but you're with me so don't worry about it."

"Are you sure?"

"I'm positive. Chef Javier's gone and even if he was here, I'd break his face."

She was still a little hesitant to smoke her first night on the job but I continued to assure her that as long as she was with me, she couldn't get in trouble. Flo knew what I was up to so she would never interfere with my game plan. By that time, I was pretty revered by Flo and the owners. Sure my work could be sloppy at times, but I was such a good worker most of the time that they swept a lot of my sins under the rug.

I ran into Kerry a few times while she was training and played it cool at first. She could only work a couple days a week because she had a full-time job at a Wells Fargo bank. On the days when she was working with us, I'd carefully throw more and more of my usual routine at her. One night while the staff was rolling silverware, I did a line from a Rodney Dangerfield movie and much to my surprise, she understood the reference. "Yea my father is a huge Rodney Dangerfield fan," she said to me warmly. I was already quite smitten with this girl but now I was completely in love. She was shy and sweet and whenever she did speak, she would usually say something cheerful and funny. I simply adored her.

Cinco de Mayo was rapidly approaching. Cinco de Mayo is a big deal for a Mexican restaurant. Jordan and Dreamy Eyes got the lunch shift and would be able to drink and party around 5 o' clock while I would be starting my shift at 4. At first, I was upset about it. Flo insisted she needed a strong server on the night shift to tickle my ego but that wasn't enough to calm me down. Then she said, "I put Kerry on the night shift." That sold me. I still had to pull the trigger and ask her out. That seemed like the perfect time to do it.

I spent most of the shift drinking because it gets to be such a madhouse on Cinco de Mayo that nobody is really paying attention as to why I was in such a happier mood than usual. After work, I invited Kerry to the bar for a drink. The rule is that you could drink at work when your shift is over but not in a Rosita's uniform shirt. She didn't have anything to change into but I had a t-shirt in the car. I scurried to my car as fast as humanly possible to get her the shirt and then we made our way to the bar. When I asked what her poison was, she said, "Jameson and ginger ale." Hands down my favorite mixed drink. The more and more I learned about her the more I saw her as perfect. "I'll have the same," I said to the bartender.

We stepped outside to the front patio and lit up a couple cigarettes. I felt in complete control of the situation. But then they started kicking all the customers out and shut down the bar. I tried to score another round but they weren't having it, not even for me. I invited her across the street to Buffalo Wild Wings and she agreed. After a couple more drinks, I started giving out way more information about myself than I previously intended. I told her about my heroin addiction in the past and crafty ways I would secure money for the habit such as robbing restaurants. Beyond that stupidity, I hadn't made a move yet. I completely froze up. I was nervous because she was an absolute goddess of a woman. I knew I didn't deserve her.

The next morning, I woke up hungover asking myself, "Why on Earth did you have to tell her all of that nonsense about yourself?"

She didn't seem to mind though.

The following Taco Tuesday I took her outside for a cigarette. "What do you say this weekend you let me take you out? See if there's some chemistry between us," I said to her.

She smiled and simply said, "Sure."

I was ecstatic. I was worried she would flake on me because she was so clearly out of my league considering how sweet and beautiful she is.

That following evening, I picked Kerry up at her sister's house. The trip was longer than it would've been because I spent the night in Staten Island to house sit for Carmine, who was on vacation. I was there to babysit Jordan and Pippen whom I loved and missed dearly. I was completely on edge the entire date. I kept telling myself things like, "don't drink too much tonight" and, "don't play your weird music." I definitely succumbed to my desire to listen to weird music. It was after all, a pretty long drive into Manhattan. The plan was to take her to a restaurant on Mulberry Street then try to get into the Comedy Cellar. I would've made reservations had I known she was really going to come on the date. I thought for sure she was going to flake on me.

I stopped at the first restaurant that didn't appear to have a wait on Mulberry Street in Little Italy. I never tried grappa before. I assumed I'd love it because I love all things Italians love. It was one of the worst tasting liquors I ever drank. I had to play it cool so I pretended to love it. We ordered our food and the conversation started off slow at first. She's a very shy and reserved person but by the time dinner was over, the conversation was flowing pretty freely.

The Comedy Cellar wasn't going to be an option. The line was already huge and nobody is guaranteed a spot. I tried my luck getting into the famous Café Wha? for some live music. I recognized the doorman from my days working at B.B. King's. He couldn't help me get in but I still got to look cool in front of Kerry by knowing a doorman at such a prestigious establishment that was once graced with performances by Bob Dylan and Jimi Hendrix. We ended up going to a bar called Off the Wagon and had a few more drinks.

As we were talking, she had such a look of enthusiasm in her eyes. She looked at me like I mattered. As if I was someone of substance. Nothing had ever filled me with such a feeling of pleasure and guilt running simultaneously. Pleasure because no girl ever looked at me that way. At least no girl as beautiful and sweet as her. Guilt because deep down I didn't feel worthy of receiving it. I was a scoundrel and I knew it. I limited myself to four drinks then suggested we head home so I could check on the dogs. The dogs were fine, it was simply my way of luring her into Carmine's apartment for some privacy.

We kissed passionately and I moved us from the couch to the bedroom. I tried to sneak her pants off but being the class act that she is, she wouldn't give in to me on the first date. I was glad she didn't because it would've ruined her whole sweet girl mystique in my eyes.

That following Friday night I took her to dinner and a movie. She told me she loved Ryan Reynolds and Deadpool 2 was coming out that night. It worked out perfect for me because I really wanted to see it myself. First, we went to the Hibachi restaurant up the road where I slugged down as much sake as I could without her suspecting I suffer from full blown alcoholism. After the movie, we went back to my apartment. We started kissing on the bed and then I tried to get her pants off again. I deliberately struggled to get them off to give her an opportunity to push me away. But she unbuttoned her pants and helped me to take them off. My stomach went into knots with exhilaration. I gently pulled her panties off next and made love to her.

On Memorial Day, my parents were babysitting my cousin Tommy Brancato's daughters Ava and Lily. Naturally, I wanted Kerry to meet them. We took them to an amusement park in Central Park. We rode rides together and had a few laughs with the girls. They were adorable as always which really reeled in Kerry a bit. As we were deciding where to eat, my mother asked Ava if the menu at a particular restaurant suited her needs. Ava assured her she would be fine. "Ava! You better be sure because you're not eating any of my food!" Lily shouted at Ava. We all laughed. "Lily's quite a little firecracker huh?" Kerry asked me. "Oh yea, Lily's a savage," I replied.

After our little Manhattan excursion, we rushed back to Kerry's house where her family was having a barbeque. I immediately felt terrible for luring her away from such a fun family gathering. They were drinking and having fun all day. When I met the father, Max, he said to me, "Hey at least you're

294   Stephen J. Sacchi

not black!" Her father and one of Kerry's uncles tried teasing me a bit but I have tough skin. I just laughed it off. I played drinking games with her siblings and step siblings. Once I was good and drunk her father hit me with it on my way to the bathroom. "So, you work at a detox huh? What's your drug of choice?" he asked me out of left field. I assumed Kerry must've told him about me so I thought honesty was the best route for me to go with. "Well now it's alcohol but it used to be heroin," I answered rather brazenly. Max is a pretty cool guy. He seemed relatively ok with the fact that I used to shoot heroin and may or may not secretly still do it from time to time. All he cared about was that I kept whatever I was into away from his daughter. That was a concern I could respect. I don't think I could get her into drugs if I tried. Nor did I want to. I was fed up with casually dating girls of no substance. I wanted to be with her because she was a nice girl. Getting her strung out was the last thing I wanted to do. "Max, I think you have to move your car. You can't park there tomorrow," Kerry's stepmother said to Max. "Ok I'll go move it," he replied. Everyone was concerned he might be too inebriated to move the car but he insisted he was fine. "I'll go with him," I said in an attempt to put their minds at ease. I don't know why I thought my presence would make a difference but it seemed to put their concerns to rest. We walked across the street to a school parking lot and got in his car. Once we were in the car, Max leaned over and said to me, "You know Kerry sees something in you. She's a very independent girl she rarely dates anybody. Let alone brings somebody here." That made me feel warm inside. "I don't take that lightly," I replied. Internally, I meant that. The part of me that was still human felt that way. But my behavior due to alcoholism would not reflect how much I appreciated her.

It didn't register in my brain that I had landed my dream girl, was 31 years old, and probably shouldn't be out drinking with my friends from the restaurant without her. I was flirtatious with other girls but it was only when I was so drunk that nobody would want me. There was no physical infidelity, but I wasn't behaving the way someone in a relationship ought to. Seeing as how I only acted that way when I was extremely drunk, I was able to rationalize the bad behavior in my head. The problem was that I was always drunk.

In the meantime, Kerry and I were two peas in a pod. We'd spend a lot of time at barbeques or bars with her family drinking and enjoying the summer. I'd make her watch all of my favorite weird movies. I don't think she particularly enjoyed them but would pretend to for the sake of making me happy. Whenever my parents were babysitting Ava and Lily, we'd stay at their house so we could play with the girls.

One day we went to a trailer park in Pennsylvania because Kerry's aunt and uncle rented one there for the summer. They had a nice little barbeque and I proceeded to get wasted. Her family was drinking too but they seemed to pace themselves a bit better than me. Except for Max, he was knocking them back that day. He coerced some random stranger into wearing a bear costume for his personal amusement. Kerry's step brother explained to me that this was his modus operandi. "You better be

296   Stephen J. Sacchi

careful, he may make you wear it one day," he said. I would've been honored. At some point, Kerry and I were drunk. At least I was drunk. She seemed to be immune to alcohol. She could put down countless Jameson and ginger ale's and seem unaffected by it. After two I'm acting like a buffoon. We found ourselves lying on a hammock together. "I'm gonna go ahead and call you my girlfriend. Do you have an objection to that?" I asked as we lay together. She shook her head no. At some point, I became too wasted to carry on. I was instructed by her family to take a nap in the trailer. Kerry came with me to keep me company. I inappropriately tried to fool around with her in the wrong place and at the wrong time but when I'm drunk, I can't help myself. Not that her relatives were in the trailer with us but they could've come in at any moment. The next day I apologized but she didn't seem too upset about it.

For the most part, I hadn't used opioids since my last over-dose. But here and there I would take a Suboxone and noticed that since I didn't have a solid opioid habit, it would actually give me a nice buzz without making me nod out. A server at Rosita's always had Suboxone so I would find myself drinking all afternoon Friday. Then I'd come in for my 5 o' clock shift at Rosita's and have him sell me one so I could sharpen back up for my shift. That irritability that comes with opioid use was creep-ing into my behavior again. I never expected it to emerge from occasional Suboxone use but it was definitely there and I could recognize it. I would constantly be agitated and take it out on people at work no matter which job it was.

Kerry's sister Brianna and her fiancé Phil were soon to be married and were having a little house warming party. Max was there and he seemed to suspect that I was succumbing to opioid addiction again. I had, in fact, taken some Oxycodone that night and he whispered to me, "Don't get my daughter mixed up with any of that shit." I insisted I wouldn't and then he said, "Ok I love ya," which I found adorable. I loved him too. Even though they were all very welcoming, I felt like an alien around her family. They were all inherently good people and I felt like a selfish monster. I never wanted to admit it to myself then but I knew deep down I didn't deserve Kerry. She definitely deserved better than a drug addict/alcoholic who works three dead end jobs and still struggles to get by week to week. She was a queen and I only cared about myself.

One night after work, the Rosita's gang was going to this server Emma's house. Emma was only 19 years old so the crowd was on the younger side. I didn't care. I was just there to get drunk with Jordan and Dreamy Eyes. When I got there, I proceeded to get drunk and made an inappropriate comment about a 15-year-old girl's cleavage. "Girl's got a beefy set of tits on her," I said to the guys. Before you call Chris Hansen, it should be noted that I was drunk and had no idea she was that young.

The next day I realized that the Cult, Bush, and Stone Temple Pilots were playing at the PNC Arts Center. I immediately called Kerry and asked if she would like to come and if she could be ready in time on such short notice. "Of course," she said. It occurred to me that she never met Ron and I knew he would've loved to see those bands. He agreed to meet us there as well. At the concert, I drank an ungodly amount of alcohol. I can barely remember the Stone Temple Pilots' set. Apparently, I was playing with some woman's baby in front of us. How or why she would trust me to play with her baby in that condition is beyond me but it definitely did happen. Kerry recorded a video of me dancing with the baby in my hands.

Sometime before the Stone Temple Pilots' set, Jordan called to tell me the gang was going to Headliner. "They're filming an episode of Jersey Shore tonight," he said. By that point, I was completely wasted.

I had the brilliant idea to pick a fight with one of the cast members so I could get on television. I thought it was a perfectly reasonable way to seek fifteen minutes of fame at the age of 31. Kerry was mortified.

"You really think it's a good idea to pick a fight," she said. She dropped me off at home because she refused to be a part of such insanity. I fell asleep immediately. About an hour later, I woke up in the middle of the night to call her and apologize. She forgave me and said, "Hey not bad for our first fight."

The next day I thought about getting sober and returning to the sober fellowship. I called Kerry and said, "Listen, I think I need to get sober again. I just want to let you know I'm going to go back to the sober fellowship." She was ecstatic to hear that news.

Kerry went ahead and put in her two-weeks' notice at Rosita's. Between working at the bank and there it was getting to be too much for her. I was elated by this. I figured it meant that none of my past sins at Rosita's could come to the light as I had often feared. But on her last day it happened. Emma explained to her all the stupidity I was exhibiting at her party. That day I had to do the health food deliveries. On my way back she wasn't answering my texts. When I got there to drop the van off, I was told she went home for the night. I knew something had happened. Nobody was giving me a straight answer. Finally, I asked Jordan. I could see by the look on his face that he had bad news that he was reluctant to share with me but was going to nevertheless.

"Look if I tell you, you got to promise not to do anything," he said.

I agreed but I was lying.

"Emma told her that you were trying to pick up a young girl at her party," he added.

Upon hearing the news, I was furious. I marched into the dining room, pulled Emma aside, and snapped on her. Eventually, I calmed down and realized I couldn't disrespect the restaurant any further and started to drive home. On my way home I let out a primal scream that seemed to stretch for an eternity.

Kerry refused to answer my calls. I took the night off at Rosita's the next day and waited for Kerry to finish work at the bank so I could try and explain myself. I thought she'd be pissed off that I waited for her in the parking lot at her job but she was relatively ok with it. I somehow managed to talk my way back into her good graces. It took a lot of charm but I managed to do it. I assured her that I was going to return to the sober fellowship, move out of Long Branch, and go back home to my family.

"You're the only part of New Jersey I want to take with me," I told her. As if New Jersey was to blame for my insanity.

After things settled down, I took Kerry out on a double date with Carmine and Lauren. I thought it might be good for Kerry to see that I was friends with a seemingly normal happy couple. It was a nice night. We ate at some trendy spot in Red Bank and after Carmine and Lauren left, I took Kerry to the boardwalk in Point Pleasant. We rode rides and I made children and Kerry laugh on the bumper cars. All in all, it was a beautiful evening and my sins seemed to be forgotten for the moment.

I tried to do everything I could to salvage the relationship. I put in my two-weeks' notice at Rosita's and I left the apartment in Long Branch. Kerry never confronted me about it but I knew sooner or later she would no longer tolerate me living with another girl. Vinny resented Anna so to give him a small victory, I left without warning so she would be screwed on the rent. Her father probably covered my end but it still brought Vinny joy knowing that she'd have to go through the pain and embarrassment of having to ask. I had nowhere else to go but my parents' house but they let me back home with open arms. I explained to my mother that my relationship was in danger but I omitted certain details.

I stayed sober for the most part at first. Here and there I'd have little slips but it was whenever I wasn't with Kerry. I would hang out with Tony at his apartment in Brooklyn. That way I could drink and do drugs without it ever getting back to her. It's ironic. I used to drink and do drugs in New Jersey so my job in Brooklyn wouldn't find out about it. Then I had to drink and do drugs in Brooklyn so my girlfriend in New Jersey wouldn't find out about it. I had no idea that the drug and alcohol abuse was still showing up in my behaviors. Even though I would remain sober around her, I wasn't exactly sober. All the tendencies were still there and she could sense it. I was looking for a job to replace Rosita's but got nowhere fast. Watching me struggle took a toll on Kerry.

Eventually she called me to have the talk. I met her at Freehold mall. She said she was hungry so we went to Chili's on highway 9. There she laid it on me. She wasn't happy, she had lost all trust for me.

"I can't continue to watch you struggle to find another job and get your shit together because I'm there suffering with you," she said. I tried begging her for some more time. I insisted that eventually things would turn around now that I was "sober." I knew sobriety could cure all her concerns but I had to actually make a decision to get sober sooner than later. She firmly held her stance.

"Did you know that on two occasions after we had sex you fell asleep on me? You have any idea how terrifying that was for me? The first time I thought you were dead!" she said.

I had no recollection of this. I was mortified. The whole time I really had it in my head that my drinking wasn't that bad. Compared to the days when I was shooting heroin daily, it seemed like I was holding it together relatively speaking. When I heard that I fell asleep on her on two separate occasions, I realized just how far down the rabbit hole I had gone.

After dinner we spoke some more in the parking lot. She mentioned again how seeing me struggle to find work was taking a toll on her. I mentioned how my criminal background and checkered past was holding me back to which she shouted, "You let it define you!"

At that moment I broke down. I started to tear up and said, "If you leave me now, then it does define me."

Seeing my vulnerability got to her. She started to cry too and began easing up a little bit. We decided to go for coffee at the Starbuck's in Barnes & Noble. The mood lightened a bit and she started to let me make her laugh again. As we looked at books, I started spewing my useless knowledge about certain authors.

"Are you like, well read?" she asked me.

"I used to read quite a bit actually. Believe it or not I once wanted to be a writer. Hey, if I become a New York Times best-selling author will you take me back?" I asked.

She smiled and said, "Oh yea of course." We both laughed. Why'd she have to be so funny as I was losing her? Not to mention she wore these sexy eyeglasses that night. I never saw her

SAVAGE - A Journey Through the Opioid Epidemic - 303

wear them until then. The movie "A Star is Born" was being released that Friday. Andrew Dice Clay had a small part in it so I casually mentioned my desire to see it.

"I'm impressed. You want to see a chick flick?" she said.

"Well Dice is in it," I replied.

She agreed to see it with me that Friday despite our relationship seemingly being on the rocks.

The movie didn't do me any justice. It's about an alcoholic, drug addicted rock star who ruins his relationship and then commits suicide. It really wasn't painting a great picture for me. The one time I needed Hollywood to deliver a chick flick with a fairy tale ending I got a huge dose of reality. After the movie, I walked Kerry to her car. We chatted a bit and before she drove off, I said, "I'd kiss you goodbye if I thought I could get away with it."

She gently grabbed my hand and pulled me in for a kiss. I was hopeful that all was well but it wasn't.

Her sister Brianna was having her bachelorette party in Nashville, Tennessee that following weekend. I spent the entire weekend drinking and getting high with Tony. I barely called or texted her that weekend. I was worried if I contacted her, she'd be able to tell I was off. She confronted me on this lack of communication and I attested it to me just wanting to back off and let her have fun with her sister. She wasn't buying it. The truth was that I didn't want her to hear me slurring my speech. She dumped me for real that time. I childishly cursed at her and said things that didn't even make sense. I was playing the victim and tried to make her feel as if she was being unreasonable but the only one being unreasonable was me. I had a complete break from reality. My behavior was disgusting.

The next day was Ava's birthday party. I can't even recall the car ride to where my cousin Tommy lived in Babylon, Long Island. I met my family at an Italian restaurant for dinner near his house. God only knows how I made it there and back. I still had a few bags of heroin left from a bundle I copped in Asbury Park. I was operating on automatic pilot. Everyone could see I was a train wreck but I thought I was concealing it well. At dinner, I was falling asleep at the table. My parents, Tommy, his wife, my cousin Dominic, and friends of theirs were all witnessing this. After dinner, we went to my cousin's house and, unbeknownst to me, I dropped a bag of heroin in the driveway. The bag itself was wrapped in a piece of paper with my name on it. There was no getting out of it. In 24 hours, I managed to alienate myself from the people I cherished most on God's green Earth. None of them wanted anything to do with me. My cousins had mercy on me at first. When I went into the house, I fell asleep on the couch for a couple hours. I said goodbye to everybody and nobody confronted me but Tommy did it with his eyes. Everybody else looked at the floor as I said goodbye but he glared into my soul. As I was walking out the door, I said goodbye to Dominic who asked, "What's the matter bro? You're tired?" with a sarcastic tone. "Yea man I'm exhausted," I said back. I was once again house sitting for Carmine that weekend. Jordan and Pippen weren't enough to lick my wounds. I was broken. I thought of committing suicide. Instead I did more heroin to try and forget about it. The next afternoon I thought of Tommy's glare and Dominic's comment. I was terrified that they found the missing bag.

Then I received a phone call from my father. He confirmed my fears. My parents screamed at me over the phone for about fifteen minutes. I couldn't even argue with them. I had no excuse. I had brought my foolishness to a child's birthday party. I snorted some more heroin and nodded out on the couch. Carmine had a camera to watch Jordan and Pippen on. "I saw you on that couch and just felt an overwhelming sense of sadness for you. Get your shit together," he said.

I went back to the sober fellowship that following Monday night. Father John was speaking at the first meeting I went to and I felt a wave of safety and security wash over me. We got together a few times but I didn't stay sober right away. I went for a few days then helped myself to a few drinks. Once I got a buzz going, I went to Rosita's to drink more and I started flirting with a new bartender's girlfriend. He punched me in the face and I realized the next morning that I had enough. I couldn't swing it anymore. No matter where I went or what I did, if there was alcohol or drugs in my system, I was destroying everything in sight.

Twenty-Five - Reborn

I admitted to Father John that I slipped again and I decided to get to work. We started reading the sacred text from the sober fellowship together. I was spiritually bankrupt. I was desperately clinging to the notion that these miracles they all speak about might happen for me this time. Desperate to reclaim my life, I went over to the College of Staten Island and enrolled in school. It was an impulsive move but usually when I act on impulse, I end up with a needle in my arm. The way I saw it, I was moving up in the world if my impulses led me to the long overdue continuation of my education.

After losing Kerry, I was in desperate need of a rebound. I needed somebody to distract me from the heartache. The only attractive girl in the sober fellowship was this girl named Victoria. She was a personal trainer and Puerto Rican so she suited me just fine. Because of all that exercise, her body was perfect. She tended to associate with the overly spiritual crowd in the fellowship. Not my forte but I knew how to play the part. She had what I perceived to be foolish notions about spirituality and new age philosophy. I could talk in those terms all day even though I secretly found most of it to be nonsense. Her dream was to teach the law of attraction in Tulum. I saw, "The Secret" and on paper that law of attraction rhetoric sounds fun and I'd really like to believe it. But I couldn't help thinking what a starving Ethiopian might say if you told him there's an unlimited source of abundance and all you need to do is think positive. I played along though because I had to have her.

I made my first initial move at the Spiritual Breakfast. The Spiritual Breakfast is an annual event held by the sober fellowship at The Vanderbilt catering hall. I had quite a line up at my table. Ron was with me but there was also his ex-fiancée Valerie, her new husband Hesh, and Ron's father Dennis who was trying to get sober but failing miserably. Dennis showed up high on Xanax. As I passed Victoria, I said to her, "Just to give you a brief inventory of what's going on. Ron is seated at a table with his ex-fiancée, her new husband, and his dad who's completely fucked up and I'm loving every minute of his pain." She laughed and we chatted for a moment or two. I decided to sit down with Ron's father. As much as Ron resented his father for being an alcoholic, ex-convict, and all-around maniac, I couldn't help but love the guy. He was hysterical to me. Victoria passed by our table and Dennis said, "Oh I like her!" I then told him, "Hey old man, back off! She's mine and you don't want to compete with me my friend. I'm a sexual fucking maverick!" Dennis snickered and said, "Oh excuse me maverick." Then he fell asleep at the table.

The food at the Spiritual Breakfast was so awful I would have to be morally compromised to feed it to my dogs. I invited Victoria and Ron to Royal Crown so we could eat some real food. Victoria rode with me and Ron took his own car. After we ate, I made my move as I was dropping her off. "I know I'm still early in sobriety but I gotta tell ya flat out, you are a fucking goddess. What do you say you let me take you out sometime?"

She insisted I should have a little more sobriety time before we dated. I waited patiently and continued pursuing her in the meantime. Desperate to try anything that might change my life for the better, I made a vision board just in case my attitude towards the law of attraction was completely cynical. Victoria suggested a book about the law of attraction so I ripped out the part where it said New York Times Bestselling Author and put it on my vision board. I also printed out a picture of my dream house, a Lincoln Continental, a picture of the perfect physique with my head glued over the guy's head, a restaurant that said Sancho's because I want to own a restaurant and name it Sancho Gambini's, a check written out to me for 3 million dollars, and a picture of Kerry, Me, Ava, and Lily from Memorial Day in Central Park. I desperately wanted the three girls I alienated back in my life. Just in case I completely pushed Kerry away, the picture to me was still representative of family. To the naked eye it looked like it could be a picture of a man with his wife and daughters. More than anything else on that vision board, I wanted a family of my own.

Work became an issue. I still had the job at the detox but that wasn't enough to get by. Given the nature of my sins, my parents were livid. They demanded I find my way out of their house and fast. If I was going to be able to afford an apartment, I would need to find a second job and fast. I tried calling Charlie but he was ducking me. Christmas was just around the corner and there wasn't a chance in hell I wasn't going to be able to get everybody a gift that year. I decided to drive to the new Rosita's location in Brick, New Jersey. I saw Charlie's silver pickup truck in the parking lot. One of the other owners and the head chef were inside. I goofed with them for a bit and asked to speak to Charlie. They directed me to the office where I found a fully bearded Charlie. "What's with the beard?" I asked. "No shave November," he said. Once we got past the beard I asked if I could get my job back. "I don't think that's a good idea dude," he said. I twisted his arm a bit. I told him I went back to the sober fellowship so he wouldn't be getting Sacchi the goofball, he'd be getting clutch Sacchi.

I started selling him on it. "I'll tell you what. I'll run it by the new manager Joe and then I'll get back to you," he said.

"Charlie, I just want you to know that the new beard is looking tough and I'm not just saying that because I want my job back," I told him.

He laughed and I was on my way. I was not expecting a phone call from them but a couple days later, the call came in. It was Joe the new manager. "Hey Sacchi, Charlie says he thinks if you're really on the up and up these days you'd be a great asset to the new location so I'd really like to have you come on board," he said.

It was about an hour drive away but I didn't care. I needed money and I couldn't fathom working for anyone else at that time. I was too early in recovery to take orders from someone I didn't already know well. I was completely on edge. I had experienced early sobriety before but it was never that bad. Without drugs and alcohol, I felt like a vampire out in the sun anytime I was thrust into any part of society.

One night after work I invited this girl Sheridan out to eat. She had blonde hair so she wasn't my type but she exhibited a little promiscuity around me. We went to some restaurant up the road and Sofia was coincidentally the new manager of the place. Seeing her prevented me from working up the nerve to seduce Sheridan for some reason. Sofia and I always discussed the Rocky movies because she loved them and my impressions. We even went to see Creed 2 together with her mother. As Sheridan and I were finishing our food, Sofia said, "I went to the Rocky steps in Philadelphia with my new boyfriend!" I felt like a dagger went through my heart.

"This may sound crazy but you going to the Rocky steps with a new boyfriend almost feels like you're cheating on me."

Sofia laughed and said, "You aren't my boyfriend, you're more like my boyfriend on the side."

I smiled and replied, "Babe, that's all I ever wanted."

My mother was insisting I apologize to my cousin Tommy for what had happened. I was way too ashamed and embarrassed to make that phone call. I told her I had to work on Christmas which was a lie. I just figured it'd be easier to sit that one out instead of making everyone uncomfortable. It was a coward's move but it had to be done. I think I would've thrown up if I tried to force myself through the anxiety of facing up to that right away. I made myself sick to my stomach anytime I thought about it. I did make sure I got Ava and Lily Christmas gifts though.

After the holidays, I spent a lot of time working with Father John. I was slowly starting to feel better. We'd hang out at his condo in Jersey, not far from where I was staying in Long Branch. As I was making progress in my recovery, I was making progress with Victoria as well. After a few platonic dates I finally managed to convince her into kissing me. From there it wasn't a long stretch into sex. There were plenty of hiccups along the way. Some dusty old biker from the sober fellowship who dresses like Indiana Jones and looks like Russell Crowe was trying to court her as well. He was constantly trying to impress her with all his Zen biker bullshit. They'd talk about the law of attraction, manifestations, and other hippie wizardry. At first, I thought maybe I was just being crazy and insecure. Just in case I was insane, I decided to be polite to the man, even when it seemed blatantly obvious that he was trying to maneuver around me.

One day after one of our meetings he invited her to the Z-One diner when we already had plans to go to the Staten Island Diner. "Oh, we're already going to the Staten Island Diner," she told him. I drove her over to the Staten Island diner and he was there waiting for us. He must've ditched whomever he was going to the Z-One diner with to attend to his relentless pursuit of Victoria. I took a deep breath and decided to remain calm. If I started acting upset by his presence it would only make me look weak. Besides, I still wasn't sure if he was just being a nice guy. All signs seemed to point to him being predatory. On our way out I shook his hand but I looked him dead in the eyes with a territorial stare that said, "She's leaving with me. Back off!" He seemed to get the message.

I vented about my frustrations with him to Father John over breakfast one morning. Because of his vow of celibacy, it was shocking to him that a girl would even consider dating an older man.

"Do girls really go for older guys?" he asked.

"I mean John if you hung up the collar you could probably clean up," I jokingly replied. One of the things they stress in the sober fellowship is that resentments are one of the most detrimental things to our sobriety. I often wrestle with that concept. Upon honest reflection of one's self, you come to the realization that if you were to hold yourself up to the same standards as you hold others, you don't quite fit the bill. I had a lot in common with the biker. I had been guilty of predatory sexual behavior. I also could easily see myself at age 60 courting a beautiful 28-year-old if I'm not married then. But when you take on a persona of someone with deep spiritual wisdom and parade around the fellowship claiming to have a profound relationship with God, I can't help but feel your personal relationships would reflect that. A man of God wouldn't find himself constantly scouring the sober fellowship for impressionable girls half his age. That's a charlatan if I ever heard of one.

George reached out to me at some point to let me know he was coming home. I didn't even answer his texts. I heard he was sober but I was determined to stay sober myself. Whenever we got together, sobriety wasn't guaranteed. Billy reached out to me as well. He was still in Florida and he was in such bad shape that he resorted to asking me for money. The first time he asked, I sent him $50 through Venmo. The second time I had to show him tough love. When people are looking for a handout, you know the situation is grim.

New Year's Day I turned over a new leaf. I was out to rectify all of my other bad habits on top of drug and alcohol addiction. Education was soon to be covered. I signed up for LA fitness to get into better physical shape for the first time in my life. I started praying and meditating daily. The sober fellowship insists that we pray and meditate daily but I never really went for that. This time around I was willing to try a few things differently. At first, I dragged my feet through the process. I would lie in bed when I prayed and meditated. I was depressed and praying and meditating felt like a chore then. You're supposed to kneel when you pray and sit in a lotus position when you meditate. Gradually I started snapping out of it and doing it right. I even quit smoking with the help of a vape. I vowed to not only start eating better but to start cooking all of my own meals. You see I always spent money like a black kid with a hit record. I was desperately seeking to become an adult. I realized how much you could save by going grocery shopping. Dom, Carmine's old partner in the bearded dragon business, was moving out of his place so Ron and I were waiting to take it over. Dom made a fortune with an

Instagram meme page he put together called Hardcore Comedy so he and his wife were moving into a new home.

School started in late January. I look and feel pretty young. You would never guess I'm in my thirties. When I looked in the mirror, I didn't see a 32-year-old. But then I went back to college and realized, "Damn, I am old!" I was taking prerequisites for the nursing program but quickly realized there was no way I was going to do well enough to get into the nursing program. I switched majors to psychology in hopes that one day I'd be addressed as Dr. Sacchi. I didn't even care if I got a decent job. If people have to address me as Dr. Sacchi, I've won the game of life.

School quickly proved to be difficult. I was constantly taking off shifts at Rosita's to study. Something was off at Rosita's. Not only was I sober but my penchant for mischief and womanizing was nonexistent. Working at the new location wasn't fun like the Marlboro location. It was a job. I decided I needed a change. I reaffirmed all of my New Year's resolutions once Ron and I moved into Dom's old place. I was cooking for myself and trying to fit in daily exercise but the reality of my situation started to sink in. Victoria and I were constantly arguing. In my head, I really thought that she was being argumentative but really, I was just so on edge that I was attracting conflict everywhere I went. There were times where she was looking out for me and I would turn it into an argument. Years of drug and alcohol abuse fried so many circuits in my brain that I was too prone to getting upset easily.

One day I had to go to The Metropolitan Museum of Art for my art history class. We were going to look at some art and then write a paper that counted as a third of our grade. I couldn't find the professor anywhere. I scoured the entire museum looking for him to no avail. I took a few pictures and even kept my ticket with the date and time on it.

As I was searching the building, Victoria was on the phone with me saying, "Look, professors want you to pass this isn't the end of the world."

I insisted this professor was a whack job and I was definitely in trouble. She was merely trying to give me sound advice but I turned it into a screaming match because I was certain the worst-case scenario would materialize. The following class, I showed him evidence that I was there and he yelled at me. I tried to plead my case but he raised his voice even louder. I almost punched the guy out. I took a deep breath, decided I would just drop the class, and walked back to my seat.

Then he walked up to me and said, "You can make the paper up, you just have to go to the museum yourself." I breathed a sigh of relief and asked him, "Why didn't you just open with that?"

The fact that I was in college at age 32 and getting overwhelmed by the classes felt completely pathetic. I was desperately trying to overachieve each day and I ended up just burning myself out. I slipped even further into my depression and temporarily put a hold on everything. I stopped exercising. I dumped Victoria. I quit working at Rosita's once and for all. I stopped hanging out with Father John and barely hung around the meetings. The only thing I managed to keep on doing was I stayed sober and finished that semester of school. My finances were a disaster. Even though I was cooking at home and curtailing my spending drastically, quitting Rosita's set me back quite a bit. I did randomly receive $2,000 in the mail. It was a tuition refund. I qualified for a grant for school and I was given more than what was needed for tuition. I just assumed they covered the semester. I didn't think they were going to just throw me free money in the mail.

I had avoided my friends from New Jersey for quite some time. I missed them but I was scared I would drink. I felt foolish going out with them but one night I mustered up the courage to keep the friendship alive. I met Jordan, Dreamy Eyes, and a few of their friends. I felt like a fish out of water. Jordan ended up tickling my heart in the sweetest way. We ended up at some seedy strip club where the girls were so disgusting that I never even considered getting a lap dance. I spent the entire time making the guys laugh at the strippers' expense. The Staten Island in me makes it impossible to speak without making elaborate hand gestures. I moved a Heineken bottle out of my way so I could continue making those hand gestures comfortably. Jordan got nervous thinking I drank the beer. "No, I just moved it out of my way," I told him. He wasn't convinced so he started asking the guys if I drank it. It meant the world to me to know that he took my sobriety seriously. I was always worried that my friendship with those guys were strictly predicated on partying. To know that he actually cared about my well-being warmed my heart to no end.

Carmine and Lauren were getting married in Saint Lucia. On top of the anxiety I was feeling from everything else, the thought that I might not be able to afford attending their wedding was weighing on me. The tuition refund saved me from that and I was able to secure my plane and hotel. When all was said and done, I managed to get pretty decent grades much to my surprise. A bunch of A's and one C. The C was in biology and that was the best I could possibly hope for. What do I know about mitochondrias? I still have no idea what they are. The weekend after school ended, we went to Saint Lucia. I was completely on edge because I quit the vape a week prior so I could be completely nicotine free and early sobriety didn't help much either. I was about six months sober, I wanted to drink, I was broke, and the little money I did have went to watching my friend get married in another country. I was just in a terrible mood and only worried about myself. I found out there was a casino on the island so I made it my mission to get there. Ron and I took a cab through this third world country of an island to find out the casino wasn't like your usual casino. It was sketchy at best. It wasn't much bigger than the size of someone's basement. The cab ride there and back cost me a small fortune. There was nothing fun for a single guy to do on this island.

Once I returned home, I reaffirmed my commitment to self-improvement. I got back into the gym on a regular basis and started paying better attention to how I was eating. I started going to meetings with a vengeance and decided to get a new sponsor. I went with Spiritual Jason. The decision was no reflection on Father John. For some reason I felt more comfortable explaining to Spiritual Jason that I had been working at a detox and lying about my clean time. Most importantly though, I started writing the first draft of this book. Since I was a kid, I wanted to be a writer but never really tried. This stretch of sobriety I made a commitment to change my life. Part of that was taking action instead of procrastinating about it like I always had. I always had the artistic temperament but never went anywhere with it. I can play a few instruments, I get lots of good ideas about writing, and I've always wanted to be a standup comedian but never really devoted the time and energy to any of those things despite the passion I felt for them. I decided the easiest thing I could do creatively is tell my own story. It would turn out there was nothing easy about it but here we are. Reliving my most cringe worthy moments was not as easy as I thought it'd be.

Carmine and Lauren had me babysit Jordan and Pippen for their honeymoon. I was always called upon to babysit them because they know and love me. They were gone for about a month. When it came time to give them up, I got depressed all over again. Coming home to seeing Jordan's bulging eyes and Pippen jumping six feet into the air with excitement brought me so much joy. A few weeks after their return, Carmine offered to let me babysit them again. I jumped at the opportunity. Ron and I hung out outside with them and I felt no need to put them on a leash because I never saw them run away before. One thing I

hadn't counted on was them attacking another dog. Some old lady was walking her dog and Jordan went ballistic and attacked it.
Pippen followed suit to back her up. They gnawed at this dog's
ears until Ron and I collected them. The lady was in hysterics.

"Oh my God! Get them off!" she screamed. We apologized up
and down as best we could. I had no idea they would behave
that way. There's a veterinarian right across the street from our
apartment. She went there to have her dog checked out. In the
meantime, I called Carmine to let him know what happened and
that he should probably pick the dogs up because if there was
any real damage done, we could just play stupid and say, "What
dogs?"

I gave him the rundown nervous as all hell thinking he'd be
mad.

"No fuck it, you want to just keep them?" he asked.

"Are you serious?" I asked. I thought for sure he was just kidding around. "Yea I thought about it for a whilenow and they
seem happier at your place. Lauren and I are working constantly
so if you want them, they're yours." he said.

"Of course I'll take them. Hey if I would've known you'd give
em up I would've set Jordan loose on a neighborhood dog
months ago!" I told him. From that point on, Jordan and Pippen
were officially my babies. They couldn't have come at a better
time. In order to establish all of my new habits I had become a
bit of an antisocial recluse so I wouldn't have any distractions.
Their good company kept me from going insane. Ron locked

himself in his room every moment he could so he wasn't any sort of company.

Mid-summer I was dragged out of my solitude due to a pool party held by some girl from the sober fellowship. I hadn't really hung out much with the young people from the fellowship but I decided to force myself into this uneasy social gathering. This newcomer couple who hadn't been dating more than a few weeks announced they were pregnant. Everybody congratulated them while I decided to go with a dose of realism. "You know most people come to this fellowship to make their lives better not ruin it," I told them. Everybody complained to me for saying that but it was the truth.

This guy Steve was there smoking a cigar. I never liked cigars but I figured I might like one since I hadn't smoked anything in a month. I figured you don't inhale cigars so it should be fine. This led to full blown cigar addiction. It got to the point where I was smoking three a day and spending way more money on cigars than I ever did on cigarettes. By the end of the summer it got to the point where I was literally depriving myself of food and nourishment in order to afford more cigars.

That summer itself was boring. I wanted to drink but couldn't. Here and there I'd hang out with Jordan and Dreamy Eyes out in Jersey and feel awkward because I wasn't drinking. I couldn't get laid because I decided I wasn't going to be predatory anymore. The sober fellowship's sacred text tells us that if we continue to engage in sexual behavior that hurts others, we will drink again. I made a decision that casual sex just wasn't for me anymore. The only way I'd try and court a girl was if I could actually see myself in a relationship with that person. Make no mistake about it, guys know if a woman is girlfriend material immediately. Anytime I met a girl of that caliber I'd mess it up or never even work up the nerve to make an approach. The confidence I developed over the years had become non-existent. You see, when it came to courting the opposite sex, I never had much confidence to begin with. So, I carefully constructed a mask over the years. A façade if you would.

I stole things from various influences when I carefully constructed that mask. There's some Vince Vaughn in there, some Andrew Dice Clay, Carmine, and a whole lot of Diamond David Lee Roth. I got so accustomed to wearing that mask to face just about anything. Not just with girls but life in general. I barely knew who I was. That all may sound cliché but I really had no idea what the genuine Stephen even looked like.

I decided to keep focusing on myself and try and figure out who Stephen is. I approached recovery with a fervor that I never had before. They say alcoholism and drug addiction is a threefold disease. Physical, mental, and spiritual. Basically, we're all PMS'ing. I always thought disease was a strong word for our affliction but it's definitely a mental illness and I was in the worst shape physically, mentally, and spiritually when I ruined Ava's birthday party. The exercise routine helped with the physical. Re-enrolling in school at age 32 was to help the mental. Meetings were to help the spiritual side along with prayer and meditation. The one area I was lacking in though, was getting involved in the meetings. I wasn't raising my hand and I would only share if I was called upon. I was trying my best but I still wasn't feeling much better. If I did say anything to anyone, I could only wear my humorous mask because the genuine version of myself was riddled with doubt and fear. The mask itself no longer felt comfortable on my face anymore. It felt heavy. It didn't work the way it used to anymore. But I couldn't bring myself to make the people in the meetings aware of my suffering. For one thing, I didn't want their pity. I was too proud for that. I also didn't want to take away from the meeting and give any newcomers the sense that this might not work for them. I had witnessed it work firsthand in so many damned souls' lives yet never my own. I knew it could work. I was simply frustrated that it wasn't working fast enough for me. I was 33 years old and the social clock that dictates I ought to be married with children and advancing in a nonexistent career by that point was laughing in my face.

People in the sober fellowship talk about miracles but a miracle seemed completely elusive to me. It felt as if I was in the studio of the Oprah Winfrey Show working as a janitor and she's just shouting to the audience, "If you look under your seat, I've given everyone a MIRACLE! YOU GET A MIRACLE! AND YOU GET A MIRACLE!" All I get is to clean up after these people who just had these miracles effortlessly bestowed upon them. When was God going to show up to help me transcend the pitiful existence addiction had thrown me into? When was I going to be worthy enough to receive such a miracle?

Mark got married that fall to his fiancée, Judith. I drove Tony over to the reception. He was wasted and making everybody laugh but, for the most part, everybody was laughing at him and not with him. I could tell he was in pain. He was making me laugh more than anybody but it was coupled with an uneasy feeling. I saw my past self in him that night. I was always making people laugh but internally feeling miserable. I would constantly feel the need to perform like a dancing monkey. I still wanted to be funny but I didn't want to kill myself to make people laugh anymore. My thinking was constantly shifting into maturity. My heroes used to be guys like Billy and Frank because they were savages. My heroes were beginning to become guys like Mark and Carmine. They were the two best examples I had of guys who transcended the stupidity of our youth. They both had city jobs, beautiful wives, and a home. Not to mention Mark was constantly in the newspaper for his heroics within the police department.

After the wedding, we got news that Billy died from an overdose in Florida. He's probably the closest friend I had who died but, by the time it happened, I had become desensitized to watching people die. Mark and I made a pit stop at the wake but got out of there as soon as we finished paying our respects. We didn't want to run into any old friends. Mark and I made sure to express our condolences to his mother and brother first. His body seemed to be in terrible shape. "I feel like that should've been a closed casket," I said to Mark once we got outside. "It should've," he replied.

Back at school it was still summer weather and this one kid came into class in a trench coat. I thought for sure he was going to pull a Columbine so I sat right behind him. My thinking was that if he reached for a gun, I was taking him down before he could pull the trigger.

In another class I had a priest as a professor. "Hey do you know Father John?" I asked.

"Yea, he's actually my superior. Am I in trouble or something?" he asked jokingly.

"Well not yet but maybe at the end of the semester you take a look at my grade, do the right thing, and maybe you get straightened out," I told him. The class erupted with laughter wondering what planet I came from.

I had successfully avoided my cousins for a few months. Johnny was going to propose to Lena and he was coming up from Florida so we could all be there. I tried to call Tommy so I could finally apologize but he didn't answer. Then my mother said Tommy and his wife wouldn't be able to make it but his brother Dominic would. I felt a sense of relief. I was still quite nervous to face Dominic but he would be exponentially easier to face than Tommy. Johnny was proposing at a rooftop bar in Manhattan. As we all met there, I noticed that Dominic had Jordan sneakers that were in perfect condition and I also happened to know they were released over a year prior to then.

"How'd you keep those clean for so long?" I asked him.

326 Stephen J. Sacchi

He explained that he barely wore them and they were black so it was easy. As he was explaining I realized I was just stalling from addressing the elephant in the room. I decided to get on with it and make my apology. "I know it's your brother I really owe the apology to but I just want to say sorry to you as well," I said with a frog in my throat and tears starting to well up. Before I got overly emotional, he put me at ease and told me not to sweat it.

"Tommy told me you tried to reach out. Just know that he's not angry with you, he's just worried about how to handle it because he doesn't want to say anything that might set you off," he said. "Let's not worry about all that. Let's just enjoy the night," he continued.

I immediately calmed down and was able to enjoy the night with my family.

I never thought I'd say this because I'm anything but sentimental, but watching my brother propose was a beautiful moment to witness. The only thing I couldn't get over was my brother's man purse that he carried the ring in. He seems to think he's some sort of fashionista but a Staten Island degenerate has no business carrying a man purse. All the strangers who witnessed the proposal and my family erupted with applause once he got on one knee. After he popped the question we all attempted to go out to dinner. My father spent about twenty minutes on the toilet while we were waiting for a table. My mother kept insisting I check on him but every time I went downstairs to the bathroom he insisted he was fine.

"What's the matter with him?" asked my Aunt Darla.

"He saw Johnny's man purse and felt sick to his stomach," I said.

My father attempted to come back upstairs and join us but he collapsed on the steps. We called an ambulance and the paramedics were able to determine that he might be fine, he would just need some food. We tried to eat but he vomited right in the middle of the dining room. After that we insisted he go to the hospital. As the paramedics were loading him into the ambulance, I said to him, "Dad I'm letting you know right now. If you pull this shit when I finally find a woman dumb enough to accept my proposal, we're gonna have a problem!" Johnny and I had a good laugh at his expense.

"Stop! Leave him alone!" my mother said.

"Come on he knows I'm only kidding," I replied. I wasn't kidding. I've been a disaster my whole life. If I domesticate myself enough for a woman to consider spending her life with me, he'd better keep it together.

I traded up cigars for the vape once again hoping the constant nicotine would relieve the stress brought on from school. I'd also be saving money because vape juice is much cheaper than smoking two or three cigars a day. My one-year anniversary of sobriety was rapidly approaching. What kept me going in order to make it to that year anniversary was envisioning my cousin, his daughters, Kerry, and the rest of my family coming. I imagined I'd be able to convince them all to come, make a really good speech, and win all of their forgiveness in some beautiful miraculous moment.

I called my cousin a week before the anniversary to finally apologize to him. He took it better than I expected but it still felt awkward. I was completely ashamed of myself. "I can't make it to your anniversary but I want to congratulate you on your accomplishment," he said. I was hoping he'd come because my word meant nothing. A room full of people who saw me sober for a year would've spoken volumes.

I shot Kerry a text but she didn't even answer me. When it came time to celebrate I didn't even want to. I wasn't feeling celebratory. I got sober for myself but the people that I really wanted to come and see the difference in me weren't there. My presence was barely felt at the meetings. I couldn't find a speaker at all. Barely anybody had enough of an emotional attachment to me because I kept a wall up.

I decided to go with Ron and Carmine. The two of them had been in my corner throughout the years more than anybody else so it seemed fitting.

The morning of the anniversary celebration, Ron was in a bad mood because of his new girlfriend Lisa. I didn't really care for the emotional turmoil she constantly seemed to put Ron through. It wasn't all her fault though. Women subconsciously say and do things to see if men react a certain way. He'd take the bait every time and fly off the handle. He was too blind to see that he wasn't ready for a relationship. My early sobriety induced edginess probably factored into his decision to back out of speaking.

"I'm not in the mood to speak today just have Spiritual Jason do it," he said to me. I knew I could get Spiritual Jason to fill in but it felt like he spit in my face. I had been a thorn in his side since we moved in together but he understood the fish out of water feeling that people go through in early sobriety better than most. And most of my tough love was out of love.

I rushed over to the meeting and asked Spiritual Jason to fill in. I had no idea what I was going to say when I received my one-year coin. I had to find somebody to fill in the meeting leader position that Spiritual Jason was originally going to hold. I went with this guy Chris, an alumnus from my detox.

"Can I tell the story of how when I passed through your detox you were still fucked up?" he asked.

"Go ahead," I said. I was such a phantom around the meetings that I didn't think anybody even really knew who I was. I was worried people were going to say, "Who is this guy celebrating?"

They welcomed me with open arms though. They all approached me warmly and helped me feel loved. Before the meeting started, Ron came in and said "Bro I'm sorry! Of course I'll speak for you." In my eyes he already ruined that. "You've been replaced. I don't fucking need you," I told him.

As the meeting began, I noticed Spiritual Jason slipped into a blazer. I was petrified of what I was going to say. I had no game plan at first. Once I noticed Spiritual Jason wearing a blazer that he didn't have on previously, I smiled and knew exactly what to do.

Chris started the meeting and said, "When I first met Steve, he was working in a detox. I said to the other patients this guy Steve is really helping me out. Then they turned to me and said, 'You know he's fucked up right.' I told them, 'Well I don't care, he's still helping me.' Despite the fact that he was fucked up he really was helpful."

Then it was my turn to get up there and receive my coin. "I told you Chris I wasn't drunk I was just tired," I opened with. The entire room erupted with laughter and I started to feel comfortable. "This year was tough. I want to thank my roommate for putting up with me because this year I was completely riddled with restlessness, irritability, and discontentment. So much so that he backed out of speaking this morning at the last minute. It's ok though Spiritual Jason keeps a blazer in his car." The room erupted with even more laughter. It felt like I took a shotgun and blasted Ron right in his chest for backing out on a day I fought so hard for. I trudged through the celebration. I decided after that day that even though I didn't witness the miracle I was hoping for, that I was going to keep on fighting.

I would often find myself wanting to give up but I decided that I started something and I was going to finish it. I got frustrated because I figured by the time my anniversary came, I'd be spiritually centered from all the praying and meditating. I figured the exercising and dietary choices would have me looking like a GQ magazine cover model by then. I figured this book would've been ready to hit the press by then. I had an internal meltdown when it didn't all fall into place on the time frame I was hoping for. Life had been kicking my ass since I was a kid. It was about time I kicked back. The effort I had already made wasn't enough. It felt as if the entire universe was working against me no matter how hard I tried.

On Christmas Day, my family was going to Long Island to see Tommy and I felt it was safe to tag along. I realized I should've insisted to Tommy that I speak to his wife Justine and apologize to her when I called him, but it took enough of an emotional toll to simply speak with him. I was going to have to make my apology on Christmas Day. The plan was we'd exchange gifts at Tommy's house and then go out to a restaurant to eat.

When I walked into the house, I went catatonic when I saw Justine. I timidly waved at her because kissing her hello seemed far too brazen. I figured I'd wait until dinner to make my apology. It didn't seem right to open up with, "Hey, I'm sorry I dropped a bag of heroin in your driveway!" As we started driving towards the restaurant, Tommy texted my mother saying that Justine wasn't feeling well so they wouldn't be joining us. My parents assured me it had nothing to do with my presence but who knows. I could only hope that I'm not that important.

My momentum and resolve in sobriety and self-care continued but it still felt like I was going against the grain. Once I realized Kerry wasn't coming back, I decided to try my hand at dating again. The problem was that I was a nervous wreck and so completely out of the loop from not dating for a year, that I had forgotten how to go about it. I was getting turned down left and right. The enthusiasm I once had was no longer there. My libido was crushed from depression. I was beginning to think a drink would loosen me up enough to ask a girl out with some self-confidence. Then the universe started playing tricks on me. I was seeing the name Kerry everywhere. In the strangest of places too. One morning I woke up for school and as I got into my car, I saw a truck pass by that said Kerry's Landscaping. Why this was happening after all this time, I couldn't possibly fathom. All I know was I was tired of being alone. I had taken a year off from being predatory in my sex life. I started asking God in my prayers for a suitable mate because let's face it, I have needs. I had spent a year without acting out sexually and I felt God owed it to me to place someone special in my life.

One day at a meeting held by the sober fellowship, a pretty girl walked in who didn't look like Kerry but had a similar aura and was pretty well kept for someone who was newly sober.

"You should ask her out," Carmine suggested. He could see I really needed to get myself back out there.

At first, I felt reluctant to do so. I didn't want to date someone in recovery. I didn't want to date anybody to be honest. I wanted to believe Kerry was coming back but there was no evidence to support the theory that I could manifest such a miracle. As the meeting progressed, the new girl spoke. Her name was Kerry! I took it as a sign from God that this is what I was asking for. I tried to court her a bit and, in the midst of my pursuit, I found out she actually was once roommates with my cousin. At first, I was skeptical that maybe this was God giving me what I had been asking for but now I was certain. Coincidences like this usually turn out to be destiny at work. After running my usual game, I finally felt confident enough to ask her out. I was certain she'd say yes. I was certain I had God on my side.

But much to my surprise, she rejected me. I couldn't believe it. She said she had just gotten out of a relationship, she was newly sober, and she didn't think she should be dating at the moment. "Aren't you not supposed to date someone in early recovery anyway?" she asked me.

"That's just something people who can't get laid like to say," I replied.

She laughed but she wasn't going to let me take her out.

I was completely confused. I was starting to lose faith. I would still force myself to pray and meditate in the morning but when I prayed I would literally grind my teeth and yell at God. "You mind telling me what the fuck is going on?" I'd ask. I was trying so hard to live by spiritual principles but I was not seeing the kind of rewards spiritual people speak of. I was rounding up fifteen months sober. Everyone else with that amount of time talks about the blessings they receive because of their sobriety. All I knew was struggle. I kept some degree of faith. I decided I'd give it a few more months and if living right doesn't pay off I'm going to start doing things my way again. In the sober fellowship, we say that we get out of the driver's seat. We let God do the driving. Right around this time it felt like God was a sketchy Uber driver taking some strange back roads.

I was beginning to think that God had no desire to help me. I was ready to take up a crusade against him. Why would he plaster the name Kerry everywhere I looked? Why would he dangle some pretty girl named Kerry in front of me? Was he deliberately trying to tease me? Is he even in existence?

I trudged on. I gave up stressing myself about these matters. I just kept on with my routine. One morning I jumped in the shower to get ready for school. Once I stepped out of the shower I couldn't believe my eyes. It was a text from the original Kerry. It read, "Hey! Sorry I know this is very random lol. But I had the weirdest dream last night about you ha-ha so I just wanted to shoot you a text and see how you are doing." God finally showed up in epic fashion. He planted a dream about me into Kerry's mind and said to me, "I'm just gonna leave this here."

Kerry and I hit it off immediately. She agreed to meet me on a lunch break. She was working in Manhattan that particular week. I got my haircut just the way she always liked it. I cut class just to see her. That class didn't take attendance anyway. The office building had a mall downstairs. I waited nervously for her in the mall's center. Once I saw her across the room approaching me, the Earth stopped. She was even more beautiful than I remembered. I gave her the biggest hug. From there we went to Starbuck's to get coffee. I was all jittery and nervous trying to come up with meaningful conversation. Eventually, we went outside for fresh air and it all started to flow naturally. She asked me, "So have you dated anybody?"

"Not really, there was one rebound after we broke up but there hasn't been anybody since. I've been focused on myself."

"A rebound?"

"Well, that's what it was. I needed to distract my mind from losing you. How about you?"

"I dated one guy for a little while but he was such a momma's boy. I lost interest."

"Going from me to him must've been like going from speed-balls to milkshakes."

"I was with him when you texted me about your anniversary. I really wanted to go and I felt terrible but I would've felt weird going while I was with him."

"It's all right don't sweat that. How's your father?"

"Don't get me started. Him and my stepmom broke up. He's been having a bit of a midlife crisis. He's been drinking more than usual. Don't ask me how he does it but he keeps landing these hot dates. He gets all dressed up and puts on this crazy hat."

Max is from Brooklyn so I figured it was one of those really big newsboy hats. I pulled up a picture of Andrew Dice Clay wearing a really big one on my phone. I showed it to Kerry and asked, "Is that it?"

She started laughing and said, "That's actually the exact same hat."

"Knew it."

That hour was the fastest hour of my life. One of her co-workers saw us together in Starbuck's because, when she went back to work, they all gave her a round of applause. "They're all gonna think I'm some hoochie," she texted me.

I missed her sense of humor so much.

The next day she needed a ride home back to Jersey and I was more than happy to oblige. She was hungover from the night before because it happened to be her birthday and her friends drove all the way to Manhattan to party with her. She was visibly beaten from the hangover and lack of sleep. I told myself I wouldn't make my move just yet. I would just be a good friend and get her home safely and comfortably. We made a pit stop at my house so I could feed Jordan and Pippen. She started falling asleep on my couch so I offered to let her sleep for a couple hours on my bed. At first, I was really going to just let her get some rest. I figured this wasn't the time to take my shot.

But I was drawn to her like a magnet. I popped my boots off and hopped in the bed with her. I started by kissing her cheeks and she motioned her mouth towards mine and let me kiss her. After that I completely smothered her. I was ecstatic. I credit her with saving my life and I thought she'd never get to see the effect she had on me. Now she was in my arms again and I was given another shot with the most beautiful girl on the face of the Earth. I could sense God above asking, "Happy now?"

After a little love making, we ordered a pizza. Ron came home shortly after. "Uh oh, what'd it go bad with original Kerry today?" he said as he noticed the pizza box. The only time I strayed from my new diet and ate pizza was when my day was unbearable. That pizza was a victory.

I was pissed off because he said, "original Kerry" not even realizing that she was there lying in bed with me. I didn't want her to get the impression that there was anybody else because there wasn't. Just a failed attempt at scoring a date way before she even reached out. Then he came down the hallway and saw her. "Holy shit!" he said.

They caught up and Kerry was petting Jordan and Pippen and said something that alluded to her knowing them. "Oh, you've met Jordan and Pippen before?" Ron asked. Kerry nodded her head.

"I used them as bait on our first date. I was housesitting for Carmine and I pretended that I needed to check on them," I chimed in.

"Oh, so is that what happened here today?" Kerry asked me.

"No, today I really needed to feed them. I rushed out of here this morning to get you without leaving them anything. It just so happened to really work out well for me again," I said.

Once her hangover began to fade, we made a pit stop at my parents' house. My mother and Kerry were ecstatic to see one another again. After they caught up, I drove her to her apartment in Brick, New Jersey right up the street from the new

Rosita's. Her bedroom was setup really nice with all sorts of girl-ie decorations and a huge comfy bed with a plethora of pillows. "We should probably snuggle," was on the wallpaper above her bed. A feeling of jealousy emerged as I imagined her snuggling with someone who wasn't me. But I took a deep breath and found solace in knowing that that night it was going to be me. She let me spend the night and we made passionate love until we fell asleep. Then again in the morning.

"You want to get breakfast somewhere," I asked as we were getting dressed.

"Sure," she said.

We went to this adorable little diner. A few weeks prior to then, I noticed a book on my friend's coffee table called "If." It's filled with a bunch of fun hypothetical questions that I realized would be perfect conversation starters for a first date. I down-loaded the book to my phone but hadn't had an opportunity to use it until then. There was nobody else in the world I would've rather gone through it with.

"If you could go back in time and witness any tragic historical event, what would it be?" I read aloud from my phone.

Without hesitation she yelled, "Holocaust." Then she made an adorable timid face because she was embarrassed that her mind went straight to the most horrible place possible. I laughed and fell deeply in love with her all over again.

Twenty-Six - COVID-19

The coronavirus pandemic was just getting started. Kerry and I didn't really take it seriously at first. I would still take the trip down to Brick, New Jersey as they were slowly beginning to shut everything down. Kerry had always said she would've loved to hear me speak at a meeting. Coincidentally, I was finally asked to speak at one of the very last meetings held before the pandemic shut us down. Kerry couldn't make it and thank God for that because I did a horrible job. I tried to be funny but all you could hear was crickets. I tried to explain the extreme measures I went through to better myself. I brought up exercising, quitting nicotine, school, praying, and meditating. I was looking for a pat on the back and the meeting heeded no quarter. Once I realized I wasn't going to win them over with my humor, I let my guard down and shared something from the heart. It wasn't enough to save me from looking like an idiot but it definitely helped.

As the coronavirus was beginning to really escalate, Kerry called me and said, "Look I just want to be up front about this, I don't want to take away from your progress or for you to think that you haven't done enough but I can't get over the past. My whole family knows what you did and I know I shouldn't care about what they think but I don't entirely trust you and I'm not exactly ready for a relationship."

She pierced my soul. I feared this conversation would come. I remained calm. A day later I suggested we keep seeing each other in a "friends with benefits" capacity. She agreed. But it didn't last long. Right about the time everything was completely shut down, so did our romance. I didn't blame her. I understood what I had put her through. It hurt like hell but how could I be upset with her? She's undoubtedly my muse and I would've never crawled so far out of the misery of my existence if I never met her.

My classes switched to online once the pandemic hit. The detox got the green light as an "essential business" but other than working there, I had entirely too much time on my hands and zero human contact. I wallowed in self-pity for a bit. We were in the dead of winter so on top of losing Kerry again, seasonal depression was kicking in as well. I was ready to quit again. Mustering the courage to walk out of my bedroom to the computer so I could participate in my classes proved to be a daunting task. I got up, made myself a double espresso and turned my laptop on.

"Ok we actually are going to take the next week off because College of Staten Island says we're going to have a recalibration period as we adjust to online learning. But I'm already way behind in the curriculum so I was wondering if you guys would want to have class anyway?" my math professor asked.

"I need to recalibrate," I typed into the computer. The professor laughed. I was given another week to procrastinate about getting my school work done. I was bedridden most of the time.

After a few weeks of living like a bum I decided to go back on the offensive. A sudden spark came alive in me. I started by getting my school work done for the semester. Then I started exercising again. I had more than enough stuff around the apartment to stay in shape so I couldn't use the coronavirus shut down as an excuse. I did start smoking cigarettes again but I actually felt pretty good about it. It started with a few cigars but the stay-at-home order made it increasingly difficult to find them. One day I was in New Jersey and tried calling a few cigar places to no avail. Finally, I reached a place where the owner happened to be in the building but he wasn't open for business.

"I'm just trying to pick up a couple cigars man," I insisted.

"All right come by but knock on the back door," he said. A tall skinny older man in his seventies answered the door. He seemed like a fun guy to have a beer with and his demeanor reminded me of my grandfather on my mother's side. I picked up a couple cigars and was on my way. The cigars eventually led me back to cigarettes again. I had been on edge since getting sober and cigarettes seemed to heal that a bit. Cigars and vaping may have satisfied the urge but nothing beats a Marlboro light in my mind. It helped me to focus. I finally found a rhythm.

For the longest time writing this book still seemed like an impossible mountain to climb. But I decided this pandemic was a golden opportunity to finally get it done. As I started writing it felt like someone shocked me with 2000 volts of electricity. The words began to pour out of me whereas in the past I would struggle to remember things. Early sobriety shriveled my attention span to work for only an hour. But the cobwebs in my mind were clearing more and more. I finally started to feel my mental health getting better. I was more kind and loving towards people. Especially at the detox where they needed to see that side of me more than anyone. The world was turning into a dystopian society but I started using it to my advantage. When the world stopped, I was able to catch my breath and relax a bit.

I still struggle a bit and I once voiced my frustrations with not being further along to Spiritual Jason. "How long did you do drugs and alcohol for?" he asked.

"Off and on for twenty years!" I replied.

"Ok so you've gotten lost wandering in the woods for twenty years and you think you're going to wander your way out in a year?" he asked.

When he put it that way, I decided to adopt the mindset of the great Paulie Walnuts. When it comes to my, at times, seemingly futile pursuit of navigating out of the woods, I tell myself, "I ain't stopping til we hit cement."

That August I was scrolling through Facebook when I saw that my first sponsor Declan shared a picture of me, him, and George with a caption that said "Rest in Peace." At first, I thought maybe there was a false rumor that I was dead. Then I realized it might've been George. George was always seemingly indestructible. I texted Declan and he confirmed it.

I went to the wake and saw the old man from that cigar shop I stopped at a few months prior. "You knew George?" I asked rather stunned.

"Knew him. He's my nephew," he replied.

Then I approached his mother and gave her a hug. "Do you remember me? Sacchi?" I asked her.

"Of course," she said. "Have you kept in touch with him?" she asked after some small talk.

"Well I've been sober almost two years now. Last time he reached out to me, I got to be honest, I ignored him because I was worried if we got together we might slip up again," I admitted as I started to get a little teary eyed. "I feel terrible about that now," I added.

"Aw don't worry he loved you," she said to comfort me.

"I loved him too," I added.

George's death really put things into perspective for me. In my head I would often go about in pity for myself but then I was able to appreciate being alive. Billy, Angelo, George, and Nikki were all gone and I could've easily died just as they did. For some reason, I was still standing. My life may not be where I want it to be just yet but I at least have my life and I have an honest chance to build it into what I want it to be. Happier days are surely on the horizon. Johnny and Lena announced they were having a baby. Carmine and Lauren announced they were having a baby as well. I was beyond thrilled to hear that I'd become an honorary uncle and an actual uncle. I started taking solace in the uncertainty the future holds rather than being afraid of it. It's important to me to live well for my friends who can't. I'm certain they would've wanted to be here and I know they would've wanted me to find the peace they never could. For the first time in my life, I felt the sense that things were going to be alright. At least, that's my guess.

About The Author

Stephen J. Sacchi grew up on Staten Island, New York. He briefly went to Hofstra University, has performed in comedy clubs, and been a general menace to society, often in hilarious ways, thanks to one of the toughest addictions one can have. Thankfully, he beat the addiction and is sober a day at a time and now writes and works in the recovery field.

Acknowledgments

I'd like to thank Mark, Carmine, and Ron. I never would've made it this far if it wasn't for your friendship. Thank you to Father John and Spiritual Jason. I didn't always heed your advice through the years but I did absorb some of it and it's allowed me to grow into a much better person. Thank you to Genesis for not only employing me but letting me work the overnight shifts. If I would've had to work the shifts that actually require work I would've never found the time to write this. Thank you to Tony for dialing 911 instead of letting me die. I will always love you like a brother. Thank you to my parents and my brother for putting up with me through the years and loving me anyway. You never gave up on me which gave me a reason to not give up on myself. Thank you to Kerry for pointing out to me what a fool I had been. That night on highway 9 you could've simply drove off but you stayed with me awhile and took a walk into Barnes & Noble. If we never walked inside there that night, I'm not sure this would've come to fruition.

CPSIA information can be obtained
at www.ICGtesting.com
Printed in the USA
LVHW021025010421
683175LV00002B/15